MW01608701

A Few Things I Remember

Or

At Least That I'll Admit!

by

Ronald Bay Furry
Professor Emeritus
Cornell University

ISBN 978-0-9894484-6-8

Published by East River Editorial, 6373 East River Road, West Henrietta, NY 14586

Copyright ©2018, Ronald Bay Furry

Printed in the United States of America

Dedication

To my wife, Anne; children, Suzanne, Kenneth and Donna;
my parents, Edna Louise and Wesley Bay Furry; and
all of my relatives and friends who made my life
interesting, instructive and worthwhile as a
valuable and successful journey.
Thank you immensely.

The **Wave** of the future starts with a little *ripple*.

Contents

Beloved

Missing You

Thank you my children,
The loves of my life,
Brought to me tenderly
By my beautiful wife.

Thank you my loved ones
For all that you are;
I'll miss your sweet voices
And await you afar.

Away

Oh! My family, I miss you all —
The voice, the laugh, the little footsteps in the hall
When morn' has not yet come to us all.

I miss the look I give to you
When each day's work and play are through
And in your beds you dream anew.

The silence in this cavernous house
Is like a thunder upon my ears,
And drives my love to mental tears
Trying to recall what only my heart hears.

I see the toys upon the floor —
I miss the knocks upon the door —
Oh! Just to hear those little voices I adore.

Who needs who I wonder not —
I know I need you all — a lot.

In My Beginning

I was born on Thursday, October 22, 1931 in the back bedroom at 165-60th Street (formerly called Jewett Avenue), Niagara Falls, New York. My Father was Wesley Bay Furry (b. December 12, 1902-d. November 15, 1955), and my Mother was Edna Louise Brown Furry (b. February 14, 1902, d. July 25, 1984). My sister, Joanne Louise Furry, was born in that same bedroom on Friday, October 26, 1934; she died April 21, 2015. I miss them all immensely. My parents were married on September 7, 1929 in Niagara Falls, New York. The photo shows them on their wedding day with their parents.

Arthur and Catherine Brown   Edna and Bay Furry   Eliza and Roland Furry

My Father grew up on a large dairy farm in Lowbanks, Ontario, Canada, on the north shore of Lake Erie, about 35 miles southwest of Niagara Falls, Ontario. One year during harvest season a stone caused a spark in a stationary grain thresher causing a fire that burned the whole farm down. The fire was so intense and fast that the people ran into the lake for safety. The family moved to Dunnville for a short while, then on to Niagara Falls, Ontario where they started a grocery store named Furry and Son on the corner of Buttrey Street and River Road in 1921. The son was my Father, and Furry referred to his Father, Roland Hugh Furry. On June 25, 1927, the family immigrated to the United States and moved into a duplex on 57th Street in the Evershed neighborhood of the Village of LaSalle, which was incorporated into Niagara Falls, New York, in the same year. My paternal grandparents, Roland Hugh Furry (b. August 25, 1867, d. May 29, 1949) and Eliza Emma Ann Stevens (b. May 15, 1879, d. February 10, 1955), eventually settled on another farm in the German hamlet of Bergholz, New York. Roland was born in Lowbanks, Ontario, Canada; Eliza was born in Virgil, Ontario, Canada; they were married in July 1896. They were buried in the Lowbanks, Ontario, cemetery. My Father became a naturalized citizen of the United States in 1936. My maternal grandparents were Arthur Henry Brown (b. March 4, 1871, d. September 29, 1938), born in Black Rock, New York, and Catherine Eucheria Doeseckle (b. June 10, 1871, d. September 9, 1957), born in Merriton, Ontario, Canada. Eucheria means Body of Christ (Eucherist).

Furry & Son Calendar Heading for 1922.

Wesley Bay Furry CERTIFICATE OF CITIZENSHIP, October 2, 1936

My Mother, Edna Louise Brown Furry, was born in Niagara Falls, New York, the third of seven children, and grew up at 167-60th Street, right next door to where she and my Father would eventually build their home in an apple orchard at 165-60th Street on a lot that she bought from her Father, Arthur William Brown. She was a private stenographer in the office of the President of The Nabisco Shredded Wheat Company, which had its corporate offices and production facilities on Buffalo Avenue in downtown Niagara Falls. The city was a big attraction to companies that required large amounts of electric power, and the falls provided plenty of that. After Bay died in 1955, Edna worked as the Registrar for the Boy Scouts of America Headquarters in Niagara Falls and Buffalo from June 2, 1958, to her retirement on her birthday, February 14, 1967, then briefly with Andrews Ignition Service until September 15, 1967, and in her words, retired "For Good!" In 1929, when my parents were just married, they lived with my Father's parents, Roland Hugh and Eliza Emma Ann Stevens Furry in the duplex at 166-57th Street. Ever lovers of the land, Roland and Eliza would later buy a small cash crop farm in Bergholtz, New York, and move out of the city, with Roland also working as a Superintendant of Production at the Carborundum Company in Niagara Falls until his first retirement. When WW2 started, he was asked to return to work to assist in the war effort, and he did so, working there for a total of 23 years.

Edna Louise Brown Furry

My very first memory is that of "hearing" a continuous, very high frequency monotone sound and simultaneously "seeing" a distributed white light, as if being in a uniformly bright, all enveloping cloud. I have heard that same sound all of my life since then, and I attribute that "noise" to the brain's circuitry, in other words the "sound" of being alive. My personal belief is that the light and sound came from the instance of my brain switching on when I was in my Mother's womb.

The picture above is from an oil portrait that my parents had painted of them in 1929. Space was left between them for the later addition of offspring, and my portrait was added in 1932. If the artist had been thinking correctly, he would have made my portrait proportionately smaller and the spacing better so another offspring, in this case my sister, Joanne, could have been added three years later! My Mother would sometimes write Joanne as JoAnne. My Father called her Rosy.

Ron in 1934 at Home in the Living Room

Home: 165-60th Street, Niagara Falls, New York

The area in which I was born and grew up was originally the Village of LaSalle, later incorporated (1927) into the City of Niagara Falls, New York, along with several other hamlets. When talking with folks from outside the region, we were careful to distinguish between Niagara Falls, New York and Niagara Falls, Ontario, Canada. We had lots of relatives and friends in Canada, because my Father had been born on his Father's dairy farm on the northern shore of Lake Erie in Lowbanks, Ontario, Canada, and my Mother's parents also had relatives in Canada.

Our home at 165-60th Street was in the middle of an old apple orchard and there were few homes on the street, perhaps six or so. The home immediately to the north at 167-60th Street was owned by my Mother's parents, Arthur and Catherine Brown. Her Father had purchased several lots when he moved to this area, and my Mother had purchased one of the lots from him when she got married. Beyond my grandparents' home lay farmland. I can still recall watching farmer Bill Sheridan trudging along behind his "oxen" (dairy cows hitched to a walking plow), as my Mother used to call them, turning over the earth to plant acres of potatoes. At that time, for me the world seemed to end at the first row of potato plants. Later, I would shock wheat on Sheridans' farm with my neighborhood playmate, Paul Holzle. He received 25 cents for a day's work; I got 10 cents because I was younger. Shocking involved collecting sheaves, bundles of wheat that had been cut and tied by a horse-drawn mechanical harvester and deposited on the ground, to stand them upright for further drying. They would later be collected on a wagon to be taken to a stationary thresher to separate the grain from the straw. Several sheaves made a shock and it took a lot of walking back and forth over the fields to accomplish this task; and the sun was hot!

One day my Grandmother Brown invited me to sleep over at her house and I thought that was a great idea. But, it turned out to not be the treat that I expected. Her house had two stories with bedrooms on the second floor and none of the bedrooms on the north side had windows. I was placed in what to me seemed to be a giant room on a cot with no lights. When the door was shut, the room was pitch black with not a glimmer of light even from under the door. I was petrified but said nothing. I lay perfectly still and stiff as a board and eventually went to sleep. Then I started dreaming and it was a fearful occurrence. I saw two fighter planes diving down from high in the sky with their wing-mounted machine guns blazing away at my bedroom! I could clearly see the pilots — they wore bubble helmets with clear visors and oxygen masks attached to them by corrugated hoses, and had shiny flight suits. The planes were sleek, single-winged aircraft *with no engines*! (Primitive jet engines were invented in 1930 independently by an Englishman and a German. Oddly, at an ASEE meeting when I was on the faculty at Cornell I met the German inventor at one of the sessions!) I was in total fear, with every muscle of my body as tight as could be. My face was as taut as a bowstring. I survived, didn't tell anyone about my vision and never slept at my Grandmother's home again. I have no idea how my mind came up with that advanced scenario. At that age I had not yet even seen an airplane.

I spent a lot of time at my Grandma Brown's home because it was right next door and there wasn't anyone my age to play with in those days. Her youngest daughter, Florence, and her youngest son, Robert (Uncle Bob to me), lived there with her after her husband, Arthur, died in 1938. Grandma, whom we called Kate, Florence and I would play cards, principally Euchre and Hase, in her kitchen by the hour, and drink lots of tea. Once in a while she would fry whole wheat bread in bacon grease — that was a real treat to the taste buds! Cooking was no easy matter. The kitchen had a huge iron stove and no refrigerator. The stove had a large and a small oven on the left side and a bigger oven on the far right. The top of the stove had several round lid sections that could be removed to permit placement of paper, kindling and firewood to heat the stove. Heating took time, so meals had to be planned well ahead of time, and then what was being cooked had to be watched carefully and continuously. If the fire went out, restarting it could be a very smoky job! Normally, smoke from the stove was vented outside through a thin-walled metal stove pipe that had to be cleaned to remove accumulated creosote and ash, and periodically replaced because it would rust and leak. There were no automatic timers or temperature controls. Experience was the greatest factor. When her husband died, Kate took in several male borders, and feeding and caring for a small "hotel" was a big chore. There was no vacuum cleaner; rugs were swept with a broom, then covered with paper and dampened to collect dust when re-swept with the paper in place. I had several "opportunities" to clean smaller rugs that were removed, hung on clotheslines outside, and then beat to death by hand with a wire rug beater! Not a pleasant task — holding my nose to avoid breathing the dust was not something I liked. Washing the laundry was done by hand in large tubs using washboards. The whole side yard was filled with clothes lines and drying wash. Attached to the kitchen was a pantry where pots, pans, and mostly food that would not spoil readily was kept, along with Grandma's "medicine" — a bottle of whiskey that was used sparingly and mixed

with honey for various ailments. It sat on one of the highest shelves. A cool room called a "cold cellar" in the basement was used to store harvested vegetables, carrots in sand containers for example, and chopped cabbage in ceramic crocks with an inverted plate and a rock on top of it to make sauerkraut to have vitamin C during the winter. Half a hog was hung from a floor joist. Of course, any stock food that was desiccating or starting to spoil was used first. The cold room was located under the four-windowed bedroom shown in the photo taken in March 1949. Harvested apples and cabbage were stored outside against the north basement wall of our house (on the right in the photo) and covered with deep straw to mitigate freezing, but that was a pretty iffy practice and was eventually abandoned. In addition to black raspberries, we always had big gardens, raising at least corn, tomatoes, carrots, rhubarb, lettuce, strawberries, dill, parsnips, beets, onions, radishes, peppers, horseradish and asparagus. I remember a particular time when my Dad had finished spading our garden, adding chicken manure to each newly uncovered row before covering it with dirt, and had raked it smooth and ready for planting. He started planting tomato plants on one side of the garden that was separated into two parts by a narrow concrete walk that ran from the house to the chicken coop. I was just a little tyke then and watched him intently: he would open a hole in the soil, insert the tomato plant, cover its roots, then step off the distance for the next hole and repeat that procedure until he reached the end of the row. I was following very closely behind him, only one plant apart. When he reached the end of the row, he turned around and I proudly handed him every plant that he had planted! There wasn't a tomato plant to be seen in the ground. That's the only time that I can remember ever being spanked on the bottom, and it was deserved, for sure. Some of our garden crops were canned for use in the winter season, including tomatoes. We didn't raise peaches, but went over the border to Canada to a peach farm where we would pick cling-free peaches for canning. Most of the vegetables and fruit were hot packed on the stove, using one quart glass jars in large aluminum containers filled with boiling water. The smell was intoxicating and the expectation of things to come months hence was great. One of my favorite aromas was that of chili sauce cooking! My Mother stored all of her home canned goods on shelves in a small room in the basement that my Dad had walled off. There were dozens of jars on the shelves. She would also have other items there, such as potatoes, onions and carrots, and also left a gallon jug of cider on the floor to turn into vinegar. We also stored leftover cooked food there, such as cake, pies and turkey. There were no home freezers in those times. My Grandma Furry made inordinately delicious Christmas fruit cake. She made her own glazed fruit and citron peel, and stored the fruit cake for months under a whiskey saturated cloth cover. Here is her recipe for the fruit cake that my cousin, Darlene Taylor Walck, sent to me on December 9, 1998.

Eliza Furry's Christmas Fruit Cake

4 large eggs
3 cups dark brown sugar
2 cups butter (add a little extra)
2 cups heavy sour cream
½ teaspoon baking soda dissolved in hot water, also put salt to taste
    in baking soda
1 cup black molasses
1 teaspoon nutmeg

6 cups flour (leave one cup flour until after the fruit is put in)
2 pounds raisins (wash in hot water)
½ pound of lemon and orange peel
1 pound citron peel
1 pound glazed cherries (some half and some whole)
A little glazed pineapple (slice thin)
2 pounds dates
Almonds or 1 pound of walnuts may be added

Put brown paper in the bottom of tins and grease the pans with either
Crisco or Spry. Bake in 300 degree F oven or a little over for about 2 hours

I loved her fruitcake! Always ate it with milk. I haven't found any fruitcake, commercial or otherwise, that can come close to it. She also made great mince meat pie, with real meat in it. Their water supply on the farm came from a well that had so much hydrogen sulfide in it that I could barely drink it even while holding my nose. All of their water was pumped by hand. Her household water for cooking, doing dishes and the like was obtained by using a pitcher pump attached to a board in the kitchen; this water was rainwater that was collected and stored in a large cistern in the basement. A creek ran through their back yard and flooded the basement just about every year. It was a tough life. This was the time of no refrigerators so food deteriorated quickly. They bought their butter from a farmer down the road who had cows and churned the cream by hand. Without good preservation, the butter soon became rancid, and believe it or not, I actually got to like the rancid flavor! (I also loved the flavor of cod liver oil, the source of vitamin D back then to prevent rickets. I got a dropper full of it every day under my tongue.) There was a one-hole outhouse in the backyard by the garage, with the usual Sears catalog there for the necessary. Yep, it stank, so looking through the catalog didn't last long. In winter, or when the weather was foul and they preferred to stay inside, or at night, there was always the chamber pot under the bed. Sometimes the bedrooms had an "aromatic odor."

My uncle Bob was 21 years old when I was born, and we naturally became good buddies. I would visit him next door and we would play catch, and he'd tell me how the world works. One day we sat down on the ground between our two yards, with our backs resting against his garage, and he took out a cigar from his shirt pocket, stripped the cellophane wrapper from it, then took his jackknife and cut off one end. He moistened the cigar with his tongue, then put it in his mouth and lit it. The smoke smelled delicious! He then gave the cigar to me and told me how to inhale. I took a few puffs and things were fine for a couple of minutes until I started to get dizzy. I got up, went across my back yard, opened the screen door, went up the stairs into our kitchen where my Mother was working, staggered across the dining room into the living room, did three twirls and fell flat on my back on the living room floor. My Mother was more than alarmed, to say the least. When the dizziness passed and I could explain what happened, she gave her brother a good lambasting. He was laughing his head off! His first marriage was to a local girl, and he converted part of the second floor of my Grandmother's house into an apartment for them. A corner of their house nearest my house was changed from a bedroom into a living room, and this is where he kept his cans of different tobaccos. Commercially made cigarettes were expensive, and lots of folks rolled their own, including my Father. A piece of cigarette paper was held in the shape of an open cylinder between the fingers of one hand, and the other hand was used to fill it with loose tobacco from a small pocket bag or other container, such as a can of premixed tobacco. The filled paper was then rolled shut after licking one edge to keep it together, and one end was twisted shut to keep the tobacco from falling out. It was then lit and smoked. The process took some skill, and the results were always different. One day he bought a small cigarette rolling machine that made uniformly nice cigarettes. It consisted of a belt and a hand lever. Tobacco was placed in a groove on the belt with a cigarette paper; the lever was then pushed forward over a contoured surface rolling the tobacco into a cylinder. It worked like a charm! One day my sister and I went into his living room when no one was around and decided to do him a favor and make him some cigarettes. In fact, we used up all of his different kinds of tobacco and cigarette paper. The only problem was that we were not smokers and had no idea of how dense the tobacco should be.

Unfortunately, our home-rolled cigarettes were packed so tightly with tobacco that air could not be drawn through them! Uncle Bob reclaimed the tobacco by tearing apart all the cigarettes, but separating the different kinds of tobacco was not possible. Roll your own cigarette machines are available today, but are much fancier. Joanne and I were always trying to be helpful. One day we were taken to Bob's brother's home for an overnight and visit. Bill was two years older than Bob and was not married at that time and had no children with whom we could play. We soon exhausted all of our exploration resources on the premises for play, but finally found interest in his garage; Bill was outside working in his back yard. There were lots of tools around and a wood workbench with a hand-powered grinder bolted to it. We then noticed that there was a big display of screwdrivers above the bench, and we found that they were all "dull," so we sharpened each to a chisel point. Joanne cranked the grinder while I made sure that the ends were sharp. Then, we proudly took some of them to show Uncle Bill. He didn't say a word, but we never stayed overnight again.

My Grandmother's home always had a big, tall evergreen tree in the living room at Christmas time. The ceilings were nine feet high to help keep the house cool in the summers. There were double sliding doors that led to the foyer and the dining room. The inside corner of the living room was where the tree was placed. Now, this was the time when electric lights for tree decoration were not used in the home because of their great expense, even if one knew where to get them. So, the tree was decorated with real candles placed in small holders that were attached to the tree. Where they were attached was very important; a candle should obviously be located so that an overhanging branch would not catch fire from the flame. To reach the candle located on the very top of the tree, my Uncle Bob would hold my legs near my ankles and hoist me up to the top with a burning fire stick. This was done first so I wouldn't interfere with the other candles on the tree. The candles were burned for perhaps 3 or 4 minutes and then put out quickly. A bucket of water was always around for safety. Affordable electric lights for trees weren't available to the general public until the NOMA Company was formed in 1925 and lasted until 1968 when increased competition forced it out of business. I can remember my Dad and I hunting for a string of Christmas tree lights in the early 1940s and all we could find was a string of large outdoor bulbs that cost $5.00, very expensive then. They were well built and I used those lights to decorate our trees, and the outside eaves of our current house, for over 70 years. The string had one light that never worked!

I don't know who started to call me by my nickname, Son or Sonny, but all my relatives did and still do. Inside the confines of grade school and high school, I was called Ron or Ronald, except for very close friends outside of my relatives. My playmates even called me Sonny. It was interesting to have a mixture of people who called me Sonny in a conversation with those who knew me as Ronald. Neither would know who the other was talking about until someone asked who Sonny was. At Cornell, I was only called Ron or Ronald. When I went home to Niagara Falls, I was called Sonny. It's a wonder that I don't have a split personality.

The trolley line from downtown Niagara Falls on Buffalo Avenue ended at 60th Street where we lived. The trolley ran in the center of the road and was not insulated, created a great racket and was fully enclosed by glass windows. I remember the first time that my Mother took me with her to go downtown. The trolley bell clanged, and we took a seat up front where the operator stood. The seats were wooden benches with no padding. Our seat was directly over a cut-out section of the floor above the big electric drive motors. I looked down through the hole and watched the blue sparks from the buzzing motors increase in intensity as the trolley picked up speed. It was an awesome sight for a little tyke and I purposely looked away for fear of slipping down the opening and being gobbled up by the motors! Downtown Niagara Falls was equally intimidating. In those days, big trucks ran on solid rubber tires and used very heavy chain drives to transfer power from the engine to the rear wheels. The chains made a real racket and sounded something like **ZZZZZ**zzzzz**ZZZZZ**zzzzz**ZZZZZ**zzzzz. There were no safety guards or any other enclosures on the equipment in those days. The solid tires running on the brick streets had their own distinctive sound signature. They could be heard from a great distance.

Sixtieth Street was not paved, and there were no sidewalks or sewers. During rainstorms, I would plead with my Mother to let me go out in the downpours in my bathing suit to splash around in the mud puddles. There were no children around my age to play with for years, so any diversion such as this was great fun. Once a year the road was dug up with a heavy toothed implement attached to the rear of a mechanical roller to eliminate the ruts and potholes, then it was sprayed with diluted asphalt or oil to keep the dust down. In the winter, paths were made along the side of the road by a horse-drawn wood V-plow. I remember one extremely heavy afternoon blizzard on St. Patrick's Day in 1936 when the snow was so deep that men had to shovel the street by hand. There were no ubiquitous mechanical snow movers in those days. When my Dad put me up on the high pile of snow next to our driveway, I could almost reach the power lines!

I went to Evershed Elementary School on Stephenson Avenue in Niagara Falls, New York, when I was not yet five years old. My Mother had to insist that I be admitted to Kindergarten because my birthday was beyond the cutoff date for entrance. The two-story red brick school had very large double-hung windows and was located about four blocks from our house. It seemed like a long way to school, especially when the hay and weeds were taller than I when I took the shortcut through the fields. I have strong recollections of walking through the narrow path in the rain, wearing my yellow rubber rain slicker and boots and being unable to see well because of its hood — like wearing horse blinders. The smell of the rubber and the wet foliage was mixed with the noise made by the stiff garment as I moved and gave me the feeling that it was only my head that was in the shell. It was hot and humid in there, too!

When I grew tall enough, I would climb over the chain link fence that surrounded the school's playground along the alley in back of the school to get into the school yard. This was a forbidden activity, which of course made it a challenge and a lot more fun than entering from the street side. Enough of us did this so often that the chain link fence developed decent toe holds caused by our jamming the toes of our shoes into the links to expand them. The shoes suffered from this a bit, too. The trick was not to get our clothes caught on the sharp, exposed ends of the wire at the top of the fence when we went over it. Getting down was easy — jump! I don't recall the girls doing this, but we did have some daredevils there, too, and I suspect that some did take the challenging way into school, especially to save time if one were almost tardy. You didn't want to be tardy in those days!

I attended Kindergarten through sixth grade at Evershed. Kindergarten was fun — building "houses" out of modular lightweight panels, coloring, listening to the teacher read stories and the like. The activity that I liked best was pasting things on paper. The glue tasted delicious and it was all I could do not to eat it all! The alphabet was displayed in upper and lower case letters in a continuous strip at about seven feet above floor level on the side of the room opposite the big windows. I really didn't see any value in the letters, tried to ignore them (even though I wondered what they were all about), but was eventually "forced" to learn them all in the correct order. For many years I didn't question that order and took it for granted that there was no other way to "say the alphabet." When asked to say the alphabet backwards, kids would turn around and recite it with their backs to you. Then, one day when I was older, a cousin of mine, Donald Frank (the son of one of my Father's sisters, Mae Furry Frank, who lived in Niagara Falls, Ontario, Canada), posed the same challenge and really recited it backwards, from Z to A! That was it; from then on I recited it both ways. My mind was starting to see other possibilities in the routine of the traditional.

One day in Kindergarten the teacher, Mrs. Hurd, introduced the class to freehand drawing using colored crayons. She showed me how to draw packed ovals in purple to represent a bunch of grapes. She varied the color density from dark on the outer edge to light near the center for each grape to make them appear to be three-dimensional. This impressed me greatly and I was hooked on crayon drawing in simulated 3-D. This probably influenced me when I was in high school to take up freehand drawing lessons from Mr. Heinrich Feldman, a very short German Jewish artist who had emigrated from the Black Sea area. My sister took piano lessons from his wife, who was English. Money was very tight, but my Mother scraped up enough cash to pay for our lessons at $1.00 each. Going to the Feldmans for lessons had an advantage in that there was a tiny family grocery store on the corner of their street, and if a nickel or dime were available, we could occasionally liberate a candy bar to munch on the way home. My favorite candy bar was (and still is) Almond Joy. My Mother played the piano and violin and taught my sister how to play the piano, and as her life would later show, Joanne had great artistic talent, too, much, much greater than mine! She was a perfect sister and I loved her dearly. We never had serious disagreements. She married my classmate and best friend in college, David Phillip Dirksen, from Rochester, New York.

We loved dogs!

Joanne and David Dirksen

First grade: Ron in first row, 3rd from right with tie.

Second Grade: Ron in middle row, 4th from left with eyes closed

I taught her to (almost!) drive at a very early age, so early that she could barely reach the brake and gas pedal on an old, secondhand 1939 Ford sedan that my Father drove. I knew how to shift the gears, so I'd start the car in neutral, tell Joanne when to push in the clutch, then I would put it in low gear, and tell her to let the clutch out slowly. After a few stalls, she got pretty good at it. So, with her steering and operating the clutch and brake pedals, we would slowly move back and forth at engine idle speed in our driveway from almost the street up to the garage. My Dad was sitting in the backyard on a lawn chair with his elbows on his knees and his arms crossed watching us. We were doing pretty well until one time heading back toward the garage, Joanne's foot slipped off the clutch pedal when we were getting ready to stop and instead hit the gas pedal! The car lurched forward, Joanne turned the steering wheel to the left, and we collided with the left hand corner of the garage, knocking it off the foundation. The car stalled. Joanne dashed for the house as I got out of the car, went into the garage, brought out a sledge hammer, and pounded the garage sill back into place. There was no visible damage. My Dad didn't move or say a word! He was a very patient man. I still have the sledge hammer in my garage.

The engine in the Ford was starting to produce more smoke than power, and my Dad eventually had to have the engine replaced. The outside of the car was frosty-looking due to the air pollution through which it had suffered over the years, but under the hood it was like an aspiring athlete. He took great pleasure in having someone come up beside him at a stoplight, look over at us in our old jalopy, gun his engine with the clutch in, and then expect to leave us in the dust when the light turned green. That didn't happen! He could use the floor shift like a professional racecar driver and knew just when to change gears. I can still see the wry smile on his face as he cruised down the road ahead of the competition! The nice thing about this car compared with the early models of vehicles was that it had a push button starter. Gone were the bruised arms and an occasional broken bone from hand cranking a recalcitrant engine. Many folks had real choice words to say to a car that wouldn't start. My uncles next-door taught me the language very early! Unfortunately, the cars had no heaters, and the windows would ice up readily on a cold winter's day. My Father installed a rubber bladed fan on the dash to blow air onto the inside of the windshield, but it wasn't very effective. I used to stick my finger into the blades to hear the chattering noise it made. He also found and installed a gasoline heater, but, again, technology was not up to the task and we froze in the car anyway, even if you were in the front seat where the heater was installed under the dash on the passenger's side. I give him a lot of credit for trying.

17

Joanne's 1953 LaSalle High School
Graduation photo.

Her prize-winning oil painting of daisies.

Joanne Louise Furry by Ronald Bay Furry

All Heart! Joanne in 1953

At 19 years old, Joanne (standing on right) taught 3rd and 6th grades at St. John de LaSalle Church, with 39 to 54 students in a class. She had attended Fredonia State Teachers College majoring in education and music until our Father died in 1955, when she left college to attend to our Mother. She was a great teacher. She also taught elementary school and music in Middletown and Monroe, Ohio, schools after she was married, as well as piano privately.

One day I was sitting in third grade class on the right side of the room about half way back and something hit me in the forehead. I didn't see what it was, but the teacher yelled at me. We were learning new words that she had written on the blackboard and I wasn't responding properly. I didn't think anything of it, just another day in school, but my Mother saw it entirely differently when I got home. She said, "What's that on your forehead?", which of course I couldn't see. She had spotted a big splash of chalk dust across my forehead and wanted to know how it got there. I told her that I got hit in the head at school but didn't know with what or why. She grabbed my hand, marched me out of the house and straight up the street where my third grade teacher lived. She had some choice words with the teacher for her action, but a few days later I had glasses and, lo and behold, there were words written on the blackboard that I was now able to see!

A favorite way to get out of class in elementary school was to be good enough to earn a chance to clean the chalk dust out of the blackboard erasers because the lucky person had to go out of the classroom to accomplish the task. I got to do this, but it was no fun! You'd carry an armful of erasers down into the school's low-ceilinged basement, sit on the coal pile and clap them together until the dust was so thick that the only incandescent bulb in the basement was merely a glow in the cloud. And you'd come back covered with chalk dust and some coal dust to boot; shoes were a mess. Being able to breathe normally again would take a couple of minutes; coughing would be gone by the time you got back to class.

19

A good way to get notoriety was to do something forbidden, such as chewing gum in class. Of course, the edict had to be challenged. In sixth grade, my seat was about half way down an outside row next to a wall. I thought that if I kept my head low, I could get away with it — but no luck, the teacher spotted me. My punishment (cleaning erasers would have been appropriate!) was to put the bubble gum on my nose and visit every classroom in the school. My action was to knock on each door, present myself to the class and not say a word. I don't remember anyone laughing, but I'll bet it served as a deterrent to at least a few folks. I can't imagine what would happen today if students were made eraser cleaners and gum exhibitors!

Across the street from the grade school was an empty lot, and next to it was a large, ancient wooden firehouse that had been converted into a bicycle shop. Someone lucky enough to have a quarter could rent a bike and peddle around to his heart's content on Evershed Avenue, which was a paved road. My Father's younger sister, Vivian Furry Taylor, lived in a second-floor apartment next to the bicycle shop for a while. I would occasionally visit her after school and look down from the open porch at the students bustling about. Next to the apartment building was a tiny store that seemed to me to be there for only one purpose — to sell candy to the kids! Bubble gum was a favorite purchase. I didn't go in for the baseball cards that came with the gum — I liked the smell of the bubble gum more than anything else.

Behind these buildings were the multiple mainline railroad tracks that ran through Niagara Falls serving industry and commerce. The passenger station was located in downtown Niagara Falls. There were plenty of tracks to cross, and the only gated crossings that I recall were downtown in the city. In those days, you had to be attentive and keep both your eyes and ears open when you crossed the tracks because you might not hear a train's whistle or see the headlight if the weather wasn't good. One day my Dad and Uncle Bob Brown were down in the center of town and had turned off Buffalo Avenue to head north toward Main Street when our old second-hand 1939 Ford sedan stalled on the tracks. I was in the passenger's seat and looked to my right up the tracks. I thought I saw a faint yellow light in the distance — it was difficult to see a train's headlight in the daytime unless it was close. In a few seconds, it was all too evident that a train was coming toward us. The problem was to determine whether or not it was on the set of tracks where we were stalled. It was. Uncle Bob said, "Better get this thing moving, Buck!" After several unsuccessful attempts to start the engine, my Father put the car in first gear, let out the clutch, then pushed on the starter button. There was enough power left in the battery to slowly inch us off the tracks and out of the train's path. No one said anything as the train clattered by behind us. I marveled at my Father's ingenuity. If we had had an automatic transmission, the result would have been calamitous.

During my primary school years, Catholics were allowed to leave class early on Monday afternoons to attend Religious Education classes. I walked from Evershed Avenue to Buffalo Avenue to board the local bus to go to St. John de LaSalle Roman Catholic Church at 8477 Buffalo Avenue, the same church to which my Mother belonged. The fare was a nickel. About a dozen of us boys met downstairs, sitting in the pews in the church to receive religious instruction from a priest. When we completed our schooling, we received Holy Communion on May 19, 1940, with Father Maurice O'Shea, Pastor (1919–1944), officiating. It was a very warm, sunny day, and all of the children sparkled in their communion outfits; everyone was dressed totally in white, from hair ribbons to shoes. The parish was formed on May 26, 1907, the first in the Village of LaSalle and named after the explorer, St. John Baptist de LaSalle, a 17th-century French priest and educator. I selected the name Paul for my Confirmation name in 1944 because it was the name of my best friend playmate, Paul Holzle. Thus, my full name is Ronald Bay Paul Furry. I had been baptized on Christmas Day 1931 as Ronald Bay Furry.

A Taste of Minorities

My Mother learned that the Bacon Memorial Presbyterian Church on the next street, 59th Street, had a Cub Scout den, and I joined it. The den meetings were held in one of the big attic rooms in the church. I enjoyed the activities greatly and worked hard for my pins and badges, expecting eventually to be a Boy Scout. One day I went to the church, knocked on the meeting room door as usual and waited for the Leader to open it. When he saw me he said, "You can't come here anymore; you're a Catholic." I had no idea what he meant, but I understood that I was different and unwanted. My Mother was devastated. Fast forward to when my own son, Ken, wanted to join a den. He started out in Ames, Iowa, in a group organized by Anne and Marie, another wife of a graduate student in the Hawthorne Apartment complex on the campus of Iowa State

University where I was working on my PhD. Everyone was welcome. Ken is second from the right in the photo. Later, when we returned to Ithaca in 1965, he joined the Boy Scouts, and I joined as an Assistant Scoutmaster, uniform and all. Troop 5 was sponsored by St. Catherine of Sienna Church in the Village of Cayuga Heights, and Monsignor Father Donald Cleary made it known that everyone would be welcome. Father Cleary had arrived on the Cornell campus in 1936, overseeing the Cornell community as chaplain for 25 years. Under his leadership Cornell's Newman Club grew to be the largest in the United States. He was a terrific man. The scouts' fathers of Troop 5 had developed such a close relationship that I stayed on as Assistant

Scoutmaster for several years after Ken left! We used the church hall for spaghetti dinner fundraisers for the Troop, as well as the regular Monday meetings at 6:30 PM, and stored some of the troop paraphernalia there, too.

Close Calls

Playing cowboys and Indians was a favorite pastime in my day and it seemed as though every kid had a toy pistol or a bow and arrow set. I especially liked the toy revolvers that fired caps to make noise. The smoke smelled good, too. But the toy guns weren't nearly as dangerous as the bow and arrow sets. A friend of mine, Jackie Webber, who lived on the next street, and I both happened to have long bow and arrow sets at the same time. These weren't the toy rubber tipped arrows, they were metal tipped, and the bows took a real effort to pull. We would practice target shooting at the covers of bushel baskets, which were plentiful because they were widely used in selling agricultural products. We soon made a mess of available basket lids, splintering them to pieces because of the metal tips on the arrows. We decided to try a more interesting skill game, one that involved a large distance and a small target, sort of like today's ballistic missile problem. My friend lived two lots over and one lot back from my yard, and we could not see each other from our own backyards. The target in each of our yards was an old bushel basket lid. We took turns firing the arrows high into the air, over the trees and yards to see who could come the closest to hitting a basket lid. We would shout back how close the arrow came to the target. One arrow he fired landed about three feet from the lid in my yard and our accuracy was improving. It finally dawned on us that this was not exactly a safe game, so we reluctantly quit. We could have easily been severely hurt, or killed. I put the bow away, and still have it.

I've had a few traffic near misses, too, in my life. The first that I can recall was in my early teens when I was visiting my best friend, Paul Holzle, who lived on the next street, 61st. It was winter and snow was falling; plows had piled snow up along the roadsides several times, and the roads were covered with hard packed snow and ice. We decided to go to the corner of the next block, 62nd, to get a comic book – riding on bicycles! I was wary of the action, but followed Paul down the street in the snow and around the corner moving east against the traffic on Buffalo Avenue. The borrowed bike I was riding had a crooked pedal and was difficult to keep in a steady motion. I looked down just in time to see a finger of ice sticking out from the hard packed plow residue on the left and felt the bike tire slide off toward the road. The next thing I saw was the tire treads of the right front tire of a car three inches from my nose. My head was lying on the road under the car beyond the bumper. Not a good place to be. I scrambled to my feet, got back on the bike and went on. I have a feeling that the woman driving the car was greatly relieved, as was I. Paul had no idea what had transpired.

I've also had good fortune in bad weather circumstances. Once in going to Cornell with my Dad in his 1949 Nash Rambler, the car lost traction on an icy patch on the old lake road at the top of Seneca Lake, swinging the rear end to the right and sliding the car broadside down the road and into a big snow bank on the opposite side of the road. It was after we backed the car out of the snow bank and were ready to move on that we noticed that the same thing had happened to a truck carrying a load of steel; unfortunately, the driver's luck had run out and the rig had hit a tree and the steel had moved forward, crushing the cab. I had a similar skid on an Extension trip to the North Country in 1957 in a bad snow storm on a dark and very windy night. Again, no traffic opposed me. Virtually all of my Extension trips around the State involved meetings after a full day's work in the field making farm visits, so nighttime driving from one county to another was common, summer and winter. My last (and final!) broadside skid across lanes occurred on Cayuga Heights Road in the Village of Cayuga Heights after a heavy snow storm that left an icy patch at a shaded spot on a curve. This time it was a second-hand Saab that was involved, and Donna was my passenger. We came nearly around the full curve going sideways and then straightened out just as though that was the normal way to take it! In those days, the speed limit on highways was 50 mph, and 30 mph in villages, but bad weather cut travel speed down considerably from those limits. And lots of potholes made it even slower going!

On to Cornell

I graduated third in my class with a Regents College Entrance Diploma from LaSalle High School, located on Buffalo Avenue in the LaSalle section of Niagara Falls, New York on June 27, 1949. Our class was the 15th to be graduated from the school. We top three had our averages calculated to the nearest thousandth of a percent to be able to separate us by rank. I was one of 18 in a class of 147 that graduated with an Honor Diploma and was simultaneously a member of the National Honor Society for the full 3 years of high school, receiving an Honor Pin. I earned 4 Units in Sciences, 2 in Latin, 3 in English, 2 in Social Studies, 3 in Mathematics, and 2 in German. I was the only graduate to earn honors in six different subject matter areas. I was also awarded the RPI medal for excellence in science. I was President of the Delta Omega Hi-Y Fraternity, President of the Forum debating society, Associate Editor of the *Ongiara* (our Class of 1949 yearbook), Treasurer of the National Honor Society, a member of Key Club International (Junior Kiwanis), a gym leader, a swim leader, and a member of the track team, bowling team, and Graduation and Interclub Council Committees, Secretary of the Catholic Youth Council of St. John's de LaSalle Church and Treasurer of the Junior Holy Name Society. I also took ballroom dancing from professionals and loved twirling in the waltz! I was one of four seniors selected as "outstanding citizens" by fellow students to participate in the competitive Citizenship Education Conference at Syracuse University, involving 650 students from 250 high schools. As Associate Editor of our yearbook, I decided to contact retired General Dwight D. Eisenhower, who at that time was President of Columbia University, for a Dedication statement, and wrote the Yearbook Theme. He was the first President for whom I voted in November 1952. My neighbor, Dorothy Webber, was the Class Valedictorian and Beverley Bates was the Salutatorian. Our Class Motto was *"Rugged Strength and Radiant Beauty – These were one of Nature's plans; Humble toil and heavenward duty – These will form the perfect man."* The Class Colors were Scarlet and Grey. The Class Flower was the Tea Rose. Our Faculty Advisor was Miss Alice Schelosky, who was the German teacher. The Principal was Elton C. Schwinger. I was voted the one Most Likely to Succeed by my classmates. I loved high school, and knew everyone in our class. I still correspond with some of them by email. We held class reunions every five years through our 60th reunion year, 2009. One year we even held a 2 ½ year reunion in Sarasota, Florida; Niagara Falls was deemed too cold for a mid-term reunion location, and a change of scenery was in order!

The LaSalle High School Class of 1949 and their spouses at their 60th and last reunion in Niagara Falls in 2014. Anne, 3rd from left in first row, with Ron in light blue jacket standing behind her.

The Cornell University Class of 1953 and their spouses at its 65th reunion on campus in Ithaca, New York, in 2018. Ron and Anne at extreme right, standing. Yep, same blue jacket as in photo above!

Dedication

"America was born in rebellion, and rebellion against wrong and injustice is imbedded in the American temper. But whatever change our rebels of the American past may have sought, they were quick to proclaim it openly and fearlessly, preaching it from the house - tops. We need their sort,...informed, intelligent rebels against ignorance and imperfection and prejudice. But because they have sought the truth and know it, they will be loyal to the American way, to the democracy within which we live. They will never tire of seeking its advancement, however viciously they may be attacked by those content with the status quo."

Dwight D. Eisenhower

Theme

America's destiny depends upon the development of the potential powers of the modern teen-ager. Through the development of these capabilities we must obtain the leaders of tomorrow whose responsibility it shall be to advance the American heritage. Recognizing that we must not fail, we consider it fitting to design the theme of this yearbook around the modern teen-ager. It is with the utmost sincerity that we say we shall not fail in proving our ability.

Ronald B. Furry

2

LaSalle High School

This photo shows LaSalle high School on Buffalo Avenue in Niagara Falls, New York. The Niagara River was just across the street. A movie theater was next door on the right. I used to go to the movies there for 10 cents well before I went to high school. Theaters then showed a short movie (a "Short"), followed by a cartoon, then a newsreel if available, and finally the main film. Virtually all films at that time were in black and white. On Saturdays, the big attraction was the continuing serials of favorite protagonists. We watched the Lone Ranger, Flash Gordon, Buck Rogers and others. The hero would always be put in dire danger at the very end of the episode, only to be saved at the beginning of the next one by some overly simple escape technique! And the theaters would stop the movie at some point and call out a ticket stub number to have a member of the audience come up on the stage for some event. My number was called once, and I went on stage to be a contestant in a quiz. The MC asked me, "How much wood could a woodchuck chuck, if a woodchuck could chuck wood." Darned if I knew, but I answered, "As much as his tummy could hold." Not the correct answer, but it was deemed to be unique and I was given a prize of a quarter! That was big money in those days. On another occasion, I was in the audience when the title for the movie *Frenchman's Creek* came on the screen. I laughed my head off because they had misspelled Crick! Now in my neck of the woods, everyone knew what a crick was, even if it was spelled creek, and I hadn't seen it spelled out before. Why, even my Grandfather had a crick in his back yard that I knew very well. I saw my very first color movie, *Snow White and the Seven Dwarfs*, in 1938. I was enthralled by it and sat on the very edge of my seat through the whole thing! An interesting fact about movie theaters in those days was that 50 Hertz (cycles per second) power was used, and I could actually see the incandescent lights dim and re-brighten whenever I went into the dark lounge area. I also remember the power company changing all of the electric motors in our home when the switch was made to 60 Hertz power. Both 50 and 60 Hertz power are still used today; Japan uses both frequencies. You'd want to make sure that you bought an electric clock that operated on the correct frequency to assure you were on time because the power supplier's frequency is used to keep the clock accurate to within a few seconds. Also, without Time Error Correction (TEC) by the utilities, an electric clock would be off by several minutes until manually reset. What a pain!

In 1948, I was selected to be the Chairman of the Soviet Delegation in a model United Nations assembly, convened at the State Teachers' College in Buffalo, NY. The assembly included 145 students from 35 schools, representing 35 nations in the UN. I had three committeemen representing economic and finance, political and security, and regionalism sectors. Each delegation had to assume completely the policies of the nation that they represented. Our USSR delegation met with the satellite countries of the Soviet Block to formulate procedural plans. Important issues included the North Atlantic security pact, control of atomic energy, and the admittance of Spain to the UN. As the Soviet Delegation, we successfully stated our viewpoints and delayed action on these problems. As a final representation of how the Soviet Delegation acted in those days, I gave an explosive anti-western speech on the floor, and then walked out of the meeting with my delegation and the Soviet Bloc! And it seems as though nothing has changed much! As President of the Delta Omega Hi-Y, I was also a delegate to the National Hi-Y Convention that met in the New York State Senate Chambers in Albany, NY. We stayed at the

Wellington, Albany's only "Garage-In" hotel at the time, but I didn't have a car! As a member of the Key Club, I was a delegate to the Sixth Annual Convention of Key Club International, March 25-26, 1949, staying at the Hotel Annapolis on 11th to 12th and H Streets, N.W., in Washington 5, DC. This hotel boasted that it had "400 Rooms with Bath and Radio"! Having grown tired of dropping water filled balloons on people from the upper stories of the hotel, we wanted to do some sightseeing, but lacked transportation, so we took a $12.00 tour of the city, but it was a rip-off. The next option was to rent a car; however, we were underage! Nevertheless, one of us was able to convince the car rental service that he was an experienced driver and he was just about to have a birthday. So, off we went with maps and guide pamphlets to see Arlington Cemetery, George Washington's tomb and plantation at Mount Vernon, and other sites, such as the presidential memorials and the Smithsonian Institution. I remember the big change from Niagara Falls – very warm, humid and lots of different smells in the south.

Hotel Marilyn   Ithaca, N. Y.

The Niagara River was just across the street from the high school; I usually walked the mile or so to the high school, but my Dad would occasionally give me a ride if he got home early enough from working the night shift. There were no school buses in those days. I had received a $350.00 per year competitive New York State (Cash) University Scholarship, and in late July decided to apply to Cornell University in Ithaca, New York. I was accepted, and in September, 1949, my Father drove me to Ithaca in his green 1949 Nash to enroll in Cornell. (The car's shape resembled a beetle and its gears could be shifted without using the clutch by letting the engine idle down and then moving the gear shift on the steering column. This action was not always perfect, and occasionally the gears would clash, which made the maneuver a bit anxiety ridden at times!) We arrived just one day before the dormitories opened, and stayed overnight at the Marilyn Hotel, which was located on the northeast corner of Aurora Street at the intersection with State Street. It was very hot that night and the window was open to the street noise; I didn't get much rest. The next morning, I moved into a small, worn out single-story army barracks that was being used for male student housing on the south end of West Avenue on the Cornell campus. My roommate and his Father arrived at our dorm room only minutes after my Father and I had deposited all of my possessions, contained in one small foot locker, in the room. My roommate was John Chin from New York City. His Father did not speak English. This was a real introduction to a new racial group for me, because I had never seen a Chinese person when I was growing up in Niagara Falls. The world up to that time had been all black and white to me, and predominantly white. He was as smart as a whip and was majoring in Engineering Physics. My Dad had to get back to Niagara Falls, which took about five to six hours in good weather at that time because there were no good interconnecting roads; the New York

State Thruway had not been built and the State speed limit was 50 mph. Travel was more stop than go sometimes because of all the little towns and villages on the route. I rode to the west end of State Street with him where the sidewalk ended, said goodbye, got out of the car and walked all the way back to the dormitory. I think I stopped crying about the time that I started uphill to the campus. This was the first time I had ever been really on my own in a strange setting. I had a few dollars in cash in my wallet that would have to go a long way. I was the first in our family line to go to college. John Chin did not graduate from Cornell due to an illness, but later enrolled in the University of Illinois. He became a lifelong friend, and later, when I was married, he and his wife, Jade, travelled together with us overseas.

My freshman year was both good and not so good. I achieved the highest average of my four years, but in the Fall Semester I contracted an ear infection from taking the swimming test in the Cornell pool and had 19 massive injections of penicillin in my buttocks; the medicine was not as effective as that used today. The infection prevented me from opening my jaw and all I could eat was liquids, mostly tea. I got so thin that when I went to lectures I had to put my left hand under me because there was not enough fat and muscle to cushion me against the wood seats. Eventually, I was sent to an ear doctor downtown in Ithaca for a procedure that involved draining the Eustachian tube. This involved holding a small amount of water in my mouth until he said swallow, upon which he injected air through my nose and simultaneously tossed a weighted dart, through a stainless steel cone shaped funnel as a guide, having a sharp pointed end into my right ear to pierce the ear drum and blow the infection out. The water blocked the air from going into my lungs. I remember seeing the overhead light bulb dim as I went unconscious from the shock. When I woke up, I was soaking wet from head to foot with sweat! On my walk across Ithaca and back up the hill to my dormitory, I could hear the air whistling in and out through my ear drum. It healed fine, but the penicillin injections made the palms of my hands and the soles of my feet crack and bleed. I was given sulfa drugs for that problem. In spite of this, I had an extremely high academic average that year. Maybe the Penicillin helped!

Exploring the Environs

Ithaca was a new experience for me, as it probably was for most students, and exploring the environs was a favorite pastime. In the warm fall weather of my freshman year, my roommate, John Chin, and I decided to have a close look at the Fall Creek Gorge along Thurston Avenue on the north side of the campus. We found the path to Cornell's old hydroelectric plant and descended into the gorge floor in the early afternoon. The water level was low, so moving west picking our way along the north shore was easy. We didn't even get our feet wet. Looking up at the gorge rim and marveling at the geology of the gorge occupied more time than we expected, and we suddenly became aware of the fact that it gets dark at the bottom of the gorge rather quickly as the sun sets. We knew we had to find a way out fast and couldn't go back to our entry point, so went downstream to the area under the Stewart Avenue Bridge. John spotted a drain pipe that ran from the Stewart Avenue street level to the bottom of the gorge, and we mounted the pipe and shinnied up to the street. This was tough work! The pipe angle was steep and the diameter made holding on tricky. By the time we reached the top we were a sweaty mess with scuffed up legs; it was dark and the street lights had come on. This was our first venture to this part of the campus, and we had no knowledge at that time of the fact that a short distance ahead lay Ithaca Falls and a point of no return!

Ithaca Falls with Stewart Avenue Bridge in upper right quadrant. The falls are 150 feet high and 175 feet wide.

John Chin had an adventurous bent and was always willing to try something new. We were initiated into Company B Eighth Regiment of the National Honorary Military Society of Pershing Rifles together and performed on the Trick Drill Team in inter-college drill competitions. While practicing our Queen Anne's rifle drills, our M1's flew apart from twirling the rifle with a finger in the finger guard, so we switched to WW1 rifles for the trick drill routines. In the spring of 1950, we went on maneuvers on Mount Pleasant and were "killed" by an "enemy" in the dark of night. The "enemy" discharged an M1 right near our heads and our ears rang for hours! We had to sit out the rest of the maneuvers in the dark in an abandoned shack on the top of the mountain. We returned to our headquarters in Barton Hall on campus in the deep of night and were greeted by a machine gun shooting blanks at us as we entered the building. So much for friendly fire!

Later, on a trip to see Taughannock Falls, John wanted to see it from the top as well as the bottom of the gorge, so we hiked up the road to the observation area. Still not satisfied with the view, he decided that we should walk up the road far enough to find the falls' precipice and go down to the creek level at the top of the falls. The area between the road and the gorge is covered with bushes and trees, and locating the precipice limit was not possible by sight. He decided that we had gone far enough, left the road, and headed down to the creek. It was dark in the wooded area, and the terrain suddenly steepened, eventually causing us to run. Suddenly, John yelled, "Ron!" and I saw him grab a tree, so I did the same. I swung around the tree to find that my right leg was out in open air over the edge of the gorge! That was enough for me — we crawled back up the hill to the road, and said nothing! At 215 feet, Taughannock Falls is the highest falls east of the Rocky Mountains, taller than Niagara Falls at 170 feet. I've never sat on the crest of Taughannock Falls like some folks do when the creek feeding it dries up, but I did walk along the crest of the American Falls in 1969 when a huge cofferdam was built to divert the water so that an inspection could be made of the rock layers for possible faults. It took 1,264 trucks dumping nearly 28,000 tons of rocky fill into a cofferdam upstream of the falls to stop the flow, permitting the US Army Corps of Engineers to begin their investigation. The dry American Falls caused an increase in tourism on the American side and a decrease on the Canadian side; one weekend a total of 89,790 people visited the American park near the dry falls. Water returned to the falls four and a half months later.

The author (rear) with student friends Bob Dellers (left), John Kleske and Harry Homola at the entrance to the West Avenue barracks dormitory in Fall Semester 1949 while John Chin takes our photograph.

My roommate, John Chin, with Butch in NY City on February 5, 1950

Taughannock Falls is located on the West Side of Cayuga Lake.

At the end of the first semester of my freshman year, I took a couple of my classmates, including John Chin, home to visit my folks and show them the Niagara Falls cataract. We started out from Ithaca with blue skies, a blazing yellow sun and a gorgeous white environment following a windy, bone-chilling snowstorm the day before. I drove up Route 96 with no problems and clear roads. When we reached the level topography between the lakes, there were no snow drifts and the road was absolutely clear. But, the car started to slow down and I noticed that the speedometer hadn't! So, I stopped the car in the center of the road and we all stepped out onto the black pavement – and the wind blew us right across the road into the snow drifts! The road was clear all right, but it was covered with a very thick layer of perfectly clear ice. No wonder we hadn't seen any traffic! Fortunately, there was a set of tire chains in the trunk, and with much slipping and sliding around the car we installed them and went on our way, much slower and with a lot of chain noise. I know that I used a few monkey links for the rear chains to repair breaks before we reached my home in Niagara Falls. The next day, I took my classmates downtown to see the cataract. It was bright and sunny, and we went down the elevator on the American side so that we could walk along the shore up to the falls. It was cold and the wind was blowing mist high into the air, landing on us. The mist froze on our heads, until we looked like we were wearing white football helmets! The ice layers on our heads were over a half inch thick. We made a hasty trip to the elevator and warmed up to the drip of our melting ice caps. Viewing the cataract from above at a different location, such as Goat Island, made more sense to us by then. Of course, I related the stories of people who had gone over the falls intentionally and not intentionally, and of Jean Francois Gravelet, known as "The Great Blondin," who walked across the gorge on a tight rope and stopped in the middle to cook an omelet, among other antics, above the gorge. People have used barrels, boats, tightropes and even swimming and an airplane in their stunts. The first stunt was performed in 1859 by Blondin; the last on June 15, 2012, by Nik Wallenda, who had to show his passport when he reached the Canadian side on his tight rope. I've been to the museum across the border in Canada that exhibits some of the contraptions used. It is estimated that 5,000 people have died going over the falls, including some of the less fortunate stunters, accidental victims and those committing suicide. On Saturday, July 9, 1960, 7-year-old Roger Woodward became the first person to survive a drop over the falls wearing only a life jacket, and was picked up by the Maid of the Mist II. His 17-year-old sister was saved at the brink by tourists on the shore, but their motorboat operator perished. The crescent falls is 170 feet high, and the water is 170 feet deep just below the falls. The rapids in the gorge below the falls, the Lower Niagara River, have attracted many daredevils as well. My uncles used to fish at night with spears and lamps in the gorge; there are ten species of fish in the lower Niagara River. When Joanne and I were kids, we were told of the Devil's Hole Massacre on September 14, 1763, when Seneca Indians, who resented Europeans taking over their territory, ambushed a wagon train at the Devil's Hole along the gorge trail. With only one warrior of the 309 in the fight being wounded, the Indians killed most of the wagon train party and 81 British soldiers who attempted to come to their rescue. Many of the wagon train party, as well as wagons and horses, were forced over the edge into the deep ravine. Getting down to the river from above required caution because of the steep terrain and rocks. I think that in our first venture there we fully expected to see skeletons that had been left behind. Young imaginations can run pretty wild!

The Great Depression

I was born in 1931, so I witnessed the trials and tribulations of the Great Depression and its aftermath. My Dad worked three jobs ceaselessly. He painted houses, and did horticultural and carpentry work when he wasn't working at the Mathieson Alkali Works, which merged into Olin Mathieson Chemical Corp. in 1954, manufacturing chlorine gas from salt (brine). He eventually became a Superintendent at the plant. (Olin Hall on the Cornell campus was given by Franklin W. Olin, Class of 1886, in memory of his son, Franklin Jr.) By 1939, he was earning $1,612.00 a year. He worked shift work because it paid 5 cents an hour more than regular day work and gave him more daylight time for his other jobs. It was a difficult time, paying off a mortgage of $52.00 a month ($624.00 per year); but they didn't lose their home to foreclosure like many folks did during the Great Depression. In addition, we raised our own fruit, vegetables, chickens and rabbits. I had lots of eggnogs. I love eggnogs! An orange from Florida was a real treat in those days, usually given to us at Christmas time. The occurrence of my Father's promotion to Superintendant in 1948 meant that we had to have a phone because he was on call 24 hours a day. So, we got a party line phone. There were four customers on the same line; each assigned a different ring signal. You had to listen carefully to see if your signal was being rung. There was no privacy, and they lent themselves to great gossip. People would wait

New Telephone Rates
(EFFECTIVE OCTOBER 1, 1959)

	MONTHLY RATES
BUSINESS PRIVATE LINE	$7.40
BUSINESS 2-PARTY LINE	6.20
BUSINESS RURAL LINE	5.20
BUSINESS EXTENSION	1.50
RESIDENCE PRIVATE LINE	$4.40
RESIDENCE 2-PARTY LINE	3.80
RESIDENCE 4-PARTY LINE	3.25
RESIDENCE RURAL LINE	3.25
RESIDENCE EXTENSION	1.00

The above rates do not include Federal Excise Tax of 10%. These are the most common rates and anyone desiring the rates for other services may call our business office.

Due to the fact that the rates were approved late in the month, October's telephone bills will be mailed a few days later than usual.

Bremen Telephone Corporation

until the party being called would pick up the phone, then they would do likewise and listen in on the conversation. Each time a new listener was added the volume went down; if every party member was on the line, the conversation would be almost indecipherable. When it got too bad, you had to tell people to "Get off the line!" Some would, others would just keep on listening — you could hear them breathing! Party lines started in 1878. Most subscribers were party line users in the middle of the Twentieth Century, but party lines were abandoned by the 1980s due to technological advances that couldn't be supported on them. Our telephone number was Bu3-4173. I still remember some friends' phone numbers; area codes were introduced by AT&T in 1947 but had not reached us. A buck was a hard earned buck, and subscribing to telephone service was a luxury then because it took money away from some other family need. When something was no longer used, it was usually passed on or sold. My

Mother sold my baby carriage for $3.00 during the Depression. She had to find another one when my sister, Joanne, was born three years later in 1934; the money was more important than an empty baby carriage waiting for the next infant. In those days babies were "aired" in the outdoors, and I can vividly remember lying in this baby carriage parked on the front lawn. My Grandmother had a German Shepherd that used to lie down next to the carriage. I recall him putting his paws up on the side of the carriage and looking in at me. I guess he wanted to see what he was guarding! I love German Shepherd dogs. When the carriage was oriented so that the sun came into my eyes, I just shut them and waited for my Mother to take me inside. I didn't like the confining closeness of the inside of the dark carriage; I preferred the outdoors but I was not able to protest!

Prices were pretty low, but expensive when compared to folks' incomes. Here are a few examples for 1931 when I was born, 1941 the year before WW2, 1949 when I graduated from high school, and 1953 when I graduated from Cornell and Anne and I came to Ithaca to live. My starting salary was $3,550.00 per year paid bi-monthly over nine months. It was very difficult making ends meet.

Item	1931	1941	1949	1953
Average income, per year	$1,858.00	$1,777.00	$2,959.00	$4,011.00
New car	$640.00	$850.00	$1,420.00	$1,651.00
Gasoline	10 cents/gal.	12	26	29
New house	$6,796.00	$4,075.00	$7,450.00	$17,500.00
Rent	$18.00/month	$20.00	$42.00	$100.00
US 1st class postage stamp	2 cents	2	3	3
Sugar	5 ½ cents/lb.	6	10	9
Bread	8 cents/loaf	8	15	16
Bacon	25 cents/lb.	34	66	73
Milk	45 cents/gal.	54	84	94
Eggs	16 cents/doz.	40	69	72
Hamburger	11 cents/lb.	26	51	39
Ground Coffee	33 cents/lb.	24	55	91
Stock Market Index	78	121	179	276
Life Expectancy	60 years	63	63	68

It's easy to see that my parents were not going to get rich selling eggs, and that if it took about half of your income to buy a new car, you were going to use an old jalopy instead. My folks never had a new car. Even their last car, the Nash, was a used demonstrator. Prices started to rise sharply starting in 1941 due to the outbreak of war in Europe in 1939. They were very loving parents and always placed us first in their minds, hearts, and actions. Both were great practical teachers, steadfast workers and wonderful conversationalists. One day, Joanne and I decided to buy our Mother a gift of appreciation for a trip that our Aunt Helena Brown made with us to Port Colborne, Ontario, but we had only 25 cents between us. We searched and searched the stores for something appropriate and finally came upon a wall plaque for the kitchen that

HERE'S TO THE ONE WHO WORKS ALL DAY WITH POTS AND PANS AND GRIN SO GAY. WHO KNEADS THE DOUGH, AND COOKS THE FAT TO CONJURE UP FROM THIS AND THAT, A SCRUMPTIOUS CAKE, A TASTY STEW.... I TAKE MY HAT OFF, COOK, TO YOU!

seemed to say it all. This plaque stayed in her sight on her kitchen wall from July 26, 1945 to her death in 1985. She gave us all we ever needed and much more. I have a few items of memorabilia that I have saved over the years that keep me in touch with my family. One that keeps me close to my sister is that wall plaque. For my Father, it's some of his old tools and a green alcohol-in-glass thermometer that is now nearly 90 years old. For my Mother it is a few pieces of her Depression glass, especially her cookie jar! For my parents jointly, it's their mantle clock that was given to them in 1929 as a wedding present from their parents. I still wind it weekly and listen for its chimes, especially when I wake at night and want to know the hour without moving in bed! It chimes on the hour and half hour, but there are six times in a 24 hour period when you can't tell the time if it chimes and you only use your ears. Can you tell what they are?

Here are some of the memorabilia, still serving their intended purposes in our home.

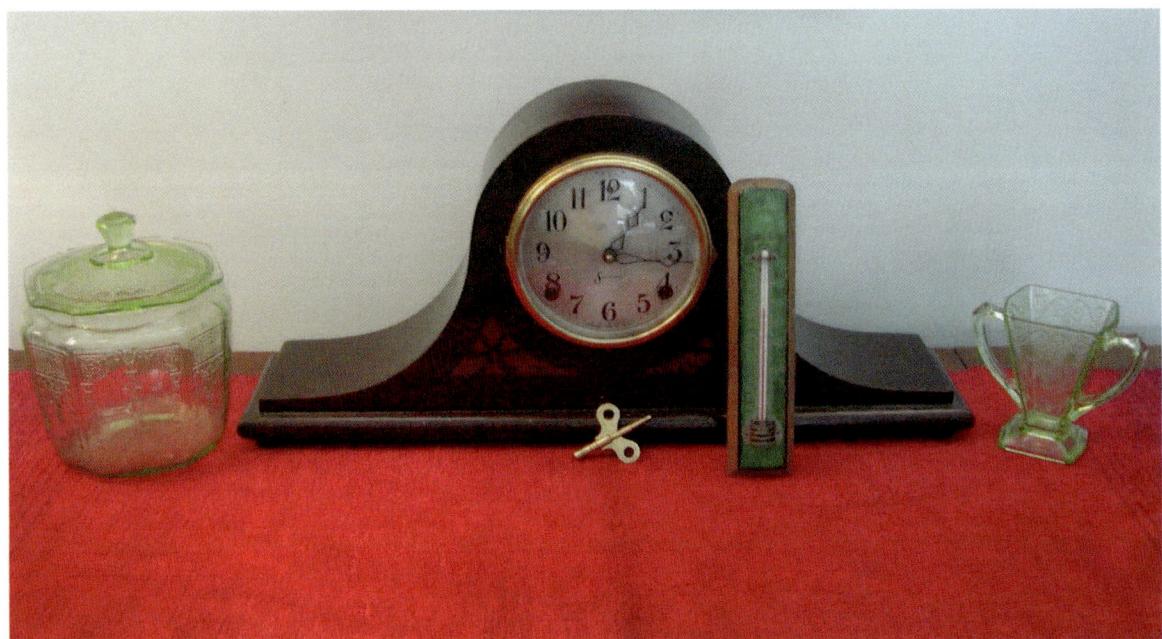

A cookie jar, wind-up mantle clock, thermometer and sugar bowl, all well-used by my family.

The Cradle

A cradle purchased in the 19th century has had a remarkable journey through time and is still in possession of descendants of the Brown family. As of this writing, it is at the home of David and Mary Beth Dirksen in Monroe, Ohio. Their two children are currently the last in the series of those who slept in it in their early childhood. The underside of the base of the cradle still shows part of the original furniture manufacturer's stencil in black letters. To reveal the original wood grain, I had the cradle refinished in 1981 to remove several layers of cherry stain that had been added over the years. In 2007, I wrote an illustrated 11-page booklet titled *THE Brown's ANTIQUE CRADLE—Nineteenth Century*, showing all of the parts and giving instructions on how to assemble and use it. David Dirksen has a copy of it. I hope the cradle survives for a few more generations!

| Me at 7 Months | At 9 Months | First Portrait | First Hot Rod |

The cradle has a unique construction that allows it to be operated without touching it. The cradle can be rocked from a standing, sitting or lying in bed position by gently pulling on a cord (see left front of cradle in the photos) to release latches on the foot board, then gently tugging on the cord to rock the cradle. There is a cord on each side of the cradle. To latch the cradle automatically, simply release the tension on the cord. <u>Warning:</u> The individual rocking the cradle may fall asleep before the baby!

<u>Those Who Slept in the Cradle</u>

1. <u>All of the following children lived in Ebenezer, New York</u>

Arthur (Brown) Witzig
Frank   "   Witzig
Edith   "   Witzig

All are Aunt Phoebe Brown's children.
Phoebe was Edna Louise Brown Furry's Father's sister.
Phoebe gave the cradle to Edna's Father, Arthur Henry Brown,
who was born on March 4, 1871, and died on September 29, 1938.

(See the section titled "Genealogy: The Brown Connection"
for information on family relationships.)

2. <u>All of the following children lived in Niagara Falls, New York</u>

<u>Catherine Eucheria Doeseckle and Arthur Henry Brown's Children</u>

John F. Brown (b. 1/8/1898, d. 11/20/1960)
Charles Roessler Brown (b. 1899, d. 1908)
Edna Louise Brown (Furry) (b. 2/14/1902, d. 7/25/1984)
Florence K. Brown (b. 3/14/1904, d. 5/16/1971)
Margaret Brown (b. 1/13/1906, d. 3/13/1931) — Margaret died
the same year that Ronald Bay Furry was born (10/22/1931).
Arthur William (Bill) Brown (b. 5/1/1908, d. 8/27/1981)
Robert Raymond (Bob) Brown (b. 6/29/1910, d. 3/11/1985)

Edna Louise Brown and Wesley Bay Furry's Children

Ronald Bay Furry — born October 22, 1931
Joanne Louise Furry Dirksen – (b. 10/26/34, d. 4/21/2015)

<u>Helen Blum and Arthur William Brown's Children</u>

Salinas Catherine Brown Manville — born November 6, 1946
Sharon Emma Brown Campione — born January 30, 1949

3. <u>Suzanne Lynne Furry and Lloyd Paul Irish's Daughter
in Burlington, Vermont</u>

Ginger Pearl Furry-Irish — born November 3, 1981

4. <u>David and Mary Beth Dirksen's Children
In Monroe, Ohio</u>

Benjamin David Dirksen — born April 4, 2007
Katherine Elizabeth Dirksen — born January 31, 2011

I also have the crib that I and my sister slept in when we were babies. It has Humpty Dumpty painted on the inside of the headboard with a castle, a wall and the King's Men, and at the other end there is a painting of a multicolored toy train and a Teddy bear. A latch allows one side of the crib to be lowered for easy access to the infant. In spite of the fact that the latch is below the mattress and springs on the outside of the crib, I learned to reach through the bars and feel around until my hand found the lever and unlatch the side. Then I would crawl over the lowered gate and slowly let myself down to the floor. The first time I accomplished this it drew a wide mouthed surprise from my Mother when I padded out to the living room. I don't know whether she was happy to see what I had accomplished or knew she now had a problem on her hands!

The disassembled crib, showing the Humpty Dumpty painting on the left
and the multicolored train and Teddy bear on the right

World War 2

I vividly remember the day that the Japanese attacked Pearl Harbor, December 7, 1941. The weather was mild for early December, and my Father and I were outside cleaning up the garden. Our neighbor, Melvin Olson, came over to talk to my Dad, and within a couple of minutes, his son Jack burst out of his house and leaped off the terrace shouting, "Dad, Dad! The Japs have bombed Pearl Harbor!" I had never heard of Pearl Harbor, let alone knew its significance, but I would spend a great deal of time for the rest of my life learning about both the European and the Pacific wars. Our worry in WW2 was being bombed by the German Luftwaffe because of our (then) industrial might located in Niagara Falls, New York, where there was abundant electric power for heavy industry and chemical factories. Germany had developed designs for an Amerika Bomber with a range of 9,500 miles that first flew in 1942. The prototypes built were the Messerschmitt Me 264, and in 1943 the Junkers Ju 390, also known as "The New York Bomber." Intended targets ranged from New York City to a variety of industrial sites in the eastern United States. The payload was to include conventional munitions and the atomic bomb that the Germans were trying to develop.

Me 264 in Flight   Ju 390 in Flight

My two closest uncles, Arthur William (Bill) Brown (1908–1981) and Robert (Bob) Raymond Brown (1910–1985), from Niagara Falls, New York entered the US Army at different times, served in different units and were both sent to fight in the South Pacific during World War 2. Bill was drafted on July 4, 1942. Bob tried to enlist, but was refused by the Niagara Falls Draft Board because he was the last living son of his widowed Mother. He then attempted to enlist in Buffalo, New York, but was refused for the same reason. Bob then joined the National Guard, which was subsequently activated, and entered service on June 2, 1943.

Both men were experienced in construction work in the chemical and other industries located in Niagara Falls, New York, where electric power was abundant because of the Niagara River and the electric power generating plants (e.g., the Schoellkopf Power Plant) that used its water. Both were experienced outdoorsmen, hunters and fishermen, and were very familiar with the Niagara River and its deep gorge. Their final military assignments in the South West Pacific Area fit their technical backgrounds very well, where…

Bill served in the…   1571st Engineer Heavy Shop Company
                          563D Engineer Boat Maintenance Battalion
                          3D Engineer Special Brigade
                          APO 920
Bob served in…   Company C
                          865th Engineering Aviation Battalion
                          APO 322

In brief, Bill supported amphibious operations (Seabees), and Bob, air operations. Both saw action in engagements with Japanese forces. In one incident, Bob spent 29 days lying on his stomach in the jungle muck with nothing to eat except an occasional fallen coconut until his unit was rescued; as a result of this experience he developed an ulcerated bacterial jungle rot disease that nearly caused the loss of both legs while in New Guinea and plagued him for the rest of his life. He was awarded the Bronze Star for "heroic or meritorious achievement of service in a combat zone." Bill's unit was nearly overrun one night by the Japanese, who had infiltrated their perimeter and turned the Americans' own machine guns on them. Neither brother knew that the other was in New Guinea. They had not seen each other for 16 months, but in January 1944, in the jungles of New Guinea, they learned that they were just 30 miles apart. Bob travelled by foot and barge along the coast to Bill's unit for a joyful reunion.

They would not see very much of each other until returning to the US mainland at the end of the war, even though they eventually were located only about a mile apart. Bob had to be hospitalized because of the severity of his jungle rot.

The island of New Guinea was strategically important because it was a major landmass to the immediate north of Australia, and its large land area provided locations for large land, naval and air bases. Of the many types of airplanes in combat in New Guinea, the P38 fighter was perhaps the most visually unusual. It is said that it essentially consisted of two P51s with the pilot's cockpit and the planes' armament in between. It would provide an interesting model for soldier "craftsmen."

Lockheed P-38 Fighter

A line of P-38 Fighters

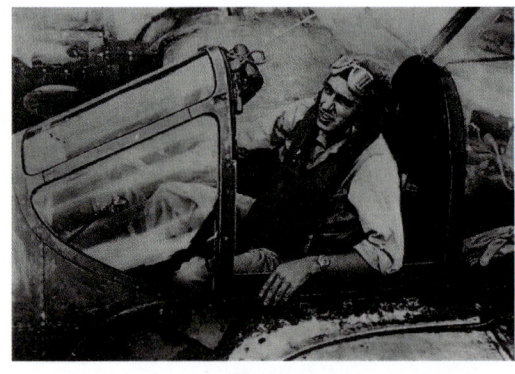

It is highly likely that Bob helped to fight for and rebuild airfields from which Niagara County, New York, farm boy John G. O'Neill flew P-38s in New Guinea. O'Neill, shown here in a P-38 cockpit, had flown in the civilian pilot training program in Ithaca, left the College of Agriculture in the spring of 1941, joined the Army and became a pilot. A daring pilot, O'Neill flew under the Golden Gate Bridge and was nearly court marshaled! Instead, he was sent overseas. He flew P-38 Lightings with the 49th Fighter Group, 9th Fighter Squadron, known as the "The Flying Knights." In 1943 he shot down 8 enemy planes, 7 of them A6M Zeros. He was the first Ace from New York State. He never came back to Cornell to finish his degree. In 2018, my 65th Cornell Alumni Reunion, the College of Agriculture and Life Sciences presented his family with a certificate of acknowledgement that made him a non-degree alumnus of the Class of 1943. The award marked the 75th anniversary of what would have been his graduation year.

As the war came to a close, the troops had more time available to pursue individual endeavors, from making music to making souvenirs. And there was plenty of natural and manmade artifacts around for conversion into jewelry and other items of utility. Jewelry was made from Australian silver coins, aircraft aluminum and other scrap, and adorned with "cat's eyes," the very colorful shells of the foot-closure, like a trap door, of a sea-snail called a Turban Shell.

Brass from shells and cartridges were plentiful. Cpl. Robert Brown used the products of battle to make P-38 fighter ashtrays. An ashtray consisted of the base of a brass 90mm anti-aircraft cartridge case manufactured in 1938, holding a 50-caliber cartridge for the support pylon for the plane. The plane was made from the cartridges and bullets of 30 and 50 caliber rounds, and the wing surfaces were fashioned from thinner flattened brass material. The plane had distinct value, in that the propellers were made from real silver Australian shillings minted in 1943. The reverse side of the coins are inscribed with "GEORGIVS VI D:G:BR:OMN:REX F:D:IND:IMP." This is Latin for "George VI, by Grace of God, King of all the Britons, Defender of the Faith." The components of a disassembled and assembled ashtray are shown below. Cpl. Bob Brown sent home captured war souvenirs, including a 25 caliber model 1905 Arisaka Japanese infantry rifle, a section cut from the propeller of a downed Japanese Zero fighter plane and a parachute strap, along with Japanese administrative record documents and a propaganda leaflet, expended cartridges, other military paraphernalia and coconuts. Bill Brown also made painstakingly crafted and exceptionally artistic jewelry, including bracelets and rings, from aircraft aluminum, coins, and "cat's eyes." The benefits of being in engineering battalions eventually paid off by providing the opportunity to use available hand tools, such as files, saws, hammers and soldering equipment. The photos show the ashtray which bears the inscription NEW GUINEA "44." I inherited it when my uncles died. The GEORGIVS VI shillings were made of 92.5% silver, and the combined weight of it in the two coins is 0.3361 Oz. The total current value of the silver is $5.19. As separate collectors' coins, they are worth about $100.00 each. A Cornell University classmate of Ken's, Steve Carter, an antique clock enthusiast, refurbished the finish on both the ashtray and my parents' mantle clock for me.

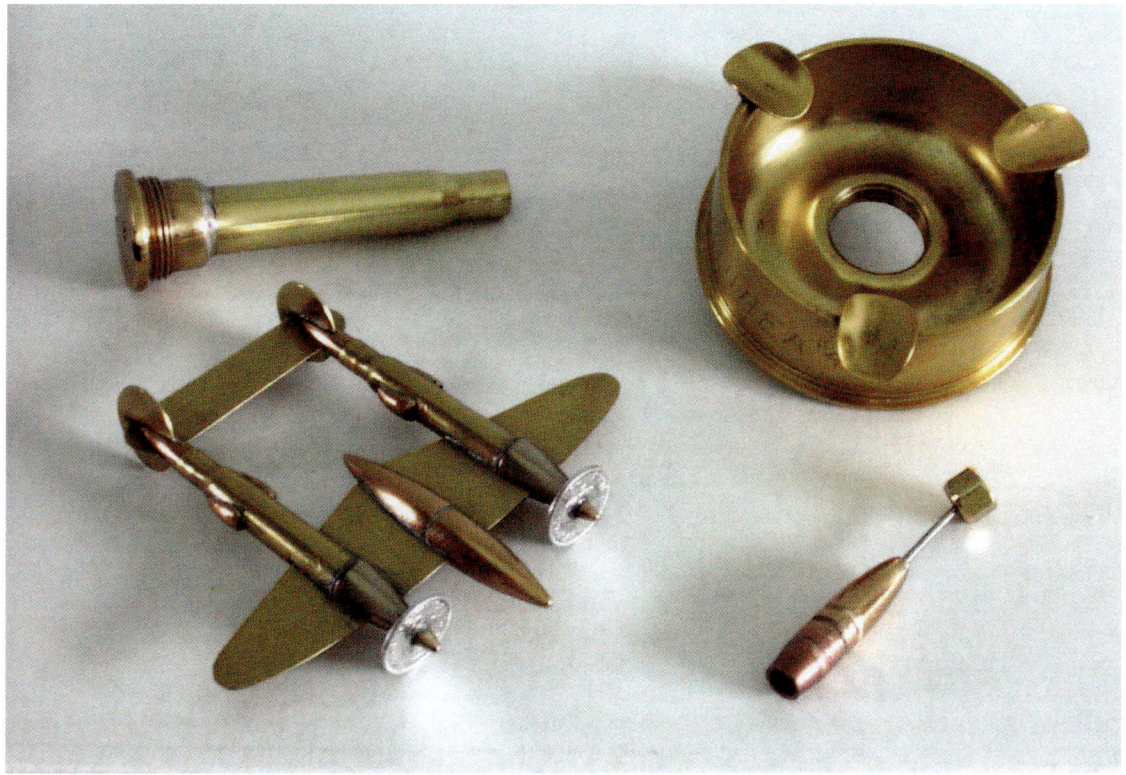

The four parts of the disassembled ashtray

Fully assembled ashtray

When Bob and Bill were overseas, we corresponded with them by V-Mail, short for Victory mail. The system was developed in England to reduce the volume and weight of shipping to provide more space for war materials. The process used a special free lightweight V-Mail letter sheet that served as both a letter and a distinctive-looking envelope. The author of a letter wrote a message in the limited space, then folded the letter, sealed it, added an address and mailed it. The letters were then microfilmed, reducing them down to about the size of a thumb-nail, with a reduction ratio of 1:37 in mailbags required, and a weight reduction ratio of 1:57 — immense savings! The microfilm was sent to a developing station near the receiver, and a facsimile was made, at about a fourth the size of the original, and delivered to the addressee. Servicemen's letters, both regular and V-Mail, were censored by their regimental officers, and you could see where sections had been cut out. Mail was an important morale booster for everyone. When we didn't hear from those on the front lines for extended periods of time, anxiety was high. Shown below are blank copies of the front and back of a V-Mail letter sheet, along with copies of V-Mails we received from Bob and Bill while they were in the South Pacific in New Guinea. No postage was required for those in the military; the serviceman wrote "Free" in the space where stamps would ordinarily be placed. Overseas military addresses had to contain an APO (Army Post Office) designation, as shown in the upper left corner of the envelope below, to facilitate delivery to a destination that may be on the move.

The envelope from a censored regular mail letter
from Cpl. Robert R. Brown to my Mother.

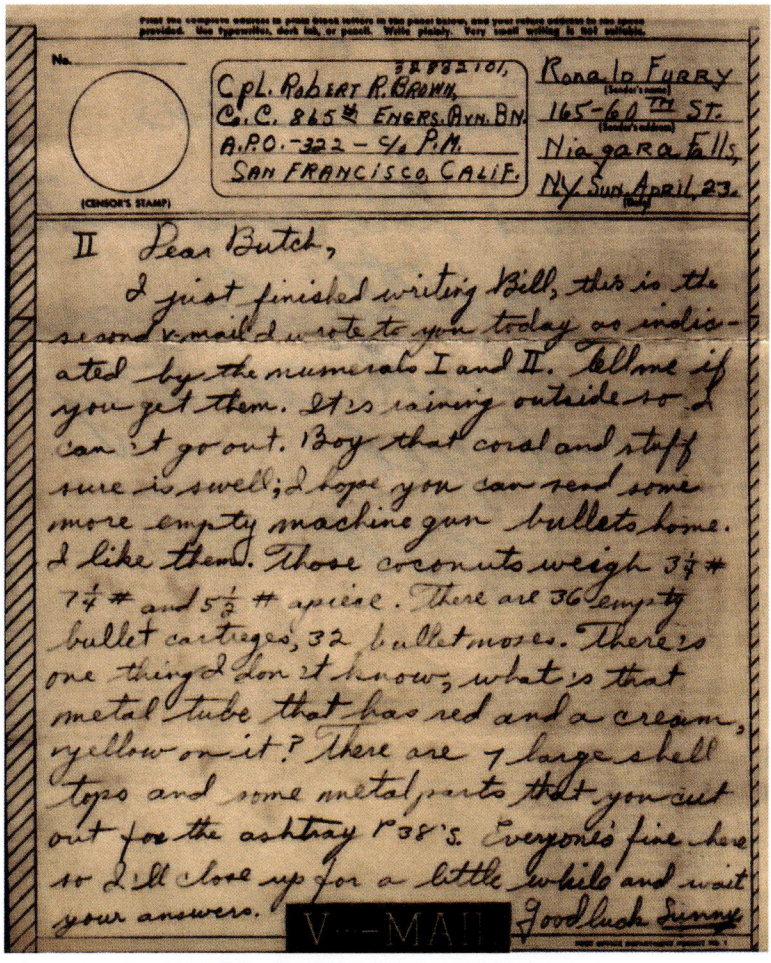

A V-Mail letter from me to Cpl. Robert R. Brown
in New Guinea on April 23, 1944

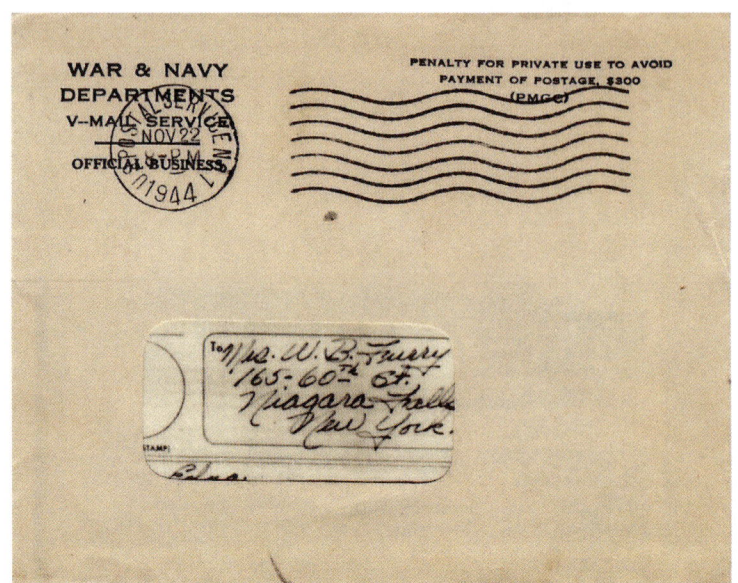

A V-Mail letter as received was enclosed in a 4 11/16" by 3 ¾" envelope and measured approximately 4 ¼' by 5 1/8" unfolded.

The **washing machines** referenced here in this V-Mail from Sgt. Bill Brown in New Guinea is military jargon for Japanese bombers, and the bursting shells are explosions from defensive anti-aircraft fire.

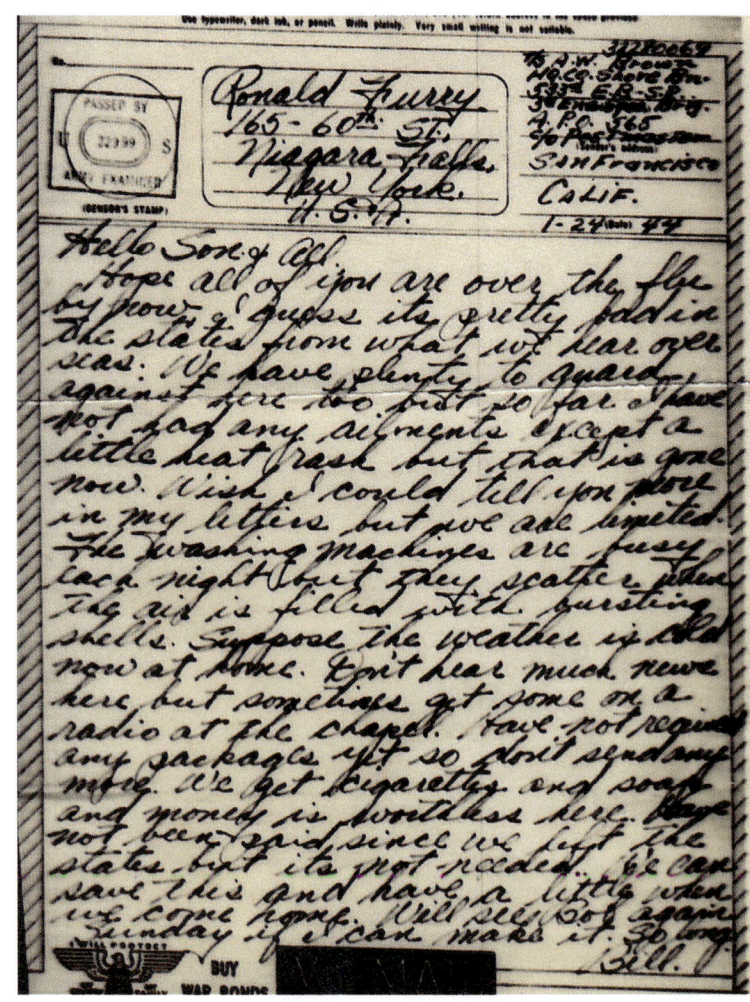

The inside message area of an original V-Mail form

41

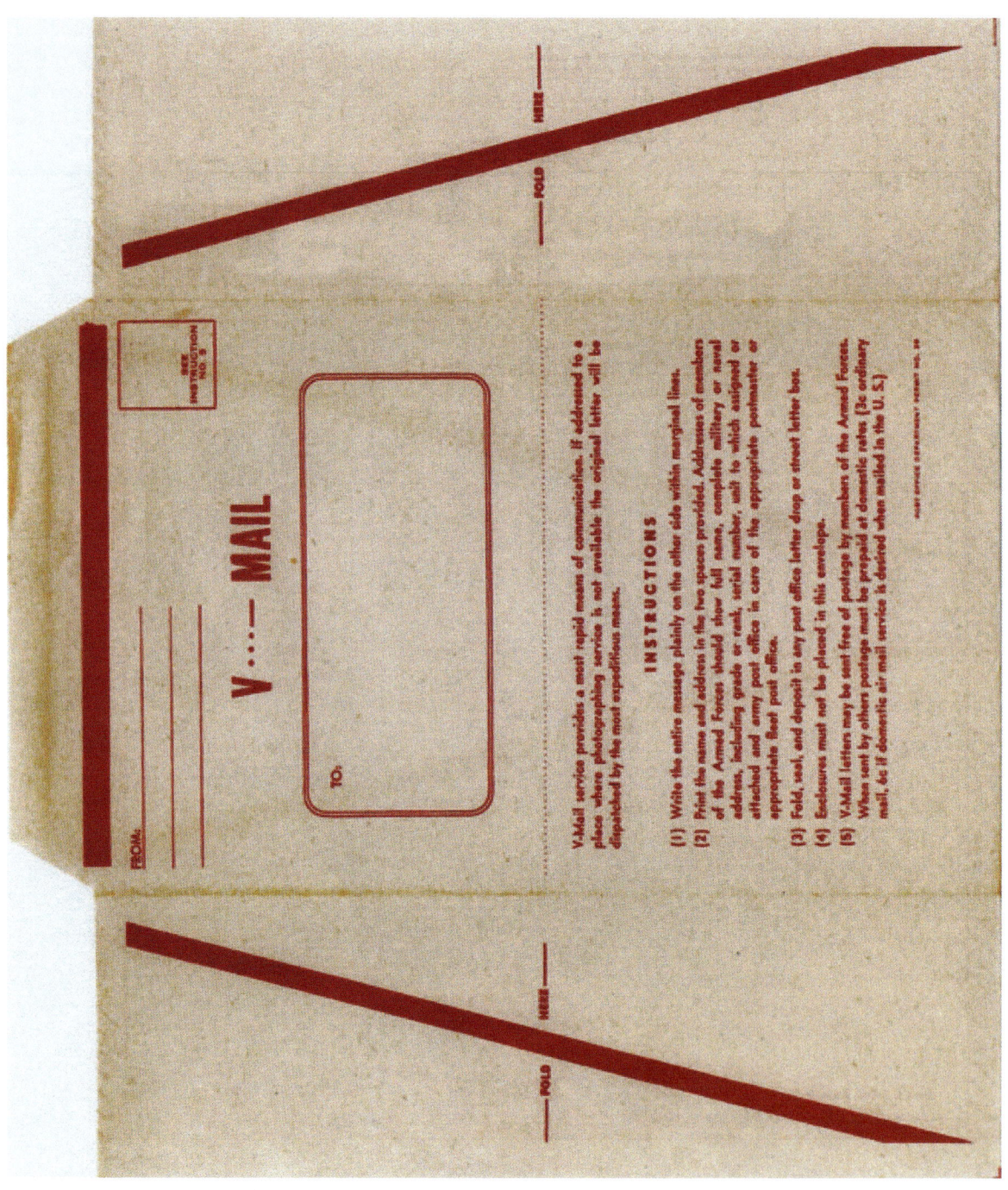

World War 2 brought rationing of everything from food to gasoline and clothing, diverting most of the materials to the war effort. Some rationing was the result of sources for material, such as rubber, being in the hands of the enemy. The amount of certain goods, such as sugar, butter, canned milk and gasoline that a person could buy was limited, and food ration cards were introduced in 1942. Restricted items included cars, tires, fuel oil, coal, firewood, nylon, silk, shoes, meat, dairy, coffee, dried fruits, jams, jellies, lard, shortening, oils, fish, bicycles, typewriters, and many others. Stickers with alphabet letters were placed on vehicle windshields to designate the amount of gasoline allowed; an A sticker, which is what we had, was the lowest designation and allowed 4 gallons of gas a week. Ration books containing removable stamps were used for food items. A point system was employed to designate allowable monthly purchases if a product was available: 48 "blue points" were required to buy canned, bottled or dried foods, and 64 "red points" were needed to buy meat, fish and dairy products. My Mother was certain that horse meat was

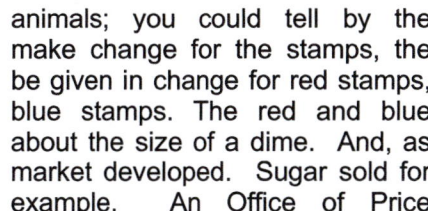

being substituted for beef and dairy animals; you could tell by the difference in the muscle fibers. To make change for the stamps, the government issued "red point" tokens to be given in change for red stamps, and "blue point" tokens in change for blue stamps. The red and blue tokens were made of fiber and were about the size of a dime. And, as might be expected, an expanding black market developed. Sugar sold for several times its normal price, for example. An Office of Price Administration (OPA) administered the rationing program, and was in effect until 1947, when restrictions on sugar were finally lifted. In addition, scrap drives were held to reclaim material, metals and rubber, for war production uses, and people planted Victory Gardens at home or on vacant lots and public parks to grow food for home consumption. As a result of a local cooperative Victory Garden, I learned that I liked Swiss chard, especially when it was loaded with butter and salt! We never planted Swiss chard in our garden. I haven't eaten it in years, though. I kept a few tokens around as souvenirs for many years after the war; the stamp books mostly disappeared as useless. Everyone had to have a Ration Card. For most people, time seemed to stand still, but the war ended the Great Depression and prosperity was in the future. It felt like a great weight had been taken off our shoulders, and we could breathe again. It took a long time for things to come back to "normal."

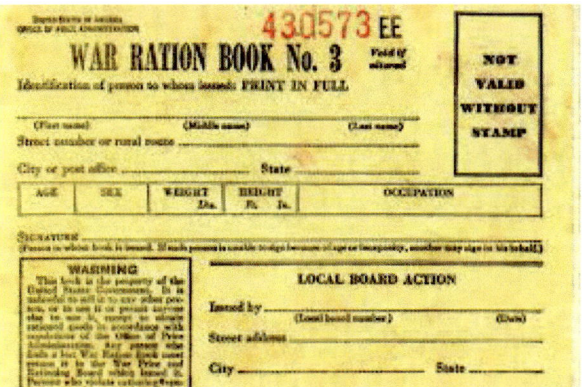

A ration book identification card

Removable stamps for rationed items

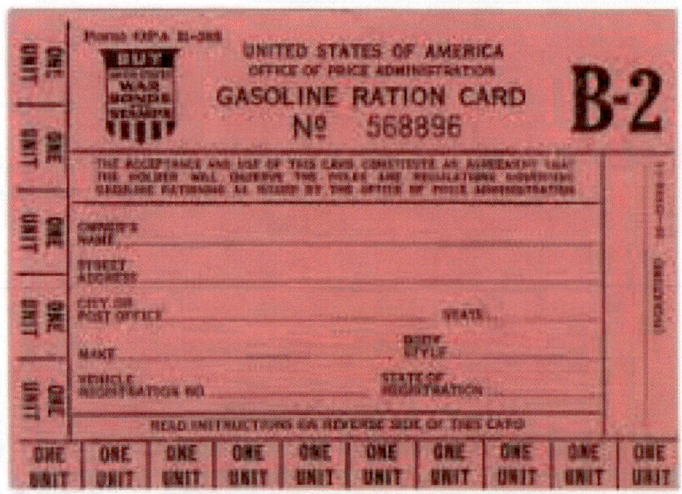

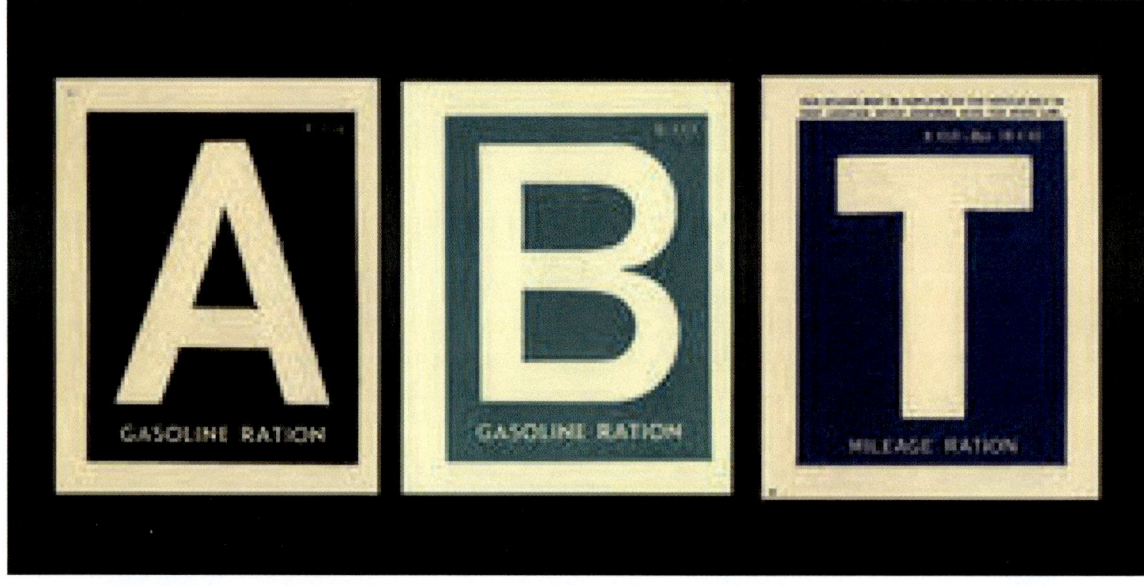

| Week of Dec. 3 to 8 | Week of Dec. 10 to 15 | Week of Dec. 17 to 22 | Week of Dec. 24 to 29 |

CUSTOMER'S SUGAR CARD

BE SURE AND BRING THIS CARD WITH YOU

This card is issued to protect our regular customers during the present Sugar shortage, and to assure them, if possible, one pound of Sugar each week.

"FOOD WILL WIN THE WAR"

Manager will punch out the dates on which the customer receives Sugar. Positively only one pound of Sugar in one week. No purchase of other goods is required. This card is not valid unless the Store Stamp and Manager's Signature appear on reverse side.

THE GREAT ATLANTIC & PACIFIC TEA COMPANY

| Week of Feb. 4 to 9 | Week of Jan. 28 to Feb. 2 | Week of Jan. 21 to 26 | Week of Jan. 14 to 19 |

Because of the heavy industry, there was heavy pollution, too. In 1949, in my senior year in high school, I wrote a petition and carried it around to homes to get signatures to support pollution abatement. Most people readily signed it, but I got a quick lesson in power politics when I presented the petition to Mr. Blackmore, a mechanical engineer in one of the factories who lived down the street from us. He said, "Sonny, I'd like to sign your petition, but if I did, I wouldn't have a job tomorrow." Pollution was so bad that if you stood under a streetlight at night, you could not see it. We used to play a team game at night with a ball that we threw over the light. If the opposite team caught it, they got a point. The ball was almost impossible to catch because of the density of the air pollution. The pollution was also toxic and corrosive. Cars left out at night would very soon lose the luster of the paint finish, and the glass windshields would become frosted.

The worst polluters would often release materials into the air at night. One such release made the entire path of the pollution laden air easy to track because all houses along the path had turned black on the exposed windward side. The affected homes had all been painted white, and in those days white lead was used in paint. The pollutant and the paint had had a chemical reaction. Denials of responsibility were standard. And it wasn't only gaseous pollution. In the summer, we had a choice of closing windows to reduce the outdoor chemical odors and sweat, or leave them open to get some "fresh air." Unfortunately, airborne particles came right through the window screens and settled in the house. I can remember lots of mornings when we would get up, walk across the hardwood floor in the bedroom and leave a sharp outline of our feet in the "dust" on the floor. And we breathed it, too. During my high school years, I would regularly drive to work on my uncle Bob's farm in Pekin, New York, and the pollution cloud could be seen all the way, over 17 miles. The Niagara River was also a common dumping ground for pollutants. There were many fish kills caused by the industrial wastes. The dead fish would of course go over the falls and pile up from shore to shore on the surface of the river water, covering several acres extending from the U.S. to the Canadian side. And then they would decay. At one time, the Niagara River was designated the most polluted river in the country. My Mother drank the Niagara River water her whole life, 82 years, and never got sick! I also remember when the abandoned Love Canal was used as a final (!) repository for waste chemicals. When I saw the canal being filled with layer after layer of 55 gallon barrels filled with chemicals, I was amazed to think that people could not see that the barrels would eventually deteriorate and crush under their own weight and the material would leak out. Around 21,800 tons of more than 200 chemicals were dumped into the canal between 1942 and 1953 by the Hooker Chemical Company. Years later, after my Father had died in 1955 and my Mother was earning money as a baby sitter, she would never take the children to the "park" that had been made to cover the canal. Still later, the area was fenced off and declared uninhabitable. These were the boom years in Niagara Falls. The population increased from 75,460 in 1930, the year before I was born, to its maximum in 1960 of 102,394, then decreased steadily to a current low of 48,623 in 2016. Niagara Falls has seen its heyday. There was another aspect of Niagara Falls to which relatives of folks who worked in the factories were attuned. Each factory had a signature whistle or other very loud distinguishing alarm signal that was used to call emergency personnel to the plant when an explosion or some other disaster occurred. There was no 911 system in those days, and the loud sound of the alert could be heard a long way, making it an almost immediate call for help, even standing out over the general hum and din of the noise of the factories. It stopped you dead in your tracks until you found out it which factory it was that made the call.

After the war, the U.S. formulated a massive rebuilding effort for Western Europe, known as the Marshall Plan, giving over 13 billion dollars (nine times that in current dollars) of economic aid in four years, starting in 1948. There was much civilian interest in helping Western Europe recover, and in 1946 individuals could purchase CARE (Cooperative for Assistance and Relief Everywhere) packages, containing a variety of food from raisins to canned soups and coffee. My folks decided to participate. I had learned from a schoolmate that she had been sending letters to students in Western Germany, and I became a pen pal (Federfreund), too. I corresponded with several German students who would write to me in English, German, or English and German, and I would write back in German. I eventually settled on corresponding with a German teacher, 42-year-old Fritz Fricke, who lived in the British Zone at (22a) Wuppertal-Elberfeld, Neue Friedrichstrasse 19,

Germany. He had also lived under the Russians and said it was brutal. Fritz would write to me in German and English and I would write to him in German script. The process went like this: I would write my letter in English, translate it into German, then rewrite it in German script and mail it to him. He would correct my German grammar in red ink and mail it back to me. He told me that I had an excellent script hand. This resulted from my very pointy English writing! We decided to send him CARE packages of our own design. I would write to tell him of when one was coming and what it contained. Invariably, when we sent coffee and other selected items, like chocolate, it would disappear from the package before it got to him. Pilfering was running rampant because everyone knew what the packages might contain. They were always hungry, and he would share what we sent with his most needy students. In return, he would send me German war memorabilia, such as medals, along with elementary school German text books, and a copy of Hitler's 1933 book, *Deutschland Erwacht* (Germany Awakened). This was the Nazi's 152-page picture album about the origin of the Nazi Party and its battle for power and victory. It contains over 200 photos that are pasted on the pages, including one 48" foldout of the review of the Nuremberg party rally of 1933. The book was originally issued with only black-and-white photos. My volume of *Deutschland Erwacht* contains all of the pictures, including those that are Agfa color prints. These books were originally issued as blank albums and when certain brands of cigarettes were purchased, the customer found a coupon inside that could be sent to the company that issued the album to receive a packet of pictures to be mounted in the book. When the book was completed, the owner would have a souvenir that chronicled the history of the Kampfzeit (struggle to power). The book measures 12 ½ x 9 ½ inches and is about an inch thick with brown, fabric-type covers. The National Socialist German Workers' Party (In German: *Nationalsozialistische Deutsche Arbeiterpartei*, abbreviated NSDAP), commonly known in English as the Nazi Party, was a political party in Germany between 1920 and 1945. Its predecessor, the German Workers' Party (DAP), existed from 1919 to 1920. The term *Nazi* is German and stems from the word *Nationalsozialist*, due to the pronunciation of Latin *-tion-* as *-tsion-* in German (rather than *-shon-* as it is in English), with German Z̲ being pronounced as 'ts'. So, now you know. The cover and the 48" rally foldout at the end of the book are shown below.

The first letter below, dated November 14, 1948 (14, 11, 48), in German script is from student Klaus Dietmar Kesper, who also lived in Wuppertal. He called me Roland, instead of Ronald. (Roland is my Grandfather's and his youngest son's first name, but he didn't know that!) Wuppertal is a city in North Rhine-Westphalia, Germany, in and around the Wupper valley, east of Düsseldorf and south of the Ruhr. It was heavily bombed on the night of May 29-30, 1943. Aspirin originates from Wuppertal and was patented in 1897 by Bayer.

The second letter, dated July 24, 1948, in both German script and English, is from student Ursula Iben in Wuppertal. Her handwriting is gorgeous! She was almost 18 years old and had lost one year of schooling due to the war. At that time, her high school class level was called Obersekunda. The students in her class were studying English, Latin and French, and she preferred French because "it is more interesting than Latin, for instance." They were reading the *Pickwick Papers* by Charles Dickens, and then were moving on to something by Shakespeare. Her twin brother was a stamp collector and very busy with his studies. She said that Wuppertal had a population of nearly 400,000 and was located about 20 miles from the Rhine River, and that 53% of it was destroyed during the war. Her family's home had been occupied by the American Army three times and they had to move to an inn. She had relatives in Milwaukee, Wisconsin, but they seldom wrote to her family, and Ursula expressed the thought that they had forgotten about them because of the war. (My Mother's oldest brother, John F. Brown, and his family also lived in Milwaukee; I wonder if they knew each other!) An envelope from one of Ursula's letters follows. German paper quality then was very poor.

Ursula's address at that time was Wuppertal-Ronsdorf (22a), Heidterstrasse 49, Germany, which was in the British Zone. This was a fortunate turn of events for her. There were four occupied zones in Germany after the war ended: American, English, French and Russian. Berlin was likewise divided into four zones.

Wuppertal-B. d. 14.11.48

Lieber Roland!

Ich warte immer noch auf einen Brief von dir. Warum schreibst du nicht? Hast du so wenig Zeit? Ich habe auch keine Zeit. Aber ich schreibe trotzdem. Also mein Junge, schreibe. Du kannst mit jedem Wort.

Morgen früh fahre ich wieder nach Köln. Die Arbeit weißt du wohl nicht ob. Ich sitze täglich 5 Stunden über dem Mikroskop, und was ich sehe, muß ich zeichnen. Und weil ich ein schlechter

Zeichner oder Naturwissenschaftler, muß ich mir viele Mühe geben. Where there is a will, there is a way. Das gilt auch für dich. Schreibe mehr von deiner Schularbeit, von deinen Lehrern, von deinen Zukunftsplänen. Du hast sicher schon von Einem Bruder gehört, daß ich Zoologie studiere. Vielleicht komme ich einmal an ein tierwissenschaftliches Institut nach Amerika. Habt Ihr in Niagara Falls einen zoologischen Garten?

Grüße Ömmi nicht und sei von mir u. sei die herzlichst gegrüßt von deinem deutschen Kameraden Klaus deinem Bruder.

Wuppertal – Ronsdorf,
July 24th 1948

Dear Ronald,

Two weeks have passed since
I received your letter. I was highly surprised to get an answer so soon. Many
thanks for it.
In the meantime we have got our holy-
days at school and to-morrow my
brother and I will drive to Hamburg.
My aunt and my uncle lived in
this town, before their house was
destroyed by an attack of air. Now
they are living in the country near
Hamburg. Another aunt and her
husband are living with them.
They are driven from the East, for
they had to leave their home-town
Danzig. — Life is better there than
at Wuppertal, for too many people

are living in our Industrial - district.

Yesterday I got a letter from a girl of England. One year ago I was to do the English correspondence with other girls, for one of each class was to do so. Now this girl had got my address by her French mistress and has written to me. You see, I have to write many letters; but I have not forgotten that your girl-friend wants to have a letter too. I shall write to her as soon as I shall have returned from Hamburg. Does she speak and write German too? I did not believe that you would be able to speak and to write our German language. 1945, when our town was occupied by American soldiers we had to leave our house three times. The first time for three days and then when we had just cleaned it, we had to leave for a week and the

last time for six weeks. For this
time we were living in one room
of an inn. There were only few
American soldiers that were able to
speak german and the interpreters
were always glad too, when hearing
that we were able to speak English.
The difference between the English
and the American language is rather
little and we were able to understand
them easily. I learn the English since
seven years. —

Vielen Dank für die Beschreibung der
Niagarafälle. Wir hatten dieses Na-
turwunder auch in Erdkunde erwähnt,
aber eine so genaue Beschreibung wur-
de uns natürlich nicht gegeben. In
Deutschland kann man sich das alles
gar nicht vorstellen, da es hier so
etwas nicht gibt. —

Nach der Geldreform hat sich das Leben
hier etwas geändert. Vorher war nur

sehr wenig zu kaufen da, und jetzt
ist alles, was es gibt, viel zu teuer.
Vor vier Jahren bekam ich die letzten
Schuhe, weil nur Flüchtlinge und Aus-
gebombte bei der Verteilung bedacht
werden. Auch jetzt sind sie noch so
knapp, daß jedes andere Familienmit-
glied verzichten muß, wenn ich welche
bekomme. Trotzdem sind die Läden
schon wieder leer, und jede neue Sen-
dung scheint teurer zu werden. Mich
soll wundern was aus der ganzen
Wirtschaftsentwicklung wird.
Für heute möchte ich schließen. Mit
vielen Grüßen, auch an die Eltern,
Schwester und Freundin,
                    verbleibe ich.
                         Ursula Iben.

I had written my pen pals about the cataracts on the Niagara River and told them about how they were illuminated at night with colored lights. They were intrigued by the size of the falls and how they were shown for tourists. They had nothing like that where they lived. All of my pen pals told me about their suspension railway, something that we don't have!

The Wuppertal suspension railway in Germany, July 15, 1948.

After WW2, students in our schools were taught to take defensive measures in case of a nuclear bomb attack by the Soviet Union. Most of the schools were constructed with large glass areas for maximum light, and obviously they were all above ground. The Office of Civil Defense promulgated Duck and Cover exercises to give people who were out of the radius of the atomic fireball a potential chance to survive the first few minutes of the explosion. But the shock wave and intense heat would have done great damage, and it is doubtful that we would have survived for long. When in school, our procedure was to rush up against the outside walls and lie on the floor under the huge windows that spread across the whole length of the classroom. Of course, there was not sufficient space for all students to do this, so it really became a futile exercise. For most of us, all we did was succeed in cleaning the floor a bit with our clothing. As the years went by, the danger increased along with the power of the nuclear devices, and the practice was dropped. There still isn't a good defense against nuclear weapons, and I don't think that the vast majority of the population even knows what MAD, or for that matter, the doctrine of Mutually Assured Destruction really means, or what supports that position. Hopefully, they won't have to. WW2 was a cakewalk in comparison. My Department at Cornell also participated in the Civil Defense Program. Professor Edwin Foss was responsible for preparation and dissemination of educational materials for the civil  defense and disaster relief programs conducted by the Extension Service. We had lots of designs for fallout shelters, and handheld Geiger counters as shown here, ready for distribution. Interest in that aspect of civil defense eventually flagged nationally, and the various civil defense agencies were replaced with the Federal Emergency management Agency (FEMA) in 1979, which became part of the Department of Homeland Security in 2002. The danger still remains.

The Work Ethic

My first job of any length when I was very young was pulling weeds from the lawn of an estate on the escarpment overlooking the Niagara River and Lake Ontario where my Father was doing yard work to make extra money. My task consisted of pulling weeds out of the lawn with bare fingers; this shortened finger nails at a rapid rate. Herbicides for this application had not yet been developed. The technique used was to mark off 100 feet or so of lawn with parallel strings spaced about three feet apart and then move on hands and knees from one end to the other. The lawn sloped toward the Niagara River and near the end the yard opened up to a spectacularly breathtaking panorama of the river and Lake Ontario. I recall just sitting there for a while, enthralled at the view. Then, back to work; I earned a penny a minute. I was very young but I had lots of relatives who worked hard and thus had many role models. My closest relatives often involved me in their work as an unpaid helper, especially when they needed someone small to get into a tight place. For example, I assisted in emptying a failed septic tank and installing a replacement, laying a sewer drain pipe, installing natural gas lines in homes, building concrete foundations, and myriad other construction and maintenance work jobs. I picked raspberries on my paternal Grandfather's farm for 3 cents a quart (adult rate was 5 cents a quart, but isn't a quart still a quart?). When I was a bit older and stronger I carried warm mash to feed our chickens in the wintertime when my Father was at work. I also shoveled chicken manure out of our chicken coop and then sprayed the inside of the building with chlorine solution until my eyes turned red and I couldn't see to sanitize it prior to populating it with a new batch of chicks. New chicks arrived in ventilated cardboard boxes in the US mail, and we started them in our attic where they were taught to drink from an inverted glass watering jar. When they were moved to the coop, we spread wood shavings on the floor and had top-loading coal fired stoves with round sheet metal hovers that directed the radiation downward to keep the chicks warm. It was a pretty sight. Adult chickens, on the other hand, are not pretty! We raised chickens both for eggs and for sale to restaurants as fryers. My Father delivered eggs to customers in the city, and my Mother sold them to neighbors at the back door. We had as many as 800 chickens in the coop at a time. In those days, everything was done manually and that number of birds kept us busy; there was no time for vacations. My Father bought some Bantam chickens for me and put them in with the large breed chickens, which were mostly single comb white Leghorns. The big Leghorns gave the Bantys no peace, and the small Bantys stayed as far away from them as possible, usually retreating to the highest roost in the coop. I recall vividly the day when one of the male Bantams had had enough. He tore into a big Leghorn that was annoying him and attacked him relentlessly. The Bantam was never bothered again. My hero! I loved those Bantams. My Mother put the egg money from the back door sales in my now unused silver baby cup and placed it on the right hand side of the first shelf of our glass-doored kitchen cupboards. One day she washed then waxed the kitchen floor, retreating from the kitchen to the back door, and went over to her Mother's house next door to wait for the wax to dry. When she came back, she noticed that the egg money was gone! But, there were footprints on her newly waxed floor. Now, in those days we had bread delivered to us by a "bread man" who used a horse drawn wagon and a helper. She surmised from the size of the footprints that it was the helper who stole the money, and she was right. The dry prints fit the helper's shoes exactly and she got the money back. My Father didn't appreciate the bread man's horse, either, because it would come up on the lawn and eat the leaves off the maple trees that he had planted near the road. My Dad also raised rabbits and when Easter or Halloween came around, he would put a couple of young Angora bunnies in a pail with some straw and show them to the kids who came to the door for treats. My sister and I also painted hard boiled eggs with gold coloring at Easter time and hid them in the chicken nests for our Father to find. It was a fun game, and we waited eagerly to get his reaction when he found them. He was always surprised of course. Good old Dad!

We also had ice delivered to our house for our ice box. Vapor compression refrigerators were not in extensive use and were very expensive compared to a small ice box. The green, metal lined ice box had an upper section and a two-door lower section where blocks of ice and tall items could be placed. An ice card could be placed in a street side window to indicate how many pounds of ice were needed, with the top number being the delivery quantity. Some folks wrapped the ice in newspaper to make it last longer, but that meant that it was not cooling the air as effectively. Saving money was very important in those days! The ice box had a narrow flap door that went across its entire width at the bottom to permit a metal tray to be placed on the floor to catch the melt water. This was difficult to manage, both in remembering to check to see how full the tray was, as well as juggle it to the sink to empty it. My Father made a brilliant adaptation: he cut a hole in the kitchen floor and ran a hose from the drain to the basement gutter, obviating the need for a tray. Our house also had a milk box. This was a small opening in the wall by the back door that had inside and outside access doors where three or four milk bottles, butter or other dairy products could be placed. The milk man knew what the regular order was, and a note left in the box would tell him what alterations to the order would be. My sister and I loved the milk box in the winter. We would get up early to race to the milk box to retrieve the frozen cream that had expanded and formed a column above the bottles with the cardboard stopper at the very top! We made our own skim milk with this practice! The milk man also delivered orange drink and great tasting chocolate milk, our favorite, but not frequent, drink. Homogenized milk lay far into our future!

When I was big enough, I took over cutting the grass in our yard. Reel push mowers were the norm; rotary mowers had not been invented. The reel mowers did a superior job of cutting the grass uniformly and my Dad loved to have the yard looking neat and tidy. I cut the grass in one direction then cut it again at 90 degrees to the original direction. It looked like a pool table! Later, I cut grass for neighbors and other folks who were in walking distance from our home. I got $1.00 per lawn. Some lawns were very difficult to cut because the homeowners did not keep their mowers in good repair or adjustment. This bothered me because I could not do a proper job of mowing, but in spite of reporting this to them, I would find the mowers in the same condition in the next and succeeding mowings.

When my Mother's youngest brother, Robert (Bob) Raymond Brown, went into WW2 on June 2, 1943, I took over the care of his car, a 4-door Buick roadster that had been set up on blocks. I started and ran the car every week for the entire time he was in the military. He came home from fighting the Japanese in the South Pacific on New Guinea, where he contracted Jungle Rot, a bacterial disease that could not be cured that affected his legs, causing open sores that penetrated to the bone. He also suffered from Battle Fatigue (N.B.: Shell Shock in WW1, PTSD now) and malaria. He bought a 96-acre farm near Pekin, New York, married a second time (Marion Beaber), and later built a house on the property and moved into it. As a high school student, I helped him evenings and weekends develop the farm before he moved there. He worked in the Niagara Falls area as a licensed steam fitter and plumber on the large industrial construction projects that were underway after WW2. During vacations, while he was at work I would work full time on the farm plowing, disking, weeding, and spraying peach trees. My sister, Joanne, three years younger than I, drove the tractor pulling the spray rig, while I walked behind covering the trees with insecticide mixes. I would come out of these episodes soaked from head to foot with spray liquid. I helped plant fruit trees, grape vines, install vine trellises, and weeded them with a tractor and disk when they were mature, plowed fields for planting wheat, and rode the combine to bag the wheat at harvest time. It was a lot of work, a lot of learning and a great experience. I earned $1.00 an hour. It was also dangerous because I was alone for most of this work, with no way to communicate if something should go wrong – no cell phones in those days! It was also hazardous. One day when I was out in a plowed field breaking up the top of a very large submerged granite boulder that kept tripping the plow out of the ground, I hit it with the sledge hammer and a sharp piece of stone broke off and penetrated the right lens of my glasses. It shattered the very center of the lens into powder, but did not penetrate to my eye. That was pure luck. Shatterproof lenses had not yet been invented; now all lenses are shatterproof.

When I was a student at Cornell, the College of Agriculture (now the College of Agriculture and Life Sciences) required all students to have farm work experience. Professor Ruben Shapley administered the program from the Farm Practice Office in the now razed Roberts Hall, which stood to the right of where Kennedy Hall is presently located. I had lots of experience with chickens, vegetables, fruit trees, grape vineyards, grain, plowing, disking, spraying, weeding and the like; however, New York State was a leading dairy state in the country, and I had no experience with cows. So, in the summer of 1950 I was sent to the farm of Henry Bauer in Angola, New York, to earn my remaining farm work credits. (Appropriately, Bauer in German means farmer!). Angola is located in Erie County, on the southeast shore of Lake Erie, so it was fairly close to home. My high school classmate, Pat Fessenden, who was also registered in the College of Agriculture, was also assigned to the Bauer farm. We shared a double bed for the summer, got up at 4 AM, ate a quick breakfast of cereal, milk, juice and toast with jam, then went to the dairy barn for the 5 AM milking. When milking was finished, the cows were turned out to pasture. Then we washed the milking equipment, cleaned the feed alleys, mangers, cow stalls and center alley in the barn, ran the gutter cleaner to load manure into the manure spreader, spread phosphate fertilizer on the center alley to make it look white and clean, then went back to the house for a real breakfast. This breakfast consisted of steak, potatoes and gravy, vegetables, fruit and juices and the like. One morning when I was brushing out the feed alley I felt something pick me up a bit and push me forward; it was the tongue of the big bull that Bauer kept on the farm to impregnate the cows! I had gotten too close to his pen and forgotten that he could stick his head through his stanchion. I was a lot more alert after that. Then, it was off to work in the fields and do other chores, such as take care of the horses, pick up baled straw and hay from the fields and store it in the barn's hay mow, build and repair fences and much more until it was dark. I mowed hay, cultivated and weeded crops with horses, spread manure on the fields and many other things. I did a lot of walking, especially when picking up bales and working with the horses. Pat and I would take an old flatbed truck to the hay fields, put it in low-low gear and let it slowly travel up and down the hills by itself while we walked quickly back and forth picking up bales and loading them on the truck. The horses were work horses, not riding horses. One was pretty lazy. When I hilled corn with it, we would start out at a good walking clip for a few rows and then it would start to slow down, and finally stop in the row. This happened repeatedly. I finally got tired of getting it to move, so when I made the turn to come back the next row I broke off a small branch from a tree at the edge of the woods, stripped it of twigs and leaves and made it into a switch. When the horse would stop, I'd rap it on the rear end and it would move on. Corn fields are big, and doing this over and over again made my arm tired, so I tried a little psychology. The switch made a whistling sound in the air when I used it, so I imitated that sound with my mouth and it worked. I threw the switch away. The Bauer farm was also a cash crop farm, raising tomatoes and beans. When the beans were ripe, I would drive an old open truck with wood sides into the city of Buffalo to pick up laborers; they were kids of all ages, waiting at prescribed street corners very early in the morning. I'd drive back to the bean field, unload them and assign them work space and then pick beans myself. It's back breaking work. I tried every position there is to keep from getting a sore back, including sitting down on the ground with my legs out in front of me and scooting along the row. Nothing worked well. I ate lots of beans, too, and you could hear me coming after awhile as I backfired down a row! The pickers got paid by the pound, and I kept records of their production, and when the truck filled up with beans, I'd drive it to the cannery, unload it, sweep the bed out, and go back to the farm. At the end of the day, I'd load up the pickers and take them back to Buffalo.

Pat and I were so dusty and dirty after a long day's work that Mrs. Bauer would not allow us to use the shower in the house because of the mess it made of the bath tub, walls and shower curtain. But Pat had found a spot in the farm creek where we could build a shallow rock dam and get the water deep enough to clean us off. So that's what we did for the whole summer. We were so brown from working out under the sun with no shirts on that the dirt didn't show that much anyway!

The milking routine was the same every day. A vacuum pipe installed along each row of stanchions in the dairy barn was connected to portable airtight milking pails. After washing the teats and checking to see if any udder quarter had mastitis using a metal cup with a strainer, teat cups were placed on the cow. Then, the cow was left to milk out while the next cow was prepared for milking, usually by simply washing the udder. I wore shoes with steel-reinforced toes because

A vacuum milking pail   A 10-gallon milk can

having a heavy 1,500-pound Holstein cow step on your foot was no pleasure. The biggest problems were avoiding a dirty tail when the cow switched away flies and not getting crushed between the cow and the metal stanchion separators when she moved sideways into you when you were down on your haunches working with the milking equipment. The milk pails were emptied into milk cans in the milk house, which were then placed into a cool-water-filled tank; they were picked up the next day and trucked to a dairy processing plant. (It's a much different system today using milking parlors, robotic milkers, bulk milk tanks and bulk milk trucks, among other labor-saving innovations!) For the 5 AM milking, when the cows were finished milking, they were let out into the pastures. For the 5 PM milking, the hunt was on! The cows were free to roam around the fenced-in pastures during the day, but we never knew where they would be. If it were very hot, they'd probably be under some trees, so we'd start there. We usually tracked them down using a surplus old WW2 Jeep, but occasionally we'd ride the work horses bareback. Herding the cows back to the barn could be a problem if the boss cow was not cooperating, but when they were let into the barn, they followed in order and went directly to their own stall where hay and grain were waiting for them to eat.

One day we arose to find cows all over the roads, in the ditches and anywhere that looked like a good place to find green feed! We tracked their escape to a broken barbed wire fence next to a cornfield and herded them back into the pasture. Then we went looking for why the fence wire had been cut and knocked down in two places. We found it — a crop duster had been using an adjacent hay field as a place to store bagged material, load his plane, then take off, dust neighboring crops, and land back in the cut hay field. Unfortunately, on his final trip he misjudged the dips in the hilly terrain, aborted the takeoff, proceeded down the field to the barbed wire fence, cut through it into the adjacent corn field, turned around in the cornfield making a mess, went back through the fence in a different spot and parked his plane. Now, barbed wire fences on dairy farms are electrified with fence controllers, which in this case were not operating due to the "accident." The cows took advantage of this lapse and the breaks. So, Pat and I got some fence posts and barbed wire and completely encircled his airplane with an electrified fence. That'll teach him!

A crop dusting
airplane in flight

A Holstein
dairy cow

I had a bad experience with a barbed wire fence. One day I was sent out to maintain the electric fence in the cow holding area adjacent to the cow barn; this is where cows were kept before allowing them to enter the barn for milking. It was mucky and slippery due to repeated use and full of manure punched up by the cows' feet. I turned off the electric fence controller, got a hammer and went along the fence making sure that the ceramic insulators that held the fence wire to prevent grounding were nailed to the fence posts. Everything went fine until I came to a right angle inside fence corner. I tapped the nail in the insulator on the corner post and suddenly found myself sitting on the ground with my back against the fence wire. The insulator had been installed improperly with no connection to the post to keep it in place when the barbed wire was under

tension. It was only a matter of time before it popped off the post, and my hammer tap did it. It was like releasing a bow string, and there was still some tension in the wire because I became a post! I looked down at my left wrist and saw that one of the barbs had penetrated my skin on the outside of my wrist and pulled the skin around and over to the inside of my wrist, fortunately avoiding the blood vessels and tendons. It took me a long time to figure out how to move my wrist to release the barbs without doing a lot more damage. When I recovered, I went to the house and asked to be taken to a doctor to get a tetanus shot. There was resistance to this request, but I insisted, and was driven to a local country doctor who had his practice in his house. He asked me whether I wanted the shot made from horse serum or egg inoculation. I asked what the difference was and he told me that horse serum tetanus cost $5.00, would cause boils, and was used for migrant laborers, and the other would not cause problems. I opted for the $10.00 serum. Tetanus bacteria can be found in dust, soil and manure – and I had plenty of the latter on me.

Henry Bauer's oldest son had graduated from Cornell with a degree in Veterinary Medicine and was practicing his specialty of large animal medicine, which, of course, included cows. One day he asked me if I wanted to accompany him on his rounds, and I said I'd certainly like to do so (it got me out of farm work!). He had driven to the farm in a leased car, and I expected to go on the road in the same vehicle. Instead, he told me to wait for him in a nearby cut hayfield and drove away alone. Pretty soon I heard the engine of an airplane and saw a yellow Piper Cub

land and sputter up to me. He went on most of his farm visitations in his plane to save time; all he needed was a fairly decent field in which to land. That was my very first airplane ride. He also let me take the controls and fly it for awhile. I liked his advanced thinking. He was a very personable fellow.

Henry Bauer had promised to pay Pat and me $200.00 each for our full summer's work, plus "a few more dollars in the check" if we worked overtime on Sundays to catch up on regular farm work that wasn't getting done due to a lack of sufficient labor. This was in addition to doing the regular daily milking, feeding and cleanup chores. That summer we even painted a silo that had been on their work list for several years. But on our last day on the farm when we were ready to go back to our homes in Niagara Falls, all we got was a check for $200.00 each. We did take home some deep skin tans, though, because we usually worked shirtless in the fields and our hands were calloused to the point of not being able to remove rings for months. We also ended up being summer blondes because we never wore hats or caps in the field. His wife admitted that she had been too hard on us, too. Ironically, in the late 1950s after I had become an Extension Agricultural Engineer in the Agricultural Engineering Department, a farmer came up to me at an evening meeting that I was holding in Erie County, where Angola is located, for those interested in learning about milking parlors for dairy cattle; he told me that he had just installed a milking parlor on his farm. He had purchased the Henry Bauer farm and was modernizing it and some of the operations, and appreciated the labor saving aspects of milking parlors — no more milk pails and all that went with the in-barn milking operation. Unfortunately, this was too late to benefit Pat and me!

I was the first to go to college in our family, but with no savings for my college education, support came entirely out of current income. My folks would send me whatever they could spare in cash directly through the mail during my freshman year. Sometimes I would run out of money, so I got

in the habit of not eating breakfast or lunch. I didn't put on any weight in four years. I am deeply indebted and everlastingly grateful to my Mother and Father for their support and sacrifices on my behalf, clear evidence of true love. My first year was the most expensive, costing $1,100.00. The Cornell University Registration Fee in the College of Agriculture was $51.50 per semester! I got a job as a Teaching Assistant in mechanical drawing in the Agricultural Engineering Department, which was then located in Stocking Hall, starting in the beginning of my sophomore year. It paid $1.00 per hour, but allowed me to depend less heavily on my parents. I could work about 7 to 10 hours a week. I took a course load of 18 semester hours each semester for 4 years, graduating with 144 credit hours, and ranking at the top of my Agricultural Engineering class. I also graduated With Distinction, the highest honor awarded by Cornell University. The photo shows a student work station in the fourth floor teaching laboratory in Stocking Hall. When I joined the Alpha Zeta Fraternity in 1951, I still did not eat breakfast, but ate an occasional lunch consisting of a peanut butter sandwich and whole milk. Occasionally I would have a candy bar for lunch if I had some change. Everyone drank whole milk and the fraternity was forever running out of it! Meals were available twice on Saturday and once on Sunday. Participating in them was voluntary, so when I got low on cash I could skip meals with no penalty. The best places to eat on campus in those days were the Willard Straight Hall cafeteria, the Home Economics cafeteria in Martha Van Rensselaer Hall, and the Department of Dairy Industry cafeteria in Stocking Hall. They were a long distance apart, and there was only 10 minutes between classes; no buses in those days, either. The Willard Straight Hall cafeteria was too expensive for my budget; the best place for me was the Dairy Industry cafeteria where I could pick and choose as little as I wanted when I could get there. There was one problem with the Dairy Industry cafeteria, though. The cafeteria was located at the rear of the department's head building where the classroom and offices were located and was connected to it by a long hallway that had various milk processing and research laboratories connected to it on one side. This hallway was packed with people standing tightly against the wall each noon during the week. They were spectators watching a game called floor tennis that had been invented by a retired Agricultural Engineering Professor, Juan Reyna, a naturalized citizen from Mexico. It was played by two or four people and became more and more popular. It disrupted the noon hour traffic flow through the building so much that the game was eventually banned. I didn't see hide nor hair of the game for a long time until one day I went to the basement lavatory in Stocking Hall. There on the new gray painted floor of the lavatory were the white painted outlines of the court; the name was changed from floor tennis to latrine tennis! The ping pong balls occasionally got wet! It's a small world. Professor Reyna had been the one who started the courses in mechanical and architectural drawing in 1912 when the Agricultural Engineering Department began in the very early part of the 20th century. Reyna had degrees in electrical, mining and civil engineering. I would replace him decades later in 1953. This photo is what the teaching laboratory furniture looked like when I started teaching there — no computers, and the term computer graphics was definitely not on anyone's list of inventions! Reyna was an interesting fellow, short, thin, wiry, energetic, and he wore glasses. One day the department head asked how old he was, and he said he really didn't know, because he didn't want to retire, but he eventually was convinced to do so. He drove around in a yellow convertible and had his license revoked, but he continued to drive anyway. I found his class grade books when I took over the courses and noted that over the years the grades he gave to students increased steadily the older he got! If you were a friend, a couple of weeks before Christmas he would come around and take orders for a bottle of his homemade "wine." He made this from pure lab alcohol that he liberated from a Dairy Industry Department lab, mixed with Grand Marnier and other flavors. It was sweet (he'd ask just how sweet you wanted it) but didn't give a hangover, probably because there were no tars in the mix. Just before the University closed for Christmas recess, he would hand deliver the bottled drink to his clientele. One year on the last day of work before Christmas recess, I was leaving my office when our department's draftsman, Frank Dean, who had an office next to my teaching lab, opened his door, stepped outside and turned around to lock the door. I noticed that he had a paper bag under his arm and assumed it was a gift from Reyna. Unfortunately, it was, because the bag slipped out of his control, dropped to the floor and broke, spilling the contents in an ever-widening circle. I told Frank to go to the lavatory next door, and get a bunch of wet and dry paper towels while I got a trash can. By the time that we started to clean up the mess it had grown to over five feet in diameter, almost covering the width of the waxed cement-based finish of the floor. We eventually cleaned it up and left. After the Christmas recess was over, we came back to work to find a huge white-circled area on the hallway floor. The "wine" had done a perfect job of removing the wax and years of dirt from the floor. But it saturated the flooring, and your shoes would stick to it – you knew right where someone was when they came down the hall! It stayed that way for months. Professor Reyna died at the ripe old age of 96, and formula wine making and eventually latrine tennis disappeared from the campus. The lavatory had another use, too. My office had a single double hung window in it that I left open at the bottom on warm days to allow ventilation because it faced the east; air conditioning was not available in those days. I always locked my office door when I was not at work. At a June Cornell alumni reunion decades later, a former student who had taken one of my drafting courses came over to me and told me that he and another student knew that I kept the window partially open at night and that they had gone into the fourth floor lavatory, climbed out its window and shuffled their way around the building in the dark on the narrow ledge to my office window, intending to enter the room to steal one of the examinations that was scheduled for the next class session. That night was the only night that I had ever closed the office window and locked it on a warm day!

The Honeymoon Capital

Niagara Falls, New York, was advertised as "The Honeymoon Capital of the World" way back in the early 1900s, and had been a popular honeymooner site from 1802, so it was natural that I adopted that phrase as a location identifier when folks asked where I was from. But to me the deep gorge and the bridges over the river were just as spectacular as the falls itself. When I was growing up, there was only a single bridge over the Niagara River from Grand Island to Buffalo Avenue in Niagara Falls; it was built in 1935. We adopted the bridge as a playground because there were no playgrounds around, and in the summer swimming pools downtown in Niagara Falls were frequently closed because of the Polio epidemic. It had a single pedestrian walkway on one side, with two-way traffic on the adjacent roadbed. The drop-off between the walkway and the roadbed was over 2 feet. The bridge's length was 4,000 feet, with an elevation of 561 feet. One of the neighborhood kids had a solid wood wagon with steel wheels that was easy to move. Two of us would take the wagon to the top of the span, get in and ride down to Buffalo Avenue. Steering was loose, to say the least, the noise was awful, and the ride harrowing, especially when cars passed us on the way down. The walk made a turn to the right near the bottom of the bridge and the challenge was not to run off the walk onto the road and stop before we ran out of sidewalk. Stopping was difficult because of the kinetic energy built up due to the high elevation of the bridge at mid-span. But no one ever got hurt in this enterprise. And our parents never knew about it; no use stressing the old folks. We also used the very steep earthen slope of one of the sides near the end of the bridge as a toboggan run, except we had no toboggans and it was a summer activity! We would hunt for large discarded cardboard boxes, flatten them, and then lug them to the top of the slope, get on and ride to the bottom. It was a very rough ride over stones and weeds, but it was lots of fun. It was a race between how long the cardboard would last, and how much of a beating our rear ends could take. Sometimes we won!

What else could we do? With no formal playgrounds around, the farmland and everything else around us was fair territory for our play. A large empty lot down the street had a lot of old apple trees, and we would form teams and have apple wars when the green apple stage had developed. These apples were just the right size for throwing from our small hands – and they really stung when you got hit by one. We were alert to the green apple stage of development and would take a salt shaker and climb up into the trees to get at the fruit. We would pick an apple, lick it, then shake salt on the licked spot and eat it. I ate so much salt that my lips seemed like they were permanently pursed together. I don't remember ever getting really sick from this practice. The empty lot was lower than the properties around it, and in the spring it would fill with water and all sorts of small life would inhabit it. I was fascinated by dragonflies and watched them flitter about for hours. One of the kids brought his Father's canvas-covered folding kayak and launched it in the water for us to paddle around in our "lake." When the water dried up, the area turned into our "jungle" and we would build hiding places and create paths through the bushes, which would eventually grow taller than we. Sometimes all of the kids from several blocks would get together for team tag. We would split up into two groups and the "It" team would hunt for the other team for hours, sometimes way into the dark, roaming all over the neighborhood. When you were caught, you were out of the game.

We were always looking for places to explore. Our favorite locations were where new buildings were being constructed. Houses were great attractions, and we would play in them as soon as the workmen left for the day. We observed the progress of the construction from the time that the basement was dug to the finishing of the roof. The cut-off ends of lumber made great building blocks, and we played on the open joists of the floors as if they were jungle gyms. But our favorite practice was to look for different sized nails that had been dropped by the carpenters. We took the nails up to the main line railroad tracks, where we would place them on the rails with their pointed ends facing the direction from which the train would come. Then, we would hide in the ditch between the sets of tracks. After the train had passed, we would run onto the tracks and hunt for the nails in the rock ballast; we usually found them all. We did this because we learned that the train would flatten the nails so that they looked like miniature swords! The shank of the nail became the blade, and the head was flattened to resemble a handle. So, we had miniature sword fights. We had lively imaginations! In 1949 I flattened a penny on the trolley

Flattened Penny

tracks in front of the Blaire House in Washington, DC, while attending a Key Club convention and waiting for Prime Minister Winston Churchill and President Harry Truman to appear. Memories last a long time! Sometimes there were hidden dangers. One day I and three other friends were chasing each other in the hay fields on Sheridan's farm near where we lived and came to an old rail fence that we took in stride without stopping. I jumped down from the top rail with my knees bent and my hands open, palms down, to break the impact of the landing. The gang was close behind me and I was determined to stay ahead of them, but they were gaining on me and started shouting, so I ran faster! I ran at top speed all the way to the back door of my house and the rest of the crew was there a split second later. My heart was pounding, but I heard them yelling, "You're bleeding!" And so I was. My left hand had landed on broken glass when I went over the fence, and the glass had sliced through the heel of my hand in the grooved area hitting some blood vessels and opening up a big gash. My Mother heard the commotion and got a small towel and wrapped it around my hand. My Dad was at work and my Mother couldn't drive, but Mrs. Olson next door had heard what happened, and she drove me and my Mother down to our doctor's office in the center of the city. I was plunked down in a chair while Dr. Burheyte stitched my wound; there was no spray-on anesthetic in those days. Dr. Burheyte kept a bottle of Coca-Cola in a refrigerator behind his desk chair and he would open its door, take out the bottle, take a swig, and then put the bottle back. Many patent medicines and medical potions contained cocaine when Coca-Cola was named in 1895. Its two medicinal ingredients were extract of coca leaves and kola nuts, hence its name. By 1929, it became cocaine free, but Dr. Burhyete was old enough to have developed a liking to its original formula and couldn't give up the habit.

One day we discovered that a new bowling hall was being built on the river side of Buffalo Avenue near the bridge from Grand Island. Of course we had to inspect it, but this time it was in the dark of night with not a bit of light in the sky. We found that the basement walls had been laid but no flooring had been placed, and the only way to get from one end to the other was by walking on the 6-inch-wide steel beam that ran on steel posts the entire length of the building. It wasn't as easy as we thought. We couldn't see our feet and couldn't turn around, and didn't know what was below us in the dark area where there was probably construction equipment and lots of debris. So we didn't jump down for fear of falling on something and injuring ourselves. Calming myself, I slowly put one foot ahead of the other, heel to toe, until I reached the opposite end of the basement. Finding the end of the beam was easy — the final foot placement found air. I cautiously squatted down until I could sit on the beam, and then let myself down into the ditch surrounding the foundation. From there I could crawl back up to the ground level and be safe. No more dark side adventures for me!

Another game we played was cops and robbers using homemade pistols and rifles. We would take a nice slender piece of wood and cut it to 6 inches to a foot long for a pistol, and perhaps up to 3 feet long for a rifle. Next, we would saw a groove in the bottom near one end and place a taught strip of a bicycle tire or a car tire in the groove and pass it around the rear end of the gun and over half of a clothespin. Finally, a nail was driven into the bottom near the clothespin to act as a finger hold. Ammunition consisted of strips of bicycle or car tires stretched from one end of the gun to the top of the clothespin, with the strip being folded together and placed in the clothespin trigger. Several strips could be tied together to accommodate different gun lengths. Firing a gun was accomplished by holding the nail with the index finger and pushing the bottom of the clothespin to release the rubber bands. Some of these bands hurt when they hit one of us! We played for hours at a time. When I was old enough, I had a BB gun; all of the boys wanted one! One of our playmates had a pump-up air rifle that shot BBs that carried a long distance and was a lot more accurate than the spring powered version of the rifle; they really stung if they hit you. They were dangerous toys but no one got hurt whenever we had a BB gun war. I later fired several real guns, including 12-gauge and .410 bore shotguns, a .45 caliber pistol, and a .22 caliber rifle. I never had a desire to own a real gun and never purchased one. I went pheasant hunting once with my uncles and bagged a pheasant on my first shot; I was the only one that had any success that day.

When I was 7 years old, the 840-foot-long Honeymoon Bridge, also called the Falls View Bridge, between Niagara Falls, New York, and Niagara Falls, Ontario, Canada, collapsed on January 27, 1938, due to ice damage to the supporting structures on each side near water level. I remember it well. I stood at the edge of the pavement where the bridge used to start on the American side of the Niagara River and peered over the side at the wreckage. A flimsy low wood slat snow fence was all that separated us from the gorge edge. I can hardly imagine what the current protocol would be for a similar event; no one would probably be allowed to get within a mile of it! Eight years later, on September 20, 1946, I was standing in our living room when I noticed that the ceiling-mounted chandeliers in the dining and living rooms started to sway like pendulums. Immediately a low rumbling sound began, something like a very heavy freight train going by on the tracks at the end of the street. We had previously moved Grandma Brown's upright piano from her house, relocating it against a long interior wall of our living room; we watched it dance the entire length of the wall, playing randomly as it went, ending up blocking the doorway to the front vestibule. In a short while, the rumbling stopped, the pendulums came to rest, and the piano took a bow for its impromptu avant-garde performance. This was a result of an earthquake that had occurred that caused some damage in various places in the city, frightened a lot of inhabitants and caused a good-sized chunk of the Niagara Falls cataract to fall into the gorge. You could see mist from the water below the falls rising high into the air when such events occurred, even though we were several miles upstream from the falls. The new bridge over the gorge held up to the earthquake, and it's still there; better engineering design yields dependable results.

The Falls View Bridge deck was made of wood and was very slick when wet. In 1930, a motorist put on the brakes, lost control of his car and careened over the edge, plunging to his death in the gorge. Note the long line of cars on the far side of the bridge waiting to be processed. In addition to having driver and car identification, passengers were required to identify themselves, and the trunks were opened for inspection. If someone forgot to declare an item or purposely tried to hide something, the vehicle was pulled over for a lengthy investigation. This happened to us once when my Dad forgot to declare a basket of berries in the trunk that was purchased earlier in the day. After interrogation, we were allowed to proceed. No jail time for us. Whew!

Ice built up to over 100 feet thick and provided a great attraction to folks. An ice jam was a favorite playground for folks in "the old days." Joanne and I were never allowed to participate!

The January 27, 1938, collapse of Falls View Bridge was caused by a sudden high wind that blew ice over the falls from Lake Erie during an exceptionally cold winter, with ice piling up from shore to shore, engulfing the bridge's supports. Attempts were made to dynamite the ice jam, but they failed, and the bridge finally succumbed.

The bridge's replacement, now called the Rainbow Bridge

Illumination of the American Falls. Note the large amount of rock at the base of the falls. This falls is not the place to attempt a trip over the cataract! Use the Horseshoe Falls on the Canadian side instead, which has a 185-foot-deep plunge pool that is filled with talus to within 72 feet of the surface. Best wishes and good luck!

Reserve Officer Training Corps (ROTC): 1949-1953

All able-bodied male students at Land Grant universities, such as Cornell, were required to enroll in ROTC for their freshman and sophomore years. Following that, a student could sign up for advanced ROTC for the next 2 years and enter the service as an officer, a 2nd Lieutenant. When I graduated, the commitment was for 2 years of active duty followed by Reserve duty. I joined the Air Force ROTC at the start of my junior year and spent the summer of 1952 at The AFROTC Summer Training Camp at Wright-Patterson Air Force Base in Ohio. Having been honored in a special ceremony as the number one ranked man in my Cornell Air Force ROTC class when I graduated, I was designated a Distinguished Military Graduate of the Class of 1953, Air Force ROTC, by the Secretary of the Air Force, which gave me special consideration for Regular appointment if I should decide to make a career of the Air Force. I received my commission as a 2nd Lieutenant on June 15, 1953, and received my 2nd Lieutenant bars in front of the World War I Memorial on West Avenue on the Cornell campus, just a few steps away from the barracks dormitory in which I had resided when I entered Cornell as a freshman in 1949. I was assigned to Headquarters 3650th Military Training Wing Sampson Air Force Base in Geneva, New York and ordered to report there on August 1, 1953. On July 5, 1953, I was assigned to Headquarters First Air Force at Mitchell Air Force Base, New York. My Air Officer Service number is AO3011809, and my Selective Service System number is 30 80 31 484.

It is likely that Anne's Father, Samuel Kenneth McClure, is in this 1917 photo of ROTC students assembled on the Arts Quad at Cornell University. He attended Cornell for a year, living in College Town in the first house at the top of the hill next to the Eddy Street Gate that was built in 1896 as the original entrance to the Cornell University campus, before he entered military service in WW1 and served in the U.S. Army in France as what we now call a Medic, reaching the rank of Sergeant. I had his well-worn dog tags made into necklaces for Anne and her sister, Barbara, to wear. His service number was 1918732. In WW1, servicemen made their own dog tags using a hammer and metal stamps. A close inspection of the top of this dog tag shows that he stamped his middle initial, K, upside down; the other dog tag of the pair was stamped correctly. He was born August 23, 1896 and died August 10, 1941. His ashes are interred in the Pine View Cemetery in Glens Falls, New York, in the gravesite where the Crandells and Mills are buried, including Hubert Lee Crandell, Anne's Grandfather (1867–1954). Ken has two headstones, one of which commemorates his service in WW1.

Left: Lois Elizabeth Crandell at age 15, born November 13, 1901; *Center:* Samuel Kenneth McClure, Senior Year High School Photo, Born August 23, 1896; *Right:* Lois, Anne, her sister Barbara and Samuel McClure in their Summit, NJ, backyard, Anne's first home.

I experienced my second flight in an airplane while in AFROTC at Cornell. Our Flight Leader, Major Ferris, requisitioned a C-47 one weekend for a group of us to fly to Memphis, Tennessee. We boarded the aircraft at the Cornell University Airport (now Tompkins County Airport), took off and then circled the Ithaca area before heading for Memphis. Seeing the city and the Cornell campus from the air was a breathtaking experience! The sun was chasing us across the landscape, so the terrain was becoming less visible as we flew west. Eventually, it was night, and I was entranced watching the lights go on below us. The population density was pretty obvious from the size of the light display. When it was still light, I got a chance to fly the plane from the co-pilot's seat. What I didn't expect was to look out the window at the wing and see the metal rippling in the wind! I could count the rivets holding the metal down and watch the wavelets. I felt a little disconcerted, but it eventually passed! We turned around after flying over Memphis and returned to Ithaca where we had a great breakfast of eggs, bacon and all the fixings.

I was in AFROTC at Cornell when the Korean War started to wind down. On July 17, 1953, I was informed that my order to enter active military service had been temporarily suspended due to a "reduction in authorized officer strength." The Air Force delayed 10,000 Air Officers from entering active duty in 1953 when I graduated. I was then rescheduled to be activated between October 1, 1953, and June 30, 1954. So, I worked for the Niagara Railway Co. in Niagara Falls, New York, for the summer of 1953 building railroad tracks in local industries. I then got an appointment as Instructor in the Department of Agricultural Engineering starting in the Fall Semester and simultaneously entered the graduate school for my MS degree. In the rank of Instructor in the Department of Agricultural Engineering I had been allowed to take 2 courses in addition to teaching courses in mechanical and architectural drawing, descriptive geometry and other related duties each semester, such as overseeing the production of plans for farm structures and equipment in the Extension Plan Service where I supervised several part-time and one full-time draftsmen. My regular duty hours ran 49 hours per week, and during the teaching periods averaged 60 hours per week. Being able to take courses while working was a real benefit to my career. I requested a delay of entry into the Air Force, which was granted, and went back to school at Cornell under the aegis of USAFIT (United States Air Force Institute of Technology at Wright Patterson Air Force Base, Ohio), and earned my MS degree in 1956 before spending a short time on active duty at Francis E. Warren Air Force Base at Cheyenne, Wyoming. I had been promoted to 1st Lt. on June 14, 1956, and my 1st Lt. pay was over double what I earned when I started work on the faculty at Cornell! I was honorably discharged on December 2, 1956, as a Research and Development Officer. This ended my expectation to see the world from the military perspective. On the way out to Cheyenne, I had included an extra day for travel time in case of a car problem, and sure enough a driveshaft knuckle joint wore out and I had to spend a night and a morning in Erie, Pennsylvania, waiting to have it fixed. Because the Interstate system had not been built, it was slow going compared to today's travel times, and when I got to the rolling plains, it was downright boring with virtually no traffic on the highway and gas stations miles and miles apart. So, I would purposely drive in the left lane for a while, then back in the right lane, and repeat. Once after a long time at the wheel, when I was in the left lane I suddenly became aware of a light blinking way ahead me in a trough in the road. A trucker sitting up higher than I had spotted my car in his lane! That ended that game for me. Back to being a safe driver! When I reached Cheyenne on November 1, 1956, I stopped at a gas station, changed into my uniform and went to a restaurant for lunch. The weather was very hot, so I ordered a glass of iced tea only to be told that "the season is over" and only hot tea is available now. I then ordered a pot of hot tea and a glass full of ice and made my own iced tea. When I went to the Base entrance gate, I showed the MP my orders and asked for directions to my unit. He told me to go to the first traffic light, turn left, go through the second light and continue on over the river until I saw a fighter plane on a pylon – that's where my unit was located. I followed his directions but saw no river, no pylon and no unit. When I got to a large level area that had huge holes in the ground and large mounds of rock, I turned around and went back to the MP. I told him that I had not crossed a river and

 didn't see a fighter plane on a pylon. He laughed and said, "That river hasn't had any water in it in over 10 years!" Now, for me, a river is the Niagara River, a mile or more wide, with water in it! The Base's river was hardly a creek, with no water to boot, and filled with dead vegetation. The pylon and my unit were in a depression not seen from the road. The holes and rock piles were the beginnings of the Atlas ICBM launch sites, with this base being the first fully operational ICBM base in the Air Force. As an officer, I had a small private room with sparse furnishings and a couple of windows. One morning I got up but couldn't see outside. It had snowed and the wind had blown it into huge drifts – the ground had been bare the night before! One of my fellow officers, 2nd Lt. Dick Hiegel, saw it and was enthralled! He was from Georgia and had never seen snow. We went outside with him and the first thing he did was taste it. Upon being told about snow angels, he lay down in it and made a couple. Upon being cautioned about slippery driving conditions, he got in his car and did spins and fast sliding figure eights in the parking lot. He was a riot! The snow was gone by the next morning. One weekend we went with him to Estes Park in the Rockies and he delighted in seeing how fast he could go around the mountain curves — there were no guardrails. Amazingly, when all newly arrived officers got on Base and met for orientation, the first thing we were told was how to stay out of jail! It seems that Cheyenne had enacted some income producing traffic laws that were driving base personnel to fits because they were having to bail out groups of unsuspecting airmen every day. The first revelation was where the speed traps were located. The roads outside of town were straight as an arrow and speeding was popular to cover the long distances between towns, but folks failed to slow down enough for the speed traps. The second item related to pedestrians. Local law required all vehicles to stop any time a person was within three feet of the curb. School kids took advantage of this as a bit of fun by walking along a sidewalk then suddenly rushing up to stand on the curb. The third problem related to car parking. Meter maids were employed to check the distance from the front bumper to the parking meter support pole using a standard length aluminum rod with chalk on one end. The parking spaces were tight and unmarked, so judging distances while parking was difficult. The meter maids also

chalked the wheels in a selected spot to make sure the cars weren't being over parked. The town treasury loved the Air Base. When I left Cheyenne for Ithaca, I traveled through a black dust storm in Nevada that just wouldn't stop. I closed every air vent but could hardly breathe, and the inside air clouded up. Waves of dust were rolling off the windshield and the wipers did no good. The tail lights of a truck ahead of me had disappeared. I couldn't see to pull off the road and the shoulders were too narrow to just sit there and hope someone wouldn't run into you. So I just kept going very slowly, watching for anything to identify the road edge, and depended on the straight-as-an-arrow design to keep me pointed in the right direction. Eventually, the storm rolled on and I could breathe again. I wondered how dirty the engine's air filter had gotten, but the car didn't stop. Later on I was traveling down a very slight incline when the left front wheel cover popped off. It was pretty large and I knew what had happened right away, so I slowed down. Sure enough, the wheel cover rolled down the road parallel to the car, then crossed slowly over in front of the car, rolled down along the shoulder, then through the ditch and up the other side, travelled along a barbed wire fence and came to rest leaning upright against a fence post! I retrieved it, but put it in the back seat. I'd had enough of those shenanigans. I marveled at the fact that the roadbeds were red instead of black as in the East. Lots of sandstone out there. I brought home a pair of fancy cowboy boots for Sue!

When I came back to Cornell following my discharge from the Air Force, I took a position as an Assistant Professor in the Department, responsible for the Dairy Structures Program in New York State working as an Agricultural Engineering Extension Specialist. This involved a great deal of travel within the State, including farm visits and nighttime meetings. I usually worked on the road from Tuesday through 1:00 PM Saturday, and then spent Sunday in the office answering correspondence from Extension personnel in the field. In those days, the normal required work week was 5 ½ days long. It was a tremendous learning experience. My fieldwork revealed that there was a big deficit of readily available information for the Extension field personnel to use when advising dairy farmers, builders, lenders, suppliers and others with respect to dairy structures and related facilities. To alleviate this situation, I originated a Dairy Structures Guide that utilized 3-ring notebooks to enable monthly updates to the subject matter with categories covering all engineering aspects related to a dairy enterprise. The guides were distributed to all County Agents in the 62 counties in New York State, and the Extension Plan Service provided drawings for related construction and equipment needs. In those days, the word Service was still in the title Cornell Cooperative Extension Service, and we provided a great deal of free service directly to farmers and other folks. During the winter of 1956, one of my Department colleagues, Professor Gordon Perry, and I spent a week making visits to dairy farms needing engineering assistance that had been requested by the County Agent in St. Lawrence County. This wasn't anything unusual, but the weather certainly was! We left Ithaca in a Fleet Garage Chevrolet and made it to Canton in good time and in good weather. Our fleet cars had no radio and no armrests (to save money at purchase!), so we did a lot of talking back then. (It wasn't until our Department Extension Leader, Ev Markwardt, finally was able to convince the Extension Administration that used cars having radios and arm rests returned greater resale value than those that didn't, and at that, we were able to "rest easy" on the road!) Anyway, we went to a hotel, ate and went to bed. The next morning broke bright, clear and very cold at **−36° F**. We were not prepared for that kind of cold! So, we kept on our pajamas and put everything else we had brought over them — underwear, T-shirts, shirts, pants, and doubled up on our socks. We were still cold. We fully expected the Chevy to not start, but a single turn of the ignition key brought it immediately to life! Good old Chevy! When we drove down the street, all four tires made loud bumping noises, and the car bounced a bit because the nylon-reinforced tires had frozen flat spots on them overnight. It took several miles for the effect to work itself out. We stopped at a diner for breakfast and noticed that every car that was parked on the street had been left with the engine running and the exhaust was going straight up in the air — no wind, and no one was taking a chance of having their vehicle not start. The parking meters were frozen solid. We spent 5 days making farm visits at that temperature, and following a very windy snowstorm Friday night, on the morning of the sixth day, Saturday, headed back to Ithaca. The sky was clear and blue and the road was clear, too, right up to a point on the highway where it turned white, glistening in the bright sun, and we saw corn stubble sticking through the snow on both sides of the road. But, it wasn't corn stubble. It was full-height corn stalks that were encased in a huge wedge of packed snow blown up to a great depth. And we ran up on that wedge of snow at 55 mph! Until the engine died. All 4 wheels were now off the pavement. We opened the hood of the car but couldn't see the engine nor any part of it – packed with snow. Up ahead we could see a silo top and a column of snow going up in the air from a snow blower, so we set off looking for assistance. It was tough going because the wedge of snow got deeper and deeper. When we reached the snow blower we saw that it was a farmer's big road blower and that the snow wedge hid the whole farmstead from our view at the car. At least it wasn't snowing, and we knew why he had such a big machine. Eventually, we were able to find a garage that was open on the weekend and have them tow us in our car back to a place where it could thaw out overnight in a heated space. And again, the Chevy started on the first turn of the ignition key the next day! Good old Chevy. We got home late Sunday night, still dressed for **–36° F.**

I had started my PhD program immediately following my MS degree, but financial constraints prevented continuation at Cornell, and I waited until July 1963 to enroll in school at Iowa State University to major in Agricultural Engineering with minors in Theoretical and Applied Mechanics and Nuclear Engineering. This was made possible by a combination of a 6-month sabbatical leave coupled with my being awarded a competitive National Science Foundation Science Faculty Fellowship. I was the first in the Department to receive one. I had exactly two years to complete my PhD program and through concentrated course work and research I accomplished that. We arrived in Ames, Iowa, in early July 1963, and I finished both my French and German language examinations before classes started in Fall Quarter 1963; that took a real load off my coursework. To be able to meet the 2-year time constraint of my leave from Cornell, I took no vacations or time off. My NSF Fellowship came with a small fund to use as my PhD program Chairman saw fit, and I used that money to process my research data on a newly installed IBM mainframe computer that the University had acquired. I had been programming computers since 1957 and that gave me another advantage, being able to process my research data on the mainframe. The biggest advantage was being able to take the processed data and move it to a smaller mainframe that was dedicated to graphing the results. I produced 8 ½" x 11" graphs that could go directly into my thesis with no manual input, with a single run being 120' long. I did all of my computer work at night because punch cards were then used for data and program input and there was less competition for the facilities. These were the early days of academic computing, and not many folks knew a programming language or how to use computers. I recognized this and one fortuitous outcome of my computer expertise was that I started a **FORTRAN** (**FOR**mula **TRAN**slation) computer course in the Department for graduate students and faculty – unexpectedly, 45 people showed up! I ran this course for a full semester, and, as usual, the graduate students were the primary beneficiaries and way ahead of the faculty; faculty didn't "need" the speed! I offered a similar course when I returned to Cornell, but the people in the Department were not enthusiastic at all. In those days, the procedure at Cornell was to first write a computer program on coding forms, and then manually transfer the program to Hollerith punch cards that could be read by a special machine. The program was next compiled in a computer language and then run (processed) on a mainframe computer and the results printed on a separate device. Several programs were usually grouped and run in batches. The printed output contained cryptic information on errors in the program, if any, as well as a listing of the program and the output, if any! The cycle time from submission to receiving the results often took 24 hours. The world has changed remarkably since then! I taught several computer courses at Cornell in different computer languages and developed a large computer laboratory in Riley-Robb Hall for both mainframe and later personal computer use. One facility had a sophisticated laboratory that I used to teach computer-generated graphics using FORTRAN to our undergraduate majors. I taught computer courses both for our engineering students and social science majors and had so many students that I had as many as 23 teaching assistants (TAs) to help teach laboratories and do consulting on a one-to-one basis during the day and evenings in the computing centers. Some students had a great deal of difficulty in understanding programming and how to devise a solution and needed much personal interaction. When I taught two different computer courses in the same semester, I frequently competed with myself for the same facilities. Giving exams was also a problem because the number of students involved required reserving rooms in as many as 5 different buildings and that could only be accomplished at night. Cell phones had not been invented and runners were used to convey fortuitous explanatory information about the exam among the exam sites in the various buildings. I prepared weekly printed lesson plans for all of my computer courses to assure uniformity across my TA staff. I also had special T-shirts made that would allow students in my courses to identify their respective TAs readily. Many students were in a state of anxiety when attempting to deal with writing a computer program, then transferring it to punch cards using key punch machines, and finally submitting it for compilation and execution, only to have it fail to perform as they thought it should, and they wanted assistance immediately! Some even took to paying other students to write their programs, or steal discarded printer output from the wastebaskets by which to model their own programs. Of course, it was simple to detect this cheating and we did so. When I started teaching the computer courses, all of the TAs were men; when I finished teaching them years later, all were women.

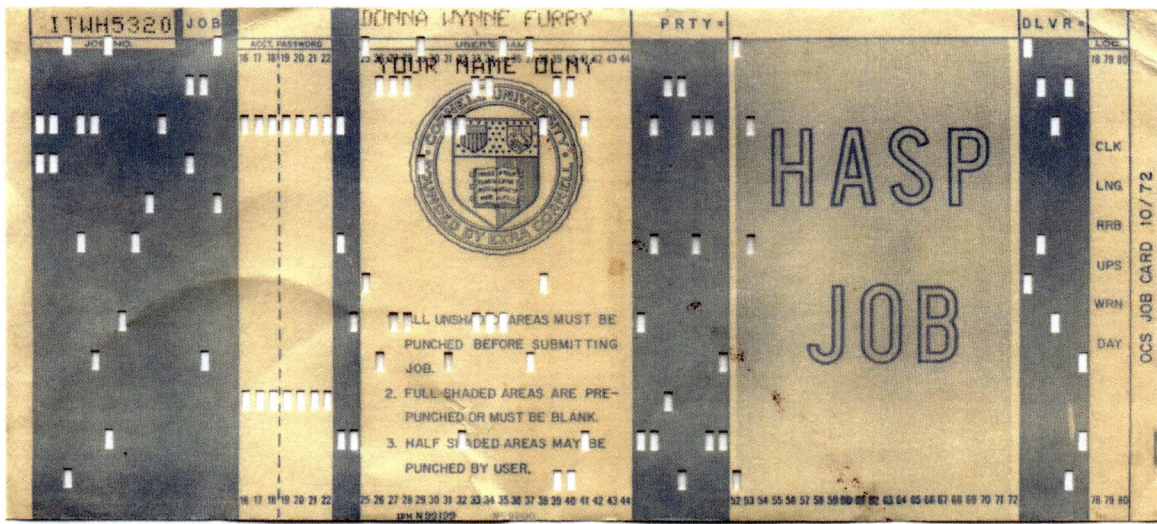

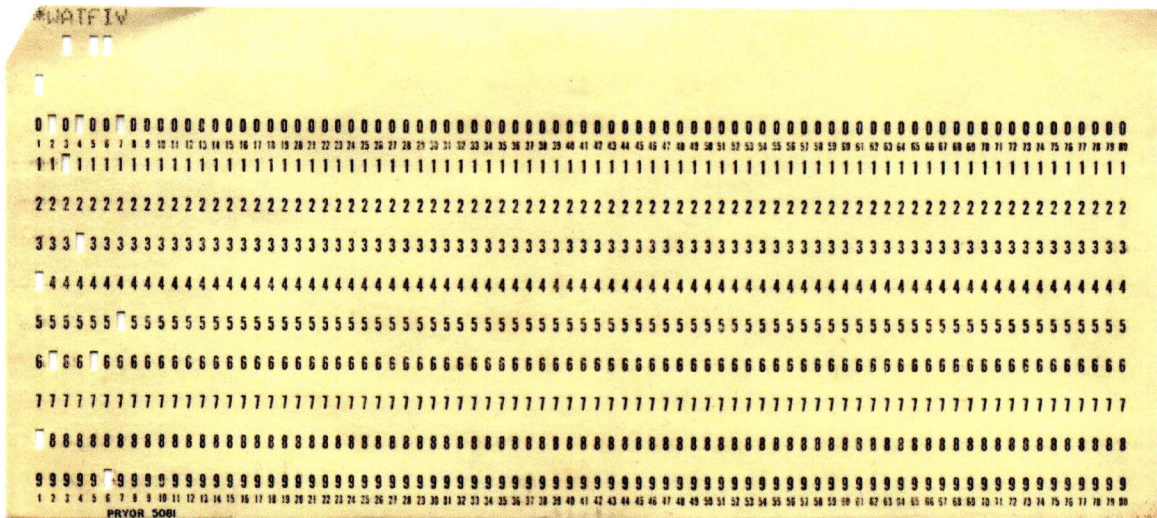

A HASP Job Card with the first card of a FORTRAN WATFIV Computer program. The related program and data set were produced by Donna Wynne Furry when she attended Ithaca High School, and then executed on a mainframe computer on the Cornell campus. Her name is visible near the upper center of the HASP JOB card, directly above the misspelled pre-printed statement that reads "**YOUR NAME OLNY**".

My Social Anchor

My Fraternity at 214 Thurston Avenue, Ithaca, New York, with a ping pong game underway.

Shown here is the Cornell Chapter of the Alpha Zeta Fraternity (AZ) House at 214 Thurston Avenue in Spring Semester 1953, the year of my graduation from college. I took this photo, then developed and printed it as part of a photography course in which I was enrolled. (Neither color film nor the digital age had arrived!) When I was a first semester Freshman I attended an orientation session in the Plant Sciences building that included a short talk by a member of AZ who explained the requirements for being considered for membership. No one was eligible in the Freshman year because a high academic average had to be earned first. That suited my interest just fine and I was determined to become a member. I lived at AZ during my Junior and Senior years at Cornell, 1951 to 1953. It became the center of my social life at Cornell. In fact, I was elected Social Chairman of the Fraternity. AZ is a national honorary fraternity based on scholarship. Only three chapters in the nation had houses, one of which is at Cornell.

The Cornell Chapter was chartered on June 11, 1901. Ezra Cornell IV, the great, great grandson of Cornell University founder Ezra Cornell, was initiated into the fraternity as its Centennial Honorary Member in 2001 at the fraternity's one-hundredth anniversary celebration. I also participated in the initiation of New York State Governor Nelson A. Rockefeller as an Honorary Member in 1962. Someone taking a walking tour around the Cornell campus will discover the names of other notable Honorary Members, such as Liberty Hyde Bailey (1901), Isaac P. Roberts (1901), Henry H. Wing (1901), John H. Comstock (1904), James E. Rice (1904), William A. Stocking (1916), George F. Warren (1929), David L. Call (1981) and Frank H. T. Rhodes (1997) displayed on plaques and buildings.

 Liberty Hyde Bailey founded the College of Agriculture at Cornell University, and was Dean of what was then known as the New York State College of Agriculture from 1903 to 1913. I joined the Faculty 50 years after Bailey became Dean, when William I. Myers was Dean.

73

Cornell held both fall and spring recreational weekends where women were invited to fraternity activities and those who lived out of town could stay on campus at the fraternities. The best part of the weekends were Crew Races on Beebe Lake and big band dances in Barton Hall, the large drill hall where ROTC classes were held and Pershing Rifles had its home. As Social Chairman, one spring I directed the construction of a huge turtle for the Beebe Lake race, and the next spring we built a huge swan for the event. Both were powered by fraternity members inside who moved the legs, neck and tail of the turtle, and the head and wings of the swan while rowing across Beebe Lake. Our AZ crews didn't win on speed, but they took first prize for originality. By far, the dances in Barton Hall were the crown jewel of the events. I just loved dancing to

the live music of Vaughn Monroe (Racing with the Moon) and Stan Kenton. Here are Anne and I at AZ in Spring Semester 1952 prior to attending one of the dances.

And this is a photograph of the AZ fraternity brothers taken in spring 1953 in a moment of "relaxation." I'm in a white shirt, sixth from the left on the first step, wearing my senior hat and chomping on a pipe.

My Father loaned me his 1949 Nash sedan during my 1953 senior year spring semester at Cornell. This photograph was taken in the parking lot of AZ. In

those days, freshmen were not allowed to have a car on campus or in Tompkins County unless they were married. One of my classmates, Bill Loper, was married and had a Chevy with a vacuum shift that we occasionally used to drive to class from Stocking Hall, where the Agricultural Engineering Department was then headquartered, to the lower campus. He delighted in showing how the car's vacuum shift would allow it to go from neutral to any gear with just a light touch on the steering wheel shift lever without having to use the clutch. My Father bought me a similar Chevy (an old 1941 model that had deteriorated from the severely corrosive industrial atmosphere of Niagara Falls) to use during my junior year at Cornell; it also had the same vacuum shift system. Campus parking permits were not required then, and the parking lots had mostly cinder surfaces. In 1953 in New York State, the average cost of a gallon of gasoline was 20 cents, and the average cost of a new car was $1,650.00. The US inflation rate was 0.82%. Our family couldn't afford new cars, and I always wanted to buy my Father a new one, but was never able to do so.

In 2001, the AZ House was rebuilt, under my direction as the Alpha Zeta Alumni Board of Directors' Facility Chairman, responsible for the planning, architectural design and all details related to razing the old structure and constructing the new $1.45 million facility and landscaping the grounds. The new structure has capacity for 33 residents. The fraternity is now co-educational. It ranks very high nationally and in the Cornell Greek system. When I was in AZ, we had 46 male members.

Life Partners and Beyond
Anne and I have a special way of relating how we met. It goes like this.

> I'm from Niagara Falls.
> She's from Glens Falls.
> We met at Taughannock Falls.
> We were married in Hudson Falls.
>
> You might say we "Fallsed" for each other!

Now, three of those statements are true. I am from Niagara Falls, she is from Glens Falls and we were married in Hudson Falls, but I did not meet her at Taughannock Falls. I met her in her bedroom at Ithaca College. And here's how that came about.

One evening when I was living in the old Alpha Zeta fraternity house on Thurston Avenue an Agricultural Engineering classmate of mine, Ray Wilkes, came to see me and told me that the Ithaca College women's dormitories were having an open house. (The Ithaca College campus on the South Hill had not been built at that time, and the College was spread out around Ithaca,

75

downtown and on the hills.) We hopped on his old motor scooter and headed for Hilliard House on the very steep East Seneca Street in College Town. The two-story dormitory was reported to have been designed by the architect Frank Lloyd Wright as a private residence, and was later converted to one of several dormitories for Ithaca College undergraduate women. In those days, men were not allowed above the first floor lounge in women's dormitories except for one evening in the Fall Semester. The dormitory was packed with curious undergraduate men, mostly from Cornell! I went up the stairs to the second floor and as I was entering the broad hallway, I spotted a pretty, jovial co-ed lively conversing with three males in her bedroom. I saw her for barely a second but was instantly smitten. I conspired with my classmate to rout the men talking with her and learned her name and the telephone number of the dormitory. Ray and I were wearing our Junior Year Cornell blazers which we convinced Anne were standard garb for airmen stationed at Sampson Air Force Base located north of Ithaca on the east side of Seneca Lake! From that evening on I gave my attention to tying up the phone line to her dormitory and isolating her from other influencers. It worked. Here we are across the years. One of the new dormitories on the Ithaca College campus is called Hilliard House to commemorate the early facilities used by "The townies."

Lois Anne McClure in 1936

Ronald Bay Paul Furry in 1937

July 22, 1953 — Wedding Day

July 22, 2018 — 65th Anniversary

Upper left: Anne McClure at 15 years old

Ithaca College Graduation, 1955   *Lower right:* High School graduation, 1951

In addition to her beauty, Anne had a superb singing voice, a terrific personality, talent galore and was highly intelligent. She was a marvelous social animal, as was proven time and time again in her professional career. She graduated cum laude from Ithaca College in 1956, with a BS in Music Education with concentrations in voice and piano, raised our 3 children, taught piano privately for 16 years, was a professional Vocal Soloist for churches for 25 years, and taught and administered the Music Education Program of the Ithaca City School District as Coordinator of Music for 20 years, retiring in 1995. She had advanced training and experience in music education and participated in several professional organizations, frequently as an officer. Anne joined organizations because she believed in them and wanted to help solve problems and make advancements. In her spare (!) time she participated in the founding of the Village of Lansing, NY in 1974, and in 1975 was elected a Trustee and Deputy Mayor. In 1981, she was elected Mayor for several terms and spent 15 years in office during the crucial times of forming the Village and defining what it was to be. Nearly all of her service was done without pay. She is the historical high vote-getter in the Village elections, even outperforming her associates in the Community Party. She continued support of the Party and the Village after her service. In later years, she turned to supporting seniors and was President of the Board of Directors of the Tompkins County Senior Citizens Council (Lifelong), and subsequently was a member of related committees. She also helped to initiate the highly successful Senior Circuit lifetime learning program at Lifelong in Tompkins County. Remembering her special relationship with Ithaca College, Anne established **The Anne McClure Furry '55 Endowment Fund for the Promotion and Support of Pedagogical Training in Classroom Music Education** at Ithaca College in 2005. She is a devoted Christian Scientist and serves the local church on the Board of Directors and supporting committees. And more! What a fortunate fellow am I!

And here
      are our
           greatest loves…

  Hi, Folks!

Sue   Ken   Donna

We are extremely proud of our children and the successes that they have made of their lives. Our grandchildren and great-grandchildren will benefit from their qualities and love of life.

Anne's poetry expresses her wisdom and attitude toward life and living in harmony with God, family, friends and nature. She has passed her values on to our children with great success.

They all love to smile!   At our 50th wedding anniversary.

Front: Ron Furry, Suzanne Irish, Barbara Bither, Meghan Tongue, Anne Furry, Denise and Ted Beane   Back: Steven Foehner, Paul Bither, Dave Dirksen, Frances Schlosstein, Ken Furry, Donna Tongue, Brad Irish, Robbyn Tongue, Scott Campione, Paul Irish, Joanne Dirksen, Pete and Sharon Campione

We celebrated our July 2003 50th wedding anniversary at Lakewatch Inn, with 110 family members, relatives and friends in attendance. This is some of our closest group.

About Abodes

I lived in the same house with my sister and parents until I was 18 years old at 165-60th Street, Niagara Falls, New York. My parents lived at her Mother and Father's home next door until their home was completed. My Father signed approval for their house design and the Bureau of Buildings in Niagara Falls approved the plans on May 12, 1930. It was a one-story house designed by Tait of Buffalo, New York, and financed through Sears Roebuck and Company. Sears then took the plans and had the house pre-cut and fitted, which saved up to 40% in construction time. All materials needed were sent directly to the building site. It had a full basement that contained a huge gravity-air coal fired furnace, a big coal bin, a set of wash tubs and a manually lit unventilated water heater. Every time we wanted to wash anything with warm water, including us, we would first have to wait for a sufficient volume to be heated. No one thought anything about the combustion gases building up in the basement! The house measured 25'-10" by 36'-1" with the narrow dimension parallel to the street, which was unpaved, and was placed in the forefront of a 40' by 210' lot. A rear alley had been proposed connecting all of the lots that were to have houses, but it was never built. The house had two bedrooms, a small bath with a tub, a living room, a dining room and kitchen with a tiny vestibule leading to a covered front porch. My Father did some of the finishing work to save money. All walls and ceilings were made of lath and plaster. The attic was unfinished until 1948 when my Dad built a single bedroom for me in the center section because that section of the attic above the dining room had a 2-window dormer in it. There was water and electricity to the property, but no sewer system then, so a septic tank was built in the front yard. The lot had plenty of yard and garden space and a place to house animals. The surrounding area was mostly farm land, so there was lots of room to roam. The soil was almost a sandy loam, with no rocks to be found. Once when my Mother was visiting Anne and me, I took her out in our current Brook Way yard to plant some young Japanese Yew bushes with me, and she asked why I was taking along a shovel and wheel barrow. I told her to just watch. She got the idea after the first hole was dug. I had to use a pick to dig into the soil, and when the hole was large enough I didn't have enough soil left to fill the hole with the root system in it. Sixtieth Street was a breeze by comparison!

When I moved to Ithaca to attend Cornell in 1949, my first stay, at the start of my freshman year, was in a battered army barracks on the south end of West Avenue on the campus. It was a single-story structure with bathroom facilities and a lounge area in the center between two halves with small double rooms along each side of a narrow, dark corridor. There were no rugs, finished floors, curtains or pleasantries in the entire building. My roommate, John Chin, and I shared a room about 8' wide by 12' long, having one window and a small length of exposed finned steam pipe for heat. The heat was turned off at 10:00 PM, and the heat pipe was so hot when it was on that you could burn yourself. We shared a bunk bed having flat wire supports and a single dresser having 4 drawers. Our study area consisted of a single shared table about 2' x 3', and one small wooden straight chair each. A single incandescent bulb hung from the ceiling, and a single lamp stood on the table. Part of the wall space ahead of the bunk bed and next to the entrance had a single 3' long rod where we could hang our clothes. Every room was the same, but mirror images of each other in terms of their layout. One night John decided to take advantage of that fact. We waited until our neighbors had gone to bed and were fast asleep, then silently drilled a hole through our wall and their wall at the same location where the upper bunkmate's head would be lying on his pillow. Then, we got a straw, inserted it through the holes in the partition wall, and squirted water into the bunker's head. At first there was surprised disbelief, then a big uproar, followed by the usual inspection to find out how he got wet. Our door was locked and the lights were out. We didn't respond, but avoided them for a few days until things settled down. So, this is how my Engineering Physics major roommate ran his Physics experiments. There were no recreation facilities around anywhere.

The second semester of my freshman year, John and I moved to a small apartment near the top of Seneca Street hill in College Town. It had a double bed with a good mattress, and was warmer, and a shared bathroom was down the hall. There was a stove that we used to just make tea. It was infinitely quieter than the dorm. We didn't spend much time there because it was a bit too far to get to during times of no classes during the day. We also noticed that the extra walking that was involved and going up and down the hilly streets was wearing the soles of our shoes out! Leather soles were pretty much the norm then, and composites were not good, if they could be found.

The summer of 1950, my old high school classmate Pat Fessenden and I shared a room and a double bed while working on the dairy and cash crop farm of Henry Bauer in Angola, New York, to earn our remaining farm work credits that were required by the College of Agriculture at Cornell.

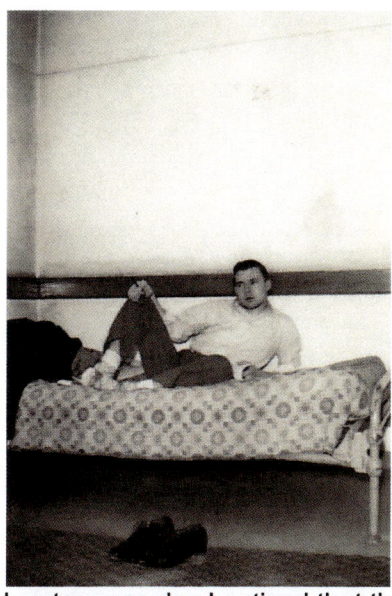

In my sophomore year, 1950-51, Pat and I shared a large room in the Kline Road dormitory on campus; John Chin was no longer attending Cornell because of illness. This dormitory was a 2-story army barracks having no amenities but very high ceilings and larger rooms, with a large shared open lavatory at one end. There were no sidewalks, lights or transportation, and it was on the hill on the northeast edge of the campus in a big field with high grass, so when you left the building the idea was to take just about everything and anything you might need with you for the day and evening — we had both evening and Saturday classes until 1:00 PM in those days. There was no supervision at all, and this was a raucous place at times. One time when a bunch of guys decided to have some fun with a couple of fellows in a room near us, they chased them into their room, which they then barricaded to defend themselves. Their antagonists then took the fire hose and squirted high-pressure water and threw fire crackers under the door. It was a noisy, wet time! Of course, the floors were old, unpainted wood, so it did little damage, just some warping. When I went into the lavatory one day I noticed that the toilets didn't seem to flush all the way and that the water closets were filling up too quickly. I took one of the water closet lids off and discovered that the tank was packed with bottled beer! There were no refrigerators in any of the dorms, so these folks were keeping their beer cold by storing it in the toilet water closets that got the most use. Must have been an engineer in the dorm someplace! One evening when Pat and I were studying, we heard a very low rumble go across our room under the building. It repeated several times and later stopped with a bang. We noticed some water coming into the hall down by the lavatory and went down to see what was going on. There was water squirting into the air from a broken toilet and pieces of the porcelain lay all over the place. We found out that a couple of the men had gotten some M-1 military fire crackers that had visco fuses that burn underwater. They would light a fuse, drop the firework in the toilet, throw in a bunch of toilet paper to make a plug, then flush the toilet. The firework would travel through the sewer pipes under the dorm until the fuse ignited it. Unfortunately, on their last attempt they used too much toilet paper for packing and the firework exploded in the neck of the toilet, breaking it to smithereens! Pat and I played less troublesome games. We had different majors, so different courses and schedules, and would seldom be in the room at the same time except at night, so we would play a continuous game of checkers or chess. The last one to leave the room would make a move on the board, then put a thumbtack on the side of the board to indicate who should move next. It was slow going!

I spent the summer of 1951 living at home in Niagara Falls and worked my Uncle Bob's farm in Pekin, New York for $1.00 an hour. One day I went to work in the morning, passing through the usual 40 mph zone on the 17-mile rural route, and came home on the same route only to be stopped for speeding. While I was working at the farm, the speed limit had been changed to 30 mph, and the local gendarme was waiting on a side road for law breakers. Surprise!

My sophomore year, 1951-52, I lived at AZ in a 4-person suite consisting of a small study room with 4 desks, a tiny bedroom with 4 bunk beds, a minuscule closet 4 feet high with no door and a single 4-drawer dresser. We were on the second floor, directly over the front porch where the brothers played ping pong. I used to start studying about 11:00 PM, so the Gnip, Gnop noise of the ball hitting the table didn't bother me too much, but the shouts of a successful smash or a victory was a decided distraction, especially later when you were trying to go to sleep! The fraternity house had been built as a private dwelling in the 1800s in the area called Cornell Heights on Thurston Avenue where all of the rich people lived. Cornell Heights was on a high promontory overlooking the entire city and lake, so the view was spectacular. The Fall Creek gorge lay across the street to the south, and a suspension bridge crossed over it to the campus. I used that bridge to get to class for the next two years. The gorge wall rose sharply at the south end of the bridge, and climbing the stairs to get to the Arts Quad level could sometimes make one breathless if you were in a bit of a rush. No fraternities or sororities were allowed in Cornell Heights until 1901 when AZ broke the ban and acquired the big house at 214 Thurston Avenue. The area now is a Historic District of the City of Ithaca. The building AZ purchased consisted of 3 stories and a stone-walled basement that contained the boiler and a very small apartment for the fraternity's caretaker. The first floor had a living room with a working fireplace, a hall with a piano, a dining room and a kitchen that spread across the back of the building. The second and third floors each had bedroom and study room combinations occupied by at least 2 people, and a lavatory. There were no straight lines in the building anymore due to differential settling, and the dark green walls and white woodwork had not been maintained in years. The stairs creaked unhappily! There was a phone on each floor level, and I spent a lot of time on the one that was in the cubby hole under the stairs on the first floor after I found Anne! Living in AZ was a whale of a lot better than living in the dormitories, and we had a common background and camaraderie to boot. I especially appreciated the fact that it was a "dry house" – no liquor was allowed on the property or at any of the fraternity's' functions. That of course has all changed with the times, but recent word from the Cornell Administration may alter that situation somewhat. The first President of Cornell, Andrew Dickson White, decided not to provide housing for all enrolled students in campus dormitories. As result, Cornell currently has 54 percent of the students living in college-owned, -operated or -affiliated housing and 46 percent of students live off campus. One-third (4,500+ students) of the undergraduate student body belongs to one of the 64 recognized fraternities or sororities. I enjoyed my life at AZ immensely. Hooray for President White!

The summer of 1952 was spent at AFROTC Summer Training Camp at Wright-Patterson Air Force Base just east of Dayton, Ohio. The barracks to which I was assigned housed 32 men on cots in a long common area with a single lavatory. Only a tall fence separated us from Route 4, which went south to Dayton and north to Springfield. It was blistering hot that summer, and the cadets would go outside with just their Jockey shorts on when we were off duty to get out of the hothouse inside the barracks. It was interesting to see the effect this had on traffic on Route 4. Girls would come zooming along in their cars, suddenly spot the undressed men, jam on the brakes, and back up to ogle and chat with the group! I never saw an accident, though. Wright-Patterson was the Air Force's research and development center, and we had lots of interaction with activities in the labs. One area I especially liked was the static load test lab that happened to have a huge 6 engine pusher 4-jet engine B-36 bomber under test. I had studied the B-36 and the selsyn (self-synchronous) fire control system for its 20 mm cannons at Cornell and was amazed to see the real thing. The load testing involved gluing strain gauges to the aircraft at selected stress points and then loading the wings with weights to simulate deflections in flight. Men were walking on the wings to accomplish this. However, the huge hanger also had a fighter ejection test seat installed at one end, and when the explosive charge under the seat went off, it surprised the folks on the wings so much that they were falling off and breaking bones, mainly legs! This problem was resolved by first sounding a Klaxon horn to warn that a shot was imminent. I thought the Klaxon's noise was almost as bad as the ejection seat explosion! After Anne and I were married, we would lie in bed at night in Ithaca and listen to the drone of B-36 bombers as they flew high over Ithaca practicing simulation flights for attacks on the Soviet Union. One time I asked her to be quiet and listen to hear the blinking wing lights on the bombers. She complied so long that I could hardly hold my laughter! The Wright-Patterson Air Force Base is very close to where Joanne and Dave lived after they were married, and he went to work for Armco Steel; they first lived in Washington Courthouse, then in Monroe, Ohio.

A B36-F: This is the bomber that carried both thermonuclear and atomic bombs during the 1950s.

My senior year at Cornell (1952–53) was spent in the same room on the second floor of AZ as the previous year. I was Social Chairman again and having a great time academically and socially.

Anne and I were married in 1953, and we spent the summer living with my parents in Niagara Falls, and I worked for the Niagara Railway Co. helping to build railroad track in Niagara Falls industrial sites. In September 1953 Anne and I moved to 410 North Geneva Street in Ithaca where I had been hired as an Instructor in the Department of Agricultural Engineering and started my MS degree work. Our total possessions were contained in one suitcase and a foot locker. We lived in a small second floor apartment that had a living room, bedroom, bath, dining room and a small kitchen. The kitchen was a converted porch whose floor sloped toward the outside of the house. One day, Anne dropped a bottle of milk, which only came in glass bottles in those days, and the bottle hit the floor and smashed to smithereens, spilling the contents. In a blink of the eye, the milk disappeared under the refrigerator! For all I know, the dried residue is still there. Anne did the wash one sheet at a time in a table top Handi-Hot clothes washer, and dried them on a pulley line from a second-floor access door. There were 2 other very small apartments in this house occupied by married Cornell graduate students Carl and Lois Hansen and Myron and Joan Watkins, along with the area occupied by the owners. The owners preferred renters that had no babies, but in less than a year there was a new baby in all three apartments! We bonded with these folks and kept in touch for the rest of their lives. The owner and his son ran an electrical business out of his 4-car garage, so there was no place to park on the property. I had our apartment rent reduced from $100.00 per month to $95.00 by agreeing to take out the garbage weekly and clearing the walks of snow. For $5.00, I rented a garage next door for a second hand 4-door Plymouth that my Father had bought for us. Carl Hansen rented a garage with double swing-out doors across the street. One day he forgot to open the doors and backed right through them with his Studebaker. He did this twice, but the insurance company paid! Anne went to school at Ithaca College in the Fall Semester, and took a leave of absence when Suzanne was born the next Spring on February 1, 1954. Sue was born prematurely and spent the first couple of weeks in oxygen in the hospital until her lungs had fully developed. This was really hard on Anne, but they both came through it well. Anne returned to school in Fall Semester 1954 and used a stroller to take Sue to a baby sitter a couple of blocks away. Jean Tripeppi, the baby sitter, charged 25 cents an hour, including lunch! A real bargain. Jean was a WW2 war bride from England and a superb individual. We still occasionally see her daughter in Ithaca. One day we were going out for groceries and Anne tripped on a ripped, loose tread cover near the bottom of the stairs to our apartment, and Sue landed on the concrete sidewalk with the fall breaking her right femur. We rushed her to our pediatrician, Dr. Thomas Mosher, and she spent the next several weeks in a cast that went all the way around her waist and down to her ankle. It was hot in the apartment that summer and the cast caused her leg to itch. She couldn't scratch the area that itched, so she would bang it with the heel of her left foot – day and night! We really felt sorry for her – and our ears at night! Later, Anne worked nights as a waitress in downtown Ithaca, and I would baby sit Sue. One hot night, I fell asleep in the chair in the living room while Sue was crawling around on the floor. I woke up to find her sitting in front of a window, studiously pulling wall paper off the wall in tiny little vertical strips! She had denuded virtually the entire area beneath the window. I glued every last one of the strips back on the wall in spite of the fact that it wasn't an easy pattern; it was full of small multicolored diamonds and zigzags. The location of this apartment turned out to be beneficial for us because it was almost in the center of the locations where Anne could walk to her Ithaca College classes, which were downtown at that time, the babysitter's home, and her waitress job on State Street in downtown Ithaca.

Anne is a nest maker. In 1956, she found a house on the corner of Aurora Street and Hillview Place on Ithaca's South Hill and convinced me to move there. This time we got Dave Dirksen to help us move with his 2-wheel trailer because we had collected a few things more by then. At this house at 517 South Aurora Street, we had the whole first floor and a small basement section for washing laundry, plus a very tiny upstairs room. Aurora Street is very steep, and the passing traffic is constant and very noisy on the brick roadbed, so we put Sue in the back bedroom and we took the front bedroom next to the street. Kenneth was born on June 1, 1956, while we lived there, so he later shared the room with Sue. The house also had a tiny full bath, a large living room that went across the full width of the house and a good-sized kitchen with a huge, heavy old-style gas stove. The bathtub had a very low side, and Ken learned to belly flop over the side into the bathwater and laugh his head off! He did it over and over again with no encouragement; this may have been a forewarning of his later prowess in swimming. A big advantage of this property was that it had a backyard with some grass that I fenced off and made into a relatively safe place where our children could play. We could also park our car in the driveway, or across the street on the south side of Hillview Place where the railroad tracks curved crossing Aurora Street to go to the Morse Chain Company. The train came right down the south side of Hillview Place in front of the houses and created quite a spectacle! Once after Ken was born, Anne went down the hill to Ithaca with Ken in the baby carriage but could hardly get back up — it was very steep. Once was enough! My Uncle Bill Brown gave us an old black-and-white TV set that I hooked up to a curtain rod on the front door as an aerial. The picture was always totally snowy, except for one day when I tuned in to the logo of a TV station in Texas! Listening to the sound was mostly impossible because the audio was overridden by the noise made by the firing of all of the spark plugs of big trucks going up and down the South Aurora Street hill. We could easily tell when the truck drivers changed gears as they were coming down the hill by the pitch and increasing frequency of the spark plugs' static. In spite of this, Anne used to watch soap operas while she was ironing! Beggars can't be choosy! In November 1956 I left for a month to go on active duty in the Air Force in Cheyenne, Wyoming. Fortunately, some of Anne's friends were around to take her shopping because she had not yet learned to drive. We bought a used 2-tone Studebaker President Classic the next year, and she learned to drive. She was free at last!

She was at it again! Anne learned that Dr. Darcy, who worked at the Cornell Clinic, and his wife were moving out of the Luce Dairy house 3 houses up the street from us on Hillview Place. This was the former family home of the owners of Luce Dairy, a local processor, bottler and distributor of milk. The milk processing plant was behind the house and there was a large paved area on one side used by bottled milk delivery trucks and refrigerated trucks delivering raw milk. Dave Dirksen helped us move again, but this time we had to rent a mover with a large truck; we were accumulating material fast! I got the small freight mover from work, and Dave and I took the legs off Anne's baby grand piano, strapped it onto the mover, and pushed it up the center of the road and into the Luce house at 410 Hillview Place. This house had 2 floors and 3 fireplaces. The first floor had a large front porch, an entry way, a living room with one fire place, a dining room, a kitchen and adjacent place for a refrigerator, a small play room and a sunroom with a second fireplace. The second floor had 4 bedrooms and a large bath (no shower), and third

84

fireplace in the rear bedroom. The attic had bats, but we didn't go up there! So, we set up house again. The owner made an off-road parking place for our Studebaker on the right front side of the lawn, but there was still plenty of grassy play space for the kids, and they learned to ride tricycle and bicycles in the paved area around the dairy plant. A small pergola adorned the side yard and I installed a picnic table there, too. We were finally away from the Aurora Street traffic noise, and the dairy only operated 5 days a week, so the local noise wasn't too bad. One problem was that the commercial refrigerated trucks that came to the dairy early in the morning before it opened would park in the paved area next to the house, and we could hear their refrigeration systems running. Probably the worst part of the house was that it was very drafty. In the winter, very fine snow would seep around the frame of a window on the landing of the second-floor stairs and pile up over 3 inches deep on the sill. I finally had to cover the outside of the window with PVC plastic film to stop it. It was still cold, though. The best part about the location was that the South Hill Elementary School was right across the street behind a row of houses with a walk straight up to the school. There were also neighborhood kids around for ours to play with, and Anne had other mothers with whom to interact. Donna was born when we lived here on June 8, 1961. Donna was musical from the start. We would sit her on the floor and say, "Dee, dee, Donna!", and she would rock back and forth from side to side!

In 1963 we sub-let the house to Howard and Carolyn Longhouse while we were in Ames, Iowa, where I was working on my PhD at Iowa State University. Howard was a staff member in the Department of Agricultural Engineering and a good friend of ours. While we were in Ames, we

lived in the Hawthorne housing complex for married graduate students. Ames had a different climate than Ithaca, and the first thing we did was buy and install a window air conditioner, primarily to reduce the humidity; the next thing we did was buy a pull-out couch for Anne and me to sleep on. Donna and Ken shared a room next to the living room and Sue occupied a room alone. The single story apartment also had a full bath and a small kitchen. One morning, Ken refused to get out of bed and I asked him why. He said the throw rug was moving. And it sure looked like it was, with hundreds of small almost translucent ants crawling all over it! So, we were off to the next phase of life in Ames, regularly taking care of the bugs. Ames had huge cockroaches! We rented a small upright piano, put it in Sue's room, and Anne taught piano lessons, as well as singing as the soloist in the local Christian Science Church. She also took singing lessons to maintain her voice. She made friends quickly with other wives of graduate students in our housing complex, which had a large grassed play area bordered by multiple single-story 4-unit apartments. It was a comfortable place to live. I bought a bicycle and rode it to my office on campus, discovering that Ames had lots of flying ants that got in my mouth and ears! There were also lots of little kids around, and the folks attributed that to the nightly train that went right by the living quarters at about 3:00 AM! I didn't take any time off when I was at ISU and finished my degree in 2 years.

When we came back to Ithaca in the summer of 1965, we again lived in the Luce house and started planning a new house. Anne was off again, now looking for a lot to purchase for a new house! We also got a puppy, with long ears, long tail and a long nose, with a downy white undercoat and long brown-black outer coat. He had a tan bow tie on his neck and the bottom few inches of each leg were tan, so we named him Spatz Arfur Furry. He was very friendly and playful. He was born February 3, 1966, and lived with us for 13 years. When he was a pup, we would chase him around the house, and he would escape from us

by hiding under the couch in the living room — until he had grown so big that he could no longer get under it. Was he surprised! He learned to say, "Hello," when we entered the house, bowing down on his front legs and trying to imitate our vocal greeting. We miss him.

In early 1966, Anne found a 1.02-acre lot in the Town of Lansing in a new, sparsely built Stormcrest Heights Subdivision that used to be the Robert Gibbs farm. The lot has Tax Map No. 45.2-1-40. It was still dairy country, and Triphammer Road was barely 2 lanes wide, intersecting the new Route 13 bypass at the same elevation with no traffic control to permit safe crossing of the divided highway. Thirteen people were killed in accidents before the State constructed a diamond overpass. She had picked out lot number 23, having a 5-sided shape, the biggest and most expensive lot in the development, away from the main road, with a stream running through the edge of the property, and a pair of ducks paddling around in a pool. It cost $2,600.00! Peanuts in comparison with prices even a few years later. So, we inquired around about local builders and hired Alex Cima to build a Bennett Lumber Corp. pre-cut home, just like my parents did in 1929, although we didn't know that then. Alex's wife was the Secretary to the Cornell University Board of Trustees and a Cornell graduate. We got along just fine and became good friends. We designed the house to have 4 bedrooms, 1½ bathrooms, a large living room, front hall, large kitchen, a full basement and an attached 2-car garage. I built a model of the living room to make certain that we got the break in the vaulted ceiling in correct proportion with the angled valance lighting on the tall wall where the floor to ceiling fireplace was to be built. The house has hardwood floors, which are now covered with carpeting. Like her sister, Anne is always writing poetry. Here's a quickie that she wrote on the back of a grocery list when the house was finished; it's to the building crew. (Note: Several years later, the Post Office changed our address to 143 Brook Way.)

Three cheers and hooray,
The house is done at 131 Brook Way.
It's been a long haul
And you've had little rest,
Alex, Eddie, Bob and Paul,
You four are the best
And please send a message
To our mason, Dick Hill,
The fireplace and cellar
Are proof of his skill.
The Furrys make this gesture —
    a sort of token,
The door at Brook Way
    will always be open.

There was no municipal water or sewer serving the development then, so we drilled a 69-foot well, and installed a septic tank and disposal field. There was so much hydrogen sulfide in the water along with sulfur-loving bacteria that we had to chlorinate the water and install an in-line filter to remove the bacteria, and replace them periodically when they became overloaded. It brought back memories of my Grandfather Furry's sulfury farm well water! This was a definite pain in the neck, and required flushing the filters every month to reduce the pressure drop in the water system. This was not alleviated until after Anne and her compatriots formed the Village of Lansing in 1974, and the Bolton Point water supply came through our area and sewer lines were installed that fed into the Cayuga Heights sewage treatment plant down on the shore of Cayuga Lake. We were able to hook up to both water and sewer service in 1982. The house originally had 1,862 square feet, but in

1996–97 we added a 21' by 22' air-conditioned sunroom with a 3-speed reversible ceiling fan, a hot tub and a Dovre DV-400 PGRN natural gas stove, giving us 2,324 square feet total. It has a

crawl space under it with a trap door entrance in the northeast corner. At the same time, we installed two ceiling fans in the living room. We also added a 14' by 16' deck attached to the house and the sunroom. Prices rise – the sunroom and deck cost more than the original lot and house combined! In October 1997, we added a large, screened oval gazebo down by the creek. Since then, we've added a water softener and a Mitsubishi Electric air-to-air heat pump with evaporator units in the bedroom and living room ends of the house. The heat pump will operate with outdoor air temperatures down to 14° F. Currently, electricity here is cheaper than natural gas for heating. We like it here, even if the deer do eat us out of house and bird feeder! Note that the deer even have watchers on guard.

Our home with the new sunroom and deck additions in Spring 1997

The Furrys Go Abroad, But Home Is Best

In addition to travel in the United States and Canada, Anne and I visited 28 countries, including England, Wales, Ireland, Northern Ireland, the Isle of Sky and Scotland on a single continuous 4,025-mile journey. We also traveled to France, Germany, Czech Republic, Slovakia, Poland, Luxemburg, Italy, Switzerland, Denmark, Monaco, Russia, Finland, Hong Kong, China, Australia, New Zealand (both the South and North Islands), Japan, Hawaii, Fiji, Anguilla, and St. Maartens (both French and Dutch parts). We enjoyed every minute of the trips, but my favorite foreign place was the isle of Fiji. Warm water and blue skies make my favorite swimming environment, and there is plenty of that on Fiji. Here I am in the big blue Pacific wearing my ultraviolet protector.

Anne likes animals and I guess they like her. Here she is in Australia with some of her friends.

With Beatrice python.   A Joey in the arms is worth 2 in the bush.   Koala bears are cuddly.

Feeding a Rosella bird in Sherbrooke Forest.   On a camel ride in Alice Springs, Australia.

But our favorite place away from home in the States is at Lake George, Anne's playground when she was growing up. In particular, we've been going to an old Adirondack-style cottage called the Kittredge Cottage since our 45th wedding anniversary in 1998, when Sue found it for us as an after-anniversary relaxer! It was built by a minister in 1916 and now doesn't have a straight line or a level floor in it! It's on a beachless shore of Harris Bay on the southeast end of Lake George in Cleverdale, New York. It sleeps 10 in not-so-comfortable accommodations, but it has great personality, sort of like almost roughing it! An Annex in the back of the lot has a full bath with a powerful shower. In good weather we spend most of the time on a dock over the water, and retreat to the fireplace in the living room when the weather gets bad. Lake George Village is 9 miles to the west, about a 19-minute drive, and this is where all of the tourists congregate. There are free fireworks displays twice a week — my favorite! We can even hear the shells burst and see the high fireworks over the hill right from the dock. Anne's Grandfather, Hubert Crandell, a very successful florist in Glens Falls at the time, owned a large beach property on the diagonally opposite side of the Bay. His property's shore had real sand and a huge two-story boathouse. It's still there, but the dwellings on the property have been remodeled and the grounds re-landscaped. We can see his former property from the Kittredge Cottage. The year 2018 was our 21st straight year of spending 2 consecutive weeks at this cottage. It has become a family reunion site. Aren't we lucky!

View looking west across Harris Bay from Kittredge Cottage. The sun sets in the lowest notch.

The Irishes, Ploofs, Furrys, and Tongues on the screened front porch

The Tongues with Neca's niece, Juliana, and Ken at a favorite lakeside pastime!

Ken Furry invents the shell phone at Lake George.

Enjoying the fire are Joanne Furry Dirksen (seated), David Dirksen, Ron Furry, Kenneth Furry, Anne Furry, Barbara McClure Foehner Bither, and Paul Bither.

The Boss takes a break.

Potato rock found on shore

Joanne Furry and Dave Dirksen's wedding, November 1, 1958. Married in St. John de LaSalle Church where Joanne previously taught. *From left:* Ronald Furry with Kenneth Furry, Maryanne Connaly, Anne Furry with Suzanne Furry, Edna Louise Brown Furry, Joanne Louise Furry Dirksen, David Phillip Dirksen, Anne L. Dirksen (Dave's Mother, Bill Dirksen.(Dave's Brother).

Our **Next Generation** generators
from **Generation Y**…

Bradshaw Irish and Sarah Dalton

Brandon Marchant and Meghan Tongue

94

Newton's First Law in Ithaca

On June 2, 1962, I joined the Ithaca Sertoma Club as a charter member. Sertoma stands for **Service to Ma**nkind. In addition to other volunteer work, we raised and donated money to support activities such as the Ithaca College Sir Alexander Ewing Speech and Hearing Clinic Mobile Audiology Unit that travelled to various locations to test people for hearing difficulties. It visited nursing homes, hospitals, schools, and the New York State Fair. The unit also made trips to Defiance, Ohio; Martinsville, Indiana; and, once, a three-week trip into Kentucky. Our club membership consisted of businessmen, professors, salesmen, engineers, policemen and a host of other professionals, all of who were willing to volunteer their labor and time to raise funds. We also held pig roast fundraisers, but our primary fundraiser was an annual sale of firewood in the Ithaca area. We would locate tracts where trees had been cut down and abandoned, then on weekends cut the logs and stumps up, and split them to fireplace size, and deliver and stack the wood at a buyer's home. One fall season we cut up and delivered a 4-foot-high stack of wood a half mile long. It was both hard work and fun and we developed a very close camaraderie. One individual in our group was Larry Kohler. Larry had come to Ithaca in 1931, my birth year, with his new bride to buy a house and start a machine shop. They engaged a real estate agent to show them houses around the county, and the first house he took them to was located across the Inlet on Route 96 (Cliff Street) at the start of the uphill part of the road just as it leaves Ithaca on the western side of the railroad tracks. They spent the whole day traveling around the area looking at houses, and Larry finally told the agent to take them back to the first home that they had seen, the one on Route 96, because it suited their needs best. The agent resisted, but they insisted and back they went. They asked why he tried to steer them away from the property and the agent told them that it was a very, very bad choice because the New York State Department of Transportation (DOT) had designated that section of Route 96 for widening and the road expansion would literally put the curb right at their front door! The Kohlers bought the property anyway, and Larry built his machine shop next to the house on the downhill side. They raised their children, had a successful business, retired, sold the property to a specialty metal business, Incodema, a short run sheet metal prototype provider at 407 Cliff Street, and moved away from Ithaca. Larry always laughed with glee at the State's road planning program — and the real estate agent who believed it so strongly. It is now 2018, 87 years after the Kohlers came to Ithaca and that section of Route 96 has not yet been touched! The DOT often takes many decades to design, develop and implement a plan for road work, but inertia works best in Ithaca.

My memories are full of contrasts. I can remember that in 1949 the very last street light when leaving Ithaca going north on Route 96 was located at what is now the Hanger Theater, and everything thereafter was absolutely pitch black at night. The same was true for all of the hills surrounding Ithaca — pitch black at night with a very dark pool that was Cayuga Lake. Now, the hills are alive with light at night, a testament to the successful effort to electrify rural America in which the department in which I worked at Cornell had a leading role in New York State (see http://ecommons.cornell.edu/handle/1813/7642), and the City glows softly in energy conserving sodium vapor lighting. An absolutely gorgeous view of the hills and the City of Ithaca can now be seen by driving south from Newfield down the hill into Ithaca. It has year 'round eye appeal, including a spectacular fall color show as the leaves blush toward winter. And there is no longer an airstrip at the (H)anger. I recall watching airplanes circling the City, getting lower and lower until they disappeared below the hills for a landing on the flats. Airplanes now circle over our house in the Village of Lansing near the Tompkins County Airport, but it is not nearly as interesting to watch – just noisier, and it's now proposed as an International Airport.

Gone is the dusty, narrow congested 2-lane road that was Route 13 to Elmira on the flats approaching Buttermilk Falls, and the annual flooding of the road in springtime. I felt sorry for the car dealers who had to wash their roadside display of vehicles that all slowly took on the same dull color when the dust billowed in clouds from passing traffic as the weather warmed. I also remember the Peters brothers relating their experience in laying brick pavers on the original State Street roadbed, and the interest The Ithaca Commons created when former Ithaca Mayor Edward J. Conley proposed converting a couple of blocks of the downtown State Street roadway into a pedestrian walkway. Ed was a celebrity at the annual New York State Conference of Mayors for a few years thereafter, and we attended because Anne was a Trustee of the newly formed Village of Lansing. Eventually, Ithaca had no true department store in the center of town and the big box stores took over. We left Ithaca for a couple of years (1963-65) to get my PhD degree at Iowa State University, and when we came back in 1965 we could hardly recognize the City, let alone find our way around the streets downtown. The Tuning Fork had been built while we were gone with Green Street and Seneca Streets now having one-way traffic in opposite directions two streets apart, but the biggest shock to our memories was to see that all of the trees along the way had been cut down to widen the roadbeds. The central core of the City was nude from east to west. It took many years for it to regain some of its original charm. We are lovers of hills, greenery and water, especially lakes, and spectacularly splendiferous multicolor sunsets. And that is why the Ithaca area attracts Anne and me, even in retirement. There may never be another devastating flood in the City like that of July 7 and 8, 1935, but I am reminded that it happened whenever I pass the high-water mark painted on the little brick building on Route 13 downtown across the street from Wegmans store. Nine and a half inches of rain fell in Ithaca in 72 hours. Across the Southern Tier, 43 people died with hundreds homeless. A series of severe thunderstorms caused streams to overflow so rapidly that people were not aware of the impending danger. One of our club members recalled canoeing in the streets in downtown Ithaca. In later years, we would experience the effects of a couple of hurricanes here, but nothing like the devastation of 1935. Driving though flooded roads in the spring to get to Loblaws to shop for groceries on the Old Elmira Road has moved well into the distant past, but we still remember. We also remember the swans at Stewart Park and the Ithaca Sertoma Club's zoo there, including penguins, and the joy of riding the carousel and the midget train, as well as swimming in the shallows of the lake. All gone, except for a refurbished carousel that was originally built in 1950, but these memories are great things to have!

Stewart Park Carousel

Professional Career: 1953–1995

My professional career can mostly be summed up by the 1990 ASAE (now called ASABE — American Society of Agricultural and Biological Engineers) **Fellow Nomination Support Information** shown in the following pages. Some information has been added to update it to 2018. *"ASABE defines a Fellow as a member of unusual professional distinction, with outstanding and extraordinary qualifications and experience in, or related to, the field of agricultural, food, or biological systems engineering. They possess a minimum of 20 years of active practice in, or related to, the profession of engineering; the teaching of engineering; or the teaching of an engineering-related curriculum and a minimum of 20 years as an active Member-Engineer or Member in ASABE."* This is the Society's highest honor. The Fellow award was made at a national meeting in 1992. I was a continuous member of ASAE for 40 years, and received a recognition certificate for that achievement in 1994. The nomination support letter for the ASAE Fellow award follows at the end of the Fellow Nomination Support Information in the pages that follow.

I worked at Cornell for 42 years, joining the faculty in 1953 and retiring in 1995. The Department's name changed 6 times since it was formed. The beginning of the present Department of Biological and Environmental Engineering at Cornell was as the **Division of Rural Engineering and Architecture**, formed when Liberty Hyde Bailey, Dean of the College of Agriculture, invited Howard W. Riley, a Cornell mechanical engineering graduate, to head it in 1907. Department status came in 1909 with the name **Department of Farm Mechanics**. In 1913 it was renamed the

Department of Rural Engineering. The name **Department of Agricultural Engineering** was adopted in 1930 and remained until July 1, 1988, when the name was changed to **Department of Agricultural and Biological Engineering**. The program subsequently evolved into two integrated focal areas, and in 2001 the name was changed to **Department of Biological and Environmental Engineering** to reflect that orientation. For nearly 50 years, the Department had no permanent home. Teaching was done at a wide variety of locations around the Cornell campus, and research was done on a catch-as-catch-can basis because of the lack of facilities. The photo below shows Riley-Robb Hall as it appeared when construction was completed and the faculty moved into its new quarters in 1956. To the right behind the head building, which has offices and lecture rooms, are two 2-story laboratory wings and a third high ceiling laboratory at the end.

Riley-Robb Hall in 1956 (above) and today (right). The building's hyphenated name honors the two founders of the Department, Howard W. Riley and Byron B. Robb.

I and one of my students, William Plevich, constructed a scale model of the entire building before it was built. The model could be taken apart floor by floor, with the space inside labeled with its functional use. The construction contractor regularly visited the model to see what the physical relationships were like in 3-D. I'm in the crowd in the left photo at the dedication of the building by New York State Governor Thomas E. Dewey on October 6, 1954.

Fellow Nomination Support Information

(A) Biographical Statement

<u>NAME</u>   Ronald Bay Furry
Professor Emeritus (Retired July 1995)
Department of Biological and Environmental Engineering
Cornell University, Ithaca, NY 14853

<u>PERSONAL</u>   Born: October 22, 1931
Niagara Falls, NY

Parents: Edna Louise (Brown) and Wesley Bay Furry

Married: Lois Anne McClure 1953 (b. March 25, 1933 New York, NY)
B.S. Music Ed. cum Laude, Ithaca College, Class of 1955
  Concentration: Voice, Piano
Permanent Certification: N.Y.S., K-12 Music
Graduate Study: Syracuse University, Music Education;
SUNY Cortland, Elementary Education/School Administration
Teacher and Coordinator of Music, Ithaca City School District
Founder (1974), Mayor, Deputy Mayor and Trustee, Village of
  Lansing, NY

Children:
Suzanne Lynne (Paul) Furry-Irish (b. February 1, 1954,
  Ithaca, NY)
B.S. Cornell University, Human Ecology 1976
M.A. Vermont College, Holistic Education 1982
Certified Librarian, State of Vermont, and
  Licensed School Library Media Specialist

Kenneth Bay Furry (b. June 1, 1956, Ithaca, NY)
B.S. with Distinction, Cornell University, Agricultural
  Economics/Business Management 1979
M.B.A. Cornell University, Johnson Graduate School of
  Management 1982
J.D. Cornell Law School, 1982
Admitted to Practice in New York and Connecticut
The Law Offices of Kenneth B. Furry, Esq.

Donna Wynne Furry (Donald) Tongue (b. June 8, 1961, Ithaca,
  NY)
B.M. Magna cum laude, SUNY Potsdam, Music Education 1983
M.M. Boston University, Voice Performance 1987
Donna Tongue Performer's Studio — Vocal Coaching in
  Acoustics and Drama

Sibling: Joanne Louise Furry (David) Dirksen (b. October 26, 1933,
  Niagara Falls, NY; d. April 15, 2015)
Fredonia State Teachers College
Elementary School Teacher, Private Piano Teacher; and
prize-winning Artist

EDUCATION

Ph.D. Agricultural Engineering   1965
      Iowa State University
        Theoretical and Applied Mechanics
      Nuclear Engineering

M.S.   Agricultural Engineering   1955
      Cornell University

B.S.* Agricultural Engineering   1953
      Cornell University
      *With Distinction

New York State Regents Diploma   1949
      LaSalle High School
      Niagara Falls, NY

FIELD OF SPECIALIZATION AND PRINCIPAL INTERESTS

Agricultural Engineering Structures and Environments
   Controlled Atmosphere Storage of Fruits and Vegetables
   Livestock Engineering
Similitude Methodology
Computer Utilization in Instruction
Student Recruitment, Undergraduate and Graduate

PROFESSIONAL EXPERIENCE

Professor Emeritus	Cornell University	1995-
Department Chairman	Cornell University	1990-1994
Professor	Cornell University	1972-1995
Associate Professor	Cornell University	1962-1972
Assistant Professor	Cornell University	1956-1962
Instructor	Cornell University	1953-1956
First Lieutenant	USAF Reserve	1953-1956
Construction Engineering	Niagara Railway Co.	1953
Undergraduate Teaching Asst.	Cornell University	1950-1953

SABBATIC LEAVE/STUDY TOPICS

1963-1965 Iowa State University   Agricultural Engineering
           Ames, IA   Theoretical and Applied Mechanics
                             Nuclear Engineering

ENGINEERING SOCIETY MEMBERSHIPS

American Society of Agricultural Engineers (now American Society of Agricultural and Biological Engineers)
     Program Chairman (National and Regional)
     Meeting Registration Chairman (National and Regional)
     Career Guidance Committee (National)
     Research Committee (National)
     Continuing Education Committee (National)
     Editor, Continuing Education (National)
     Computers Committee Chairman (National)
     Computer Simulations Applications Program Presiding Officer (National)
     American Society for Engineering Education:
     Chairman, Biological and Agricultural Engineering Division (National)
     Past Chairman, Biological and Agricultural Engineering Division (National)

Secretary/Treasurer, Biological and Agricultural Engineering Division (National)
Program Chairman/Vice Chairman, Biological and Agricultural Engineering
  Division (National)
Editor, Biological and Agricultural Engineering Division (National)

(B) Achievements

Dr. Furry participated in all three mission functions of the Department of Biological and Environmental Engineering at Cornell University. Over his 42 years on the faculty, he integrated Research, Teaching and Extension into virtually all of his activities, thus providing a broad spectrum of experience, outlook, leadership and direction for departmental programming. This wide range of interest and experience benefited not only the department, but also the larger university, local and state communities as well. A few examples are presented to illustrate the point.

Excluding normal reports, development of materials for coursework and the like, Dr. Furry produced 395 writings, including fifteen sole-author, eighteen principal-author and seventeen contributing-author papers; sixty engineering bulletins, mostly sole-authored; four manuals and guides; one book chapter; one hundred seventy articles; thirty-two agricultural structural design plan sets; and seventy-eight serial newsletters, all related to agricultural engineering subject matter topics in research, teaching, Extension, design, and student recruitment and enrollment. In addition, he developed mainframe and microcomputer engineering design application packages which he utilized extensively in his teaching program.

His principal research involvement can be summarized to reside in the following areas:
  Controlled Atmosphere/Temperature Environments for Agricultural Materials
  Harvesting and Handling of Agricultural Products
  Structures and Environments
  Improving Dairy Buildings and Equipment
  Research Project Advising

Over the years he had extensive interaction with faculty in other departments, not only in research, but in the broader context of the meaning of community. Additional examples of this involvement are presented below.

His commitment to agriculture, the Agricultural Engineering profession, and the benefit to society in the large can be illustrated by the fact that in 1960 the cabbage storage industry in New York State was moribund, in spite of the state's leading edge in total production, yields per acre and superior dry matter content of the product. Product loss in storage commonly amounted to 40% and more, producers were losing markets because they could not supply a quality product over a full year as demanded by supermarkets and the growing fast-food trade. In the early sixties, he formed and led a cooperative research program with scientists in the Departments of Vegetable Crops, Plant Breeding, and later Plant Pathology, to embark upon a twenty year research program that saved that storage industry in the State. The basic research dealt with determining optimal systems for developing and maintaining the product in long term (eight months and more) Controlled Atmosphere (CA) storage. The effort compared utilization of commercially pure gases; catalytically generated CA; controlled-ventilation CA; hypobaric storage and self-generated CA; cultivar attributes; pathogenicity; preharvest history; product maturity; temperature, oxygen, carbon dioxide and trace gas influence on storability; freeze tolerance; effects of volatiles, especially the hormone ethylene; as well as the design, construction, operation, management, maintenance and control of the physical storage system itself. After extensive laboratory and pilot chamber testing, the first full scale commercial CA storage system for the cabbage industry was constructed and placed into operation in 1974. Since that time, major commercial producers adopted the practice and a superior product became available to the public in a steady year-around supply. The results of this research were directed to benefit society at large through immediate leveraging of the technology transfer process via the Extension and teaching programs.

Dr. Furry had a long standing interest in improving farm structures and their environments, dating back to his early experience in expanding development of the Cornell Extension Plan Service, where he regularly employed ten to twelve undergraduate and graduate students to design, produce and disseminate plans for a wide variety of farm structures and equipment. Later, he also ran the Extension dairy structures program for New York State, where he developed a wide variety of technology transfer materials for field agents and dairy owner/operator use. He won several ASAE blue ribbon awards for his work. He also developed the original design for the Cornell University Animal Science Teaching and Research Center located at Harford, NY, that incorporated separate unique animal housing and production facilities for dairy, sheep, beef and swine on a 2,500 acre site, and then participated in directing its utilization. In addition, he was a leader and central designer of selected facilities in the Miner-Cornell Dairy Research Project in Chazy, NY which illustrated how new technology could be adapted and implemented in underdeveloped regions of northern New York State. This latter activity was principally directed at improving the economic well-being of a historically poor segment of the state's farm population which resided in a region having difficult-to-manage soil resources and a relatively short growing season, with little opportunity for alternative employment. The facility's principal utility was as an applied regional demonstration resource project to promote education in the dairy production industry of the region. His efforts in these and related activities originated a livestock engineering thrust at Cornell and made possible research, teaching and Extension programs by others who would subsequently join the department and utilize the facilities.

Throughout his career, Dr. Furry has stimulated and encouraged agricultural engineers. The desire to provide thorough education of students and continuing development of staff members was evident from his words and deeds. He was an ardent, dedicated educator, whether it was at the university, community or unit level. He originated or developed a variety of courses, and taught the following:

ABEN 750   Orientation for Research
ABEN 651   Similitude Methodology
ABEN 497   Special Topics in Agricultural and Biological Engineering
ABEN 498   Undergraduate Teaching
ABEN 499   Undergraduate Research
ABEN 465   Agricultural Processing Systems
ABEN 450   Introduction to Analog Computation
ABEN 401   Career Development in Agricultural Engineering
ABEN 314   Computer Data Analysis
ABEN 204   Introduction to Computer Uses
ABEN 152   Computing with Graphics
ABEN 151   Introduction to Agricultural Engineering and Computing
AgEn 105   Descriptive Geometry
MD 1 & 2   Engineering and Architectural Drafting

He enjoyed teaching at all levels, and to all audiences. ABEN 204, for example, was a computer course in Pascal/FORTRAN which he taught to non-engineers. Enrollment in this course reached as high as 328 students, and while simultaneously teaching ABEN 152, total enrollment in these two courses reached 400 students. This required training and managing a small army of 23 teaching assistants, almost all undergraduates, each year, along with developing the usual lesson plans, assignments, manuals, examinations, grading documents, etc. Fortunately, Dr. Furry enjoyed organizing efforts, fostering the development of individuals, and watching them grow into assignments bearing responsibility and accountability. He was a stickler for detail, accuracy and proper communications, which was an especially noteworthy attribute to have when teaching computer programming and literacy. Many of his undergraduate teaching assistants received lucrative positions in computer or computer related industries or businesses, including engineering and banking applications.

He designed and developed a $500,000 major college Microcomputer Center which supported undergraduate and graduate instruction for both the department and others. In addition to the general purpose computer classrooms, this facility included a special Computer Graphics laboratory that served agricultural engineering students in an engineering computing environment that supported a wide range of commercial application packages, plus special software that met specific course objectives, such as dynamic simulation of physical systems with subsequent animated 3-D color display of multi-variable dimensionless response surfaces to illustrate the concept of families of solutions, regimes of operation, and optimization in design, with full student user control for input and output, including both printed character and color graphic plotting of results. He was committed to excellence in teaching, including the proper utilization of computers.

Although he operated a successful graduate recruitment and study program as Graduate Faculty Representative, perhaps one of his most notable successes and contributions to the profession was the origination of a departmental undergraduate recruiting program (CURE). When first instituted, this program doubled enrollment in the department in one year, bringing in 1,700 requests for information from high school students in New York and selected neighboring states. He maintained contact with over 1,550 high school and transfer institutions, and received 500 recruitment related contacts a year; resulting in increased enrollments in the department's undergraduate engineering and technology programs. He proved himself to be a dedicated educator committed to the development of agricultural engineering professionals who can serve the needs of the global society.

Dr. Furry also recognized the importance of the interrelationships of engineering with the health career fields. He participated in the formation, development and operation of the Cornell University Health Careers Program, which provides a wide variety of information and services to students who anticipate entry into the medical or veterinary fields following their undergraduate program. The Biological Engineering concentration in the department's undergraduate program is the appropriate beneficiary of entering students who are recruited with this career interest in mind.

He is a staunch supporter of the Student Engineering Branch concept, having served in the offices of treasurer, secretary, and president of the local Branch as an undergraduate. He originated, developed, promulgated and administered the John W. Layer Memorial Fund endowment, the earnings from which are used to support travel for undergraduate student majors in the department to permit them to attend national and regional ASAE (now ASABE) and related meetings. The principal objectives of this fund are to promote ASAE, foster interaction between professionals and these pre-professionals, and stimulate and encourage their entry into the profession following graduation. Scores of Cornell undergraduate agricultural engineering students participated in national ASAE and related meetings as a direct result of this activity.

Dr. Furry was instrumental in moving the American Society for Engineering Education (ASEE) Biological and Agricultural Engineering Division (BAED) into a new expanded and re-directed orientation and pro-active role. He developed and planned the first all agricultural engineering division series of programs on national agricultural engineering recruitment, enrollment, curriculum and direction, and selected successors who would continue the development because of their belief, vision and commitment to education and newly developing directions for the profession. The value of shifting the BAED from virtually a totally passive to a pro-active role became readily apparent. To sustain educational development on the local level, he appointed a Coordinator of Instruction (COI) in the Department of Agricultural and Biological Engineering at Cornell to direct all departmental undergraduate studies and related operations, along with support for a related teaching assistant and funds to attend a national educational conference each year. Fostering continuity in the development of a supply of agricultural engineering professionals for the future ranked high on his list of priorities.

From the standpoint of supporting undergraduate education in general, Dr. Furry participated in a variety of committees and capacities in both the College of Engineering and the College of Agriculture and Life Sciences at Cornell. He also was active for many years in fostering academic excellence and the social environment for students. He has participated on the Board of Directors of the Alpha Zeta Corporation Board for several decades, and served as Chairman of the Board's Facilities Committee for four years. He was the leader responsible for developing plans for a combined new and renovated $1,450,000.00 house for the Cornell Chapter of Alpha Zeta and participated in the initiation of the alumni fund raising campaign to finance the construction. Many agricultural engineering students are elected to the Alpha Zeta honorary fraternity at Cornell, and Dr. Furry was also a member as an undergraduate. He was committed to providing an appropriate environment for future professionals, including one where close interaction with individuals in diverse fields is possible, such as the Alpha Zeta Chapter at Cornell provides.

In addition to voluntary service within the institutional environment, he has also been involved in public service activities, including Boy Scouts, fund drives for various agencies, and is a Charter Member of the Ithaca Sertoma Club service organization. The most notable voluntary service that he has achieved began in 1954 when he joined the then year-old Cornell Federal Credit Union (CFCU) (now the CFCU Community Credit Union). He has been a member of that organization continuously, having originally volunteered to develop a newsletter to maintain contact with a diminutive membership having an asset balance of a few thousand dollars. Since that time he has served as a volunteer on the CFCU Education Committee and the Supervisory Committee, and spent eleven years (1979-1990) on the Board of Directors, as Vice Chairman, and the final four years as Chairman. As Chairman he expanded educational emphasis and training within the organization, promoted new products and services, and at the close of his tenure as Chairman of the Board CFCU assets stood at $103,000,000.00, with 64 employees and 30 volunteers servicing nearly 38,000 members in five existing branches, and a new $3,250,000 headquarters building under construction in the Village of Lansing. (Update: Assets $1,056,836,312.00, 200 employees, 70,000 members, and several new branch offices in 2018).

(C) Professional Leadership Activities and Contributions Overview

       Professional Societies
          American Society of Agricultural and Biological Engineers (ASABE):
               Program Chairman (National and Regional)
               Meeting Registration Chairman (National and Regional)
               Career Guidance Committee (National)
               Research Committee (National)
               Continuing Education Committee (National)
               Editor, Continuing Education (National)
               Computers Committee Chairman (National)
          American Society for Engineering Education (ASEE):
               Chairman, Biological and Agricultural Engineering Division
                (National)
               Past Chairman, Biological and Agricultural Engineering Division
                (National)
               Secretary/Treasurer, Biological and Agricultural Engineering
                Division (National)
               Program Chairman/Vice Chairman, Biological and Agricultural
                Engineering Division (National)
               Editor, Biological and Agricultural Engineering Division
                (National)

American Nuclear Society, Member

Professional Service, Voluntary

Ithaca Sertoma Club (Charter Member June 2, 1962) — various offices, committees and awards, including Outstanding Regional Secretary, and Vice President

Education Committee, Cornell Federal Credit Union

Supervisory Committee, Cornell Federal Credit Union

Chairman, Cornell Federal Credit Union Board of Directors

Vice Chairman, Cornell Federal Credit Union Board of Directors

Various Community Fund Raising Activities

Committee Chairman and Assistant Scout Master, Boy Scout Troop 5

(D) Honors, Awards and Activities

General:

National Science Foundation Science Faculty Fellow

Ford Foundation Graduate Study Award to Prospective Teachers in Engineering

Phi Kappa Phi

Sigma Xi

Gamma Sigma Delta (Charter Member, Cornell University; Iowa State University)

Cornell Alpha Zeta

Distinguished Military Graduate (DMG), Cornell University AFROTC

Pershing Rifles

ASAE Fellow

ASAE Blue Ribbon Awards

Cornell Student Engineering Branch ASAE Outstanding Faculty Award

American Society for Engineering Education Centennial Award

Continuing Education Units in:

"Seminar on Understanding and Using Computer Graphics"

"Institute for Material Handling Teachers"

Departmental Committees and Activities:

Committee on Undergraduate Recruiting Efforts Chairman (CURE)

Committee on Academic Programs (CAP)

Space Committee

Coordinator of Research

Computing Needs Committee

Computer Facilities Coordinator

Livestock Engineering Program Advisory Committee Chairman

Graduate Faculty Representative

Coordinator of Graduate Instruction

ASAE Student Engineering Branch Advisor

Social Activities Committee

J.W. Layer Memorial Scholarship Fund Faculty Administrator

Various Ad Hoc Committees (tenure, promotion, advisory, etc.)

Undergraduate Student Advisor

Graduate Student Advisor

Department Chairman

University, College of Agriculture and Life Sciences, and College of Engineering Committees and Activities

University Senator

University Senate Campus Planning Committee

University Senate Minority and Disadvantaged Interests Committee Subcommittee

105

on Migrant Labor
University Faculty Council of Representatives
University Graduate Faculty
University Advisory Committee on Academic Computing
University Advisory Committee on Instructional Computing
University Subcommittee on Open Access Computing Chairman
University Health Careers Program Advisory Board
University Committee on Fraternity and Sorority Relationships
University Computing Board
CALS (College of Agriculture and Life Sciences) Computing Advisory Committee
CALS Interactive Computing Facility Committee
Computer Activities Group (CAG) Faculty Consultant
College of Engineering (CoE) Policy Committee
College of Engineering Study Committee on Freshmen Engineering Courses
College of Engineering Common Curriculum Governing Board (CCGB)
Computing and Computing Applications Committee
Chairman, Liaison Committee to Computer Science 202
Chairman, College of Engineering Materials Handling Prize Awards Committee
Chairman, CALS Faculty Committee on Admissions
CALS Animal Science Teaching & Research Center Planning Committee
CALS Animal Science Teaching & Research Center Operating Committee
Committee on Course Registration
Faculty Promotion Review Committees, CALS and CoE
Director, Alpha Zeta Corporation Board (over 50 years)
Chairman, Alpha Zeta Facilities Committee for New Fraternity House, dedicated 1993
Beta Epsilon Phi Faculty Advisor
Special Committee Assignments: Various

(E) Summary Statement on Impact of Achievements
The expanded descriptions of selected specific but representative achievements detailed in Section (B) illustrate the following.

Dr. Furry has a deep commitment to maintaining the profession and providing it with well educated, highly qualified individuals, especially those at the original entry level to the profession. The best repository of knowledge in agricultural engineering is not in the books, papers, manuals or treatises that reside in bookcases and stacks in libraries, but rather what resides as a commitment to service in the profession in the educated minds of the young professionals who are our future.

His interest in the economic and functional well-being of the agricultural industry is amply evident in his long-term involvement in technology transfer through Extension and research. His research on CA storage of vegetables literally rescued the nearly defunct cabbage storage industry in New York State, and made it possible to provide a quality product the year around, thus benefiting both the entrepreneur and the consumer public at large. Subsequent research showed that similar benefits may also be obtained for celery to meet special conditions, much as preserving the crop locally for holiday marketing at large nearby population centers. It must also be noted that his work spanned both the animal and plant industries over his career.

He was a dedicated engineering educator at both the undergraduate and graduate level. He organized conferences, served on committees and wrote papers on agricultural engineering coursework, curriculum development, model curricula, recruitment and similar topics, and conducted a model undergraduate recruitment program at Cornell for over 17 years. In addition, he perpetually developed new coursework and support systems at the cutting edge of new engineering technology. For example, he began promoting the use of computers in research and teaching when slide rules were still popular, and did not cease that effort.

He began his commitment to agricultural engineering as a freshman in 1949. He became involved in ASAE since his first attendance at a meeting of the Student Engineering Branch in that same year. During his ASAE membership years he served on a wide variety of committees and supported numerous other activities, as well as promoted ASAE to both professionals and pre-professionals. He encouraged students to join the Society and established a memorial fund to enable Cornell students to attend ASAE national meetings. He also contributed significantly to the re-birth and functional development of the Biological and Agricultural Engineering Division of ASEE, which increased the visibility of ASAE and the profession in that education directed organization. ASEE also used his program development techniques as a model for other ASEE Division Chairmen, again enhancing the visibility of ASAE and agricultural engineering in that society.

Ron describes himself as a team player. His performance and programs over the years aptly testified to that description. His final gift to the department was writing the history of its first 100 years. Titled **A Pioneering Department: Evolution from Rural Engineering to Biological and Environmental Engineering at Cornell University, 1907-2007**, the book is available free on-line as a pdf file at...

https://ecommons.cornell.edu/handle/1813/7642

The abstract that he wrote for the book follows:

"Why does a Department of Biological and Environmental Engineering exist at Cornell University and what was the vision of those who saw the need? This book explores the beginnings and growth of Biological and Environmental Engineering at Cornell University in Ithaca, NY over its first 100 years, starting with excerpts from the historic legislation that made it possible, next relating the beginning of agricultural engineering and the important contributions that Cornell University had in pointing the way in this new field, and summarizing the department's first century of service through its teaching, research and Extension programs. Also included is a description of the struggle to obtain appropriate facilities, a look at the people who helped make the Department a national and world leader in the field, along with a benchmark of current activity as the department enters its second century. Illustrations remind the reader of "the good old days", as well as how time has brought about transformations to the present."

(F) <u>Partial List of Publications (Articles, Scripted Radio Talks, Construction Plan Sets, Serial Newsletters, Administrative Publications, etc. are not included)</u>

> R. B. Furry and J.V. Bartlett. 1987. DIFFER. Turbo Pascal. IBM PC/AT with monochrome and color graphics displays, multicolor pen plotter, and dot matrix printer. Package provides authoring, solution, repetitive display, and hard copy printer and plotter presentation for sets of differential equations.
> R. B. Furry and J. V. Bartlett. 1987. GPUMP. Turbo Pascal. IBM PC/AT with monochrome and color graphics displays, multicolor pen plotter, and dot matrix printer. Package provides input specification, system modification, solution and interactive dynamic display of 3-pump/reservoir systems incorporating friction, dimensionless response surface generation and rotation, using animated 2-D and 3-D graphics with printer and color plotter hard copy.
> R. B. Furry, J. R. Hicks, M. C. Jorgensen, and J. A. Bartsch. 1984. Controlled atmosphere storage of celery. ASAE Paper #84-4038.
> R. B. Furry. 1983. Computers and computer graphics in the agricultural engineering curriculum. Proc. 983 Annual Conf. ASEE Vol. 1, pp. 1-4.

R. B. Furry. 1983. Contributor to Ventilation for horticultural crop storage, IN: Ventilation of agricultural structures, Ch. 13. ASAE Monograph #6.

R. B. Furry, G. E. Rehkugler, and H. A. Longhouse. 1982. Interactive computer graphics in agricultural engineering instruction. American Society of Agricultural Engineers, Paper No. 82-5014. 24 pp.

R. B. Furry, F. M. R. Isenberg, and M. C. Jorgensen. 1981. Postharvest controlled atmosphere storage of cabbage. Search: Agriculture. Ithaca, NY. Cornell Univ. Agr. Exp. Sta. No. 19, 22 pp.

R. B. Furry. June 1980. Perspectives and projections on engineering enrollments. Proc. 1980 Annual Conf. ASEE. Vol. 1, pp. 5-11.

R. B. Furry, J. R. Hicks, M. C. Jorgensen, and P. M. Ludford. December 1979. Effects of ethylene on controlled atmosphere storage of cabbage. ASAE Paper #79-4537.

R. B. Furry, F. M. R. Isenberg, M. C. Jorgensen. June 1979. Post-harvest controlled atmosphere requirements of cabbage intended for long duration storage. ASAE Paper #79-6011.

R. B. Furry, Editor. June 1979. Student involvement and other methods of recruiting. Symposium presented at 1979 Summer Meeting of ASAE-CSAE, Winnipeg, Canada. ASAE Paper #79-5043.

R. B. Furry. June 1979. Student recruiting in the Northeast. In ASAE Paper #79-5043, pp. 7-10.

R. B. Furry. June 1979. Perspectives and projections on engineering academe. In ASAE Paper #79-5043, pp. 1-6.

W. W. Gunkel, R. B. Furry, D. R. Lacey, S. Neyeloff, and T. G. Porter. May 1979. Development of a wind powered water heating system for dairy application. 36th Annual Progress Report to the N.Y.S. Food and Energy Council, Cornell Univ., pp. 73-84.

W. W. Gunkel, R. B. Furry, D. R. Lacey. S. Neyeloff, and T. G. Porter. May 1979. Development of a wind-powered water heating system for dairy application. Presented at the USDA-DOE Workshop — Wind Energy Applications in Agriculture, Scheman Center, Iowa State Univ.

H. R. Davis, R. B. Furry, and F. M. R. Isenberg. February 1979. Storage recommendations for northern grown onions. Plant Sciences-Agricultural Engineering 9 — Info. Bul. 148.

W. W. Gunkel, R. B. Furry, D. R. Lacey, S. Neyeloff, and T. G. Porter. Fall 1978. Development of a wind powered water heating system for dairy application. Proceedings - American Wind Energy Association,National Conference, Cape Cod, Mass., pp. 171-180.

H. R. Davis, R. B. Furry, and F. M. R. Isenberg. August 1978. Storage recommendations for northern grown onions. Agricultural Engineering Extension Bul. 428.

H. R. Davis, F. M. R. Isenburg, and R. B. Furry. July 1978. The control of natural-air cabbage storage environment. Plant Sciences-Agricultural Engineering 8 — Info. Bul. 137.

M. B. Timmons, L. D. Albright, and R. B. Furry. 1978. Similitude aspects of predicting building thermal behavior. Trans. of ASAE 21(5). (ASAE Honorable Mention).

W. W. Gunkel, R. B. Furry, S. Neyeloff, D. R. Lacey, C. J. Solat, and T. G. Porter. May 1978. Wind energy substitution at dairy milking center. 35th Annual Progress Report, N.Y.S. Food and Energy Council, pp. 67-87.

R. B. Furry, M. C. Jorgensen, and O. C. Yoder. May 1978. Postharvest storage research on cabbage. 35th Annual Progress Report, N.Y.S. Food and Energy Council, pp. 59-64.

R. B. Furry, et al. February 1978. Toward an energy self-sufficient food production system. Research Proposal with Addendum to U. S. Department of Energy. Feb. 1978. (133 pp.)

H. R. Davis, R. B. Furry, and F. M. R. Isenberg. Jan. 1978. The control of natural-air cabbage storage environment. Agric. Engr. Exten. Bul. 427.

R. B. Furry, et al. Occupational brief on the agricultural engineer. Agr. Eng. Nov. 1977. (23 pp.)

R. B. Furry, F.M.R. Isenberg and M.C. Jorgensen. Progress in research on the postharvest storage response of cabbage subjected to various diurnal freeze-thaw regimes. N.Y.Farm Electrification 34th Annual Progress Report, pp. 97-101. May 1977.

R. B. Furry, M. C. Jorgensen and F. M. R. Isenberg. Postharvest storage response of Cabbage subjected to various diurnal freeze-thaw regimes. Acta Horticulturae, Tech. Comm. ISHS No. 62. 1976.

R. B. Furry, S. T. Slack, N. L. VanDemark and R. G. Warner, Conference Coords. Proceedings of the 1976 Teaching and Research Center Outlook Conference. NYS College of Agric. & Life Sci..Cornell Univ. (69 pp.) Oct. 1976.

A.C-C. Ku, R.B. Furry, W.K. Jordan and D. Dropkin. Numerical analysis of heat and mass transfer during freeze-drying. Symposium on Development of Biological Standards. Freeze Drying of Biological Products. Vol. 36. Oct. 1976.

M. B., Timmons, L. D. Albright and R. B. Furry. Distortion effects in using building models to predict time dependent thermal behavior. ASAE Paper No. 76-4024. 1976.

R. F. Lucey, C.C. Lowe and R.B. Furry. Climate, soils and field crops. Miner/Cornell Dairy and Crop improvement Program Progress Report 1971-75. Multilithed. Feb. 1976.

W. W. Irish and R.B. Furry. Miner/Cornell dairy and crop improvement project: dairy facilities. Miner/Cornell Dairy and Crop Improvement Program Progress Report 1971-75. Multilithed. Feb. 1976.

R. B. Furry. Undergraduate recruitment reference manual. Six sections, 47 items. Nov. 1975.

R. B. Furry, E. O. Eaton, H. A. Longhouse and L. H. Irwin. Agricultural and Biological Engineering as a profession. A/V Package: 17 pp; cassette tape; 68 color slides. August 1975

R. B. Furry. Modified atmosphere storage of cabbage: application phase. 32nd Annual Progress Report, N.Y.S. Farm Electrification Council, pp. 61-63. May 1975.

R. B. Furry. Controlled atmosphere/temperature environments for agricultural materials. Agric. Engr. Res.,, N.Y.S. Coll, of Agriculture and Life Sciences, pp. 38-43. 1974-75.

A. C. Ku, R. B. Furry, W.K. Jordan, and D. Dropkin. Heat and mass transfer during freeze-drying of food products: simulation and application results, ASAE Paper No. 74-6014. 1974.

R. B. Furry. A summary of studies on the use of catalytically generated atmospheres for the storage of cabbage. 31st Annual Progress Report, N.Y.S. Farm Electrification Council, pp. 61-67. May 1974.

R. B. Furry, F.M. Isenberg, M.C. Jorgensen, and J.E. Carroll. Pilot studies on the use of catalytically generated atmospheres for the storage of cabbage, Brassica oleraceae L. ASAE Paper No. 73-3506. 1973.

R. B. Furry. Continuing Research on post-harvest storage of cabbage. 30th Annual Progress Report, N.Y.S. Farm Electrification Council, Cornell Univ., pp. 16-25. May 1973.

J. G: Riley and R. B. Furry. Simulation of the road corrugation phenomenon, Highway Research Record No. 438, pp. 54-62. Highway Research Board, National Research Council, Washington, DC. 1973.

J. F. Ourada and R. B. Furry. Application of the absorption concept for continuous CO_2 and O_2 analysis: the search for a low cost control element for CA storage utilization. ASAE Paper No. 73-366. 1973.

B. D. McLendon and R. B. Furry. Simulation of integrating sphere evaluation of diffuse reflectance of intact biological specimens. ASAE Paper No. 72-349. 1972.

R.E. Garrett and R. B. Furry. Velocity of sonic pulses in apples. ASAE Trans. 15:770-774. 1972.

R. B. Furry. Postharvest storage of cabbage: problems and prospects. ASAE Paper No. 72-877. 1972.

R.B. Furry, J.W. Layer and M.C. Jorgensen. Postharvest storage of cabbage.29th Annual Progress Report, N.Y. Farm Electrification Council, pp. 55-69. May 1972.

J. M. Allison and R. B. Furry. Diffusion of oxygen through cabbage leaf disks under controlled atmosphere conditions. ASAE Paper No. 71-346. June 1971.

Maghsood, J.R., N. R. Scott, R. B. Furry and R. Sexsmith. Finite element analysis of wood structural members. ASAE Paper No. 70-922. Dec. 1970 (39 pp.)

R. B. Furry. Controlled Atmosphere/Temperature Environments for Agricultural Materials. 27th Annual New York Farm Electrification Progress Rept. 1970

R. B. Furry. Tilt-up Concrete Insulated Sandwich Panel Walls for Farm Construction. Agr. Engr. Bul. 330 (12 pp.) 1968

R. B. Furry and T. W. Hazen. A constant temperature model of the ventilation-dilution phenomenon. ASAE Transactions l02:188-195, Aug. 1967.

R. B. Furry. Basic Arrangements of Milking Parlors with Stall Barns. Cornell Ext. Bul. 1085. 1963

R. B. Furry. PhD Dissertation – Similitude study of the change in CO_2 concentration in a ventilated enclosure. Ames, Iowa. 1965. vii, 199. illus. 28 cm.

R. B. Furry. Types of milking parlors. Cornell Extension Bulletin 1084. 1962, 16 pp.

R. B. Furry. Cooling Apples Before Storage. Farm. Research XXII[1]. Jan. 1956

R. B. Furry. MS Thesis – Vacuum and hydrocooling studies on McIntosh apples. Ithaca, New York. 1955. 112. illus.

Nomination Support Letter

October 23, 1990
Awards Department
American Society of Agricultural Engineers
2950 Niles Road
St. Joseph, MI 49085-9659

Dear Sir/Madam:

I nominate Dr. Ronald B. Furry for the grade of ASAE Fellow. As you can tell from the enclosed information he has been a strong contributor to Agricultural Engineering especially in his activities with both our Department of Agricultural and Biological Engineering and the Biological and Agricultural Engineering Division of the American Society for Engineering Education. His leadership role in our Cornell Department of Agricultural and Biological Engineering is best demonstrated by his appointment to Chairman, Agricultural and Biological Engineering Department, Cornell University, effective 1 November 1990.

To support Ron's nomination I have asked the following 20 ASAE members broadly representing our profession plus 3 non-ASAE members to provide original written statements giving their reasons for his nomination. I am aware that only 10 letters are required but some of 20 members may not be able to respond by the 1 November 1990 deadline.

James M. Allison	Donald Price
Landis L. Boyd	Mark Raabe
Wesley F. Buchele	Gerald E. Rehkugler
William J. Chancellor	John Riley
Joe T. Clayton	Paul Robillard
Denny Davis	Norm R. Scott
Roger Garrett	Larry J. Segerlind
Robert E. Graves	John C. Siemens
Andrew G. Hashamoto	M. Ray Smith
Marie Layer	Ronald W. Space
B. Derrell McLendon	Stanley A. Weeks
C. Alan Pettibone	

For your use and awards committee evaluation, I am enclosing six copies of the following information:
A. Dr. Ronald B. Furry's Biographical Statement
B. List of Important Achievements
C. Professional Activities
D. Peer Recognition
E. Support Statement
F. Statement of Sponsor
G. List of News Media

H. Signatures of Agricultural and Biological Engineering Faculty, Cornell
      University supporting the nomination of Dr. Ronald B. Furry to the grade
      of ASAE Fellow

Sincerely,

Wesley W. Gunkel
Professor, and
Coordinator of Graduate Instruction
Fellow - ASAE

Enclosures
WWG/db

As Others See Us

I found myself too engaged in what I was "doing" over the years to be able to "see" what I was doing, and I'm amazed at how other folks view me. I have never had a desire to "be something," and consequently had no master plan to follow to take me to a selected outcome. All I ever did was try to fill a need that I perceived and do a good job. This attitude took me into many activities and groups where I learned a lot and contributed what I could. The following examples cover a broad spectrum of folks who "saw" me in various ways, from my children to my work colleagues and volunteer organizations. Most are related to the occasion of my retirement in 1995. I enjoy their descriptions!

Family

A FATHER'S CONTRIBUTION (The Meaning of Fatherhood)

When I was growing up, my Dad used to tell me to "Wise up, Kenny." He'd say it with that deep, worldly, matter-of-fact tone of voice, while looking in another direction, busily engaged in some chore like stacking fireplace wood. He'd say it in response to something I'd said that displayed my naiveté, like after I'd related some sad story about how I'd been used by my friends. This statement always conveyed the message that I should have known better; it always had a small hint of exasperation in it.

My Father's "wise up" instruction exemplifies the very clear role he played in our early family life. This was back when my older sister and I knew that we knew everything; well before we had any genuine claim to questioning his authority. Dad's most profound quality then was his uncompromising refusal to give the world more credit than it deserved. This view was based on solid evidence gathered throughout his life.

My father has seen some challenging times of his own. But more importantly, from a young age he had heard the people he loved and respected, the less educated, but proud and practical men of his upbringing, describe their tough times. Bill and Bob Brown, his uncles, made an especially deep impression on him. They had grown up, the sixth and last siblings in a family of seven children in Niagara Falls, New York. From what my Dad said, and from what I myself heard, they were tough, athletic, hardworking boys, who grew up to be tough, blue-collar young men who fought in New Guinea in World War II. When I knew them, they seemed to be not only tough, but bitter, at a society they saw as unjust and corrupt, and ungrateful in its treatment of its veterans.

When he was a boy, Bob and Bill took Dad pheasant hunting. I've never wondered why they went hunting; I bet my Dad never wondered why they went hunting. That's because if you knew Bob and Bill you wouldn't have had to ask. Hunting was just something they were. They did it because they were independent, self-sufficient men. To ask them whether they enjoyed it would have been to ask the Pope if he enjoyed being Catholic.

My Dad's Mother, Edna Brown, was as determined as her brothers were. She always had a definite opinion on important family issues. She usually won. Someone once told me a story about how my grandmother reacted when her boyfriend, Bay, who was to become her husband, showed up sporting a mustache one night. She refused to go out with him unless he shaved it off. They did go out that night, and the mustache stayed behind. That's not surprising when you consider that their courtship lasted ten years.

The Browns didn't have any money. They worked hard. Edna saw to it that her children had the opportunities that she didn't have. When my Dad was 17, she packed him off to the college that didn't charge full tuition for its Agricultural Engineering program so that it could attract students. So my Dad became an Agricultural Engineer. He was the first member of his family to get a college degree, and eventually he became a tenured professor on the faculty of this college. He was able to do it because he was intelligent, he worked very hard and he was sincere. And because his Father and his Mother and all of the Browns expected him to succeed; he was their son.

So my father developed a no-nonsense attitude toward the world because he was raised by no-nonsense people who lived in no-nonsense times. And that is what he brought to his own family. Nothing fancy, nothing fake, just the stubborn conviction that you ought to be able to take care of yourself, because the world won't.

My Dad used to say something else, too. After he'd responded with his gruff "wise-up," he'd usually listen with half an ear to the rest of your story while continuing to stack wood. Then you'd finish, and wait for some sympathy.

"You'll learn," he'd say. "You'll learn."

November 1988 by Kenneth Bay Furry

KENNETH B. FURRY, ESQ.
216 East 83rd Street
New York, New York 10028

October 8, 1995

Ronald B. Furry,
 Professor
Department of Agricultural and
 Biological Engineering
Riley-Robb Hall
Cornell University
Ithaca, New York 14850

Re: An Open Letter to My Dad (Or, What I Learned
 as the Child of an Agricultural Engineer)

Dear Dad:

Congratulations once again on your retirement from the faculty of the College of Agriculture and Life Sciences at Cornell University. Your career, which has spanned more than four decades, exemplifies a depth of commitment and longevity that are all too rare.

The "ripple" effects of your retirement dinner will be manifold. One effect, for example, is that your family, as well as your friends and colleagues, will continue to hope that this small ceremony was sufficient to symbolize the vast affection that we feel for you and the respect we have for your values and achievements. We cannot imagine having a better example of fatherhood and of professional excellence.

For your part, the celebration of a long and successful career should be cause for reflection of the kind that is a never-ending process. It involves the development of a deeper understanding of what one was able to accomplish by following one's deeply held convictions as to how a professional life should be lived. The task is to gain a more

114

profound grasp of the fact that the effects of good acts are permanent, and proceed outward in ever-widening circles.

The interpretation of your years at Cornell will be one of the continuing jobs that will occupy you during your "retirement." It's not something you will necessarily consciously work at, but it will no doubt take place.

At this juncture, however, we who have been so close to you have an obligation to point out that no matter how hard you try, you will never completely comprehend all of the consequences of the choices you made and the actions you took. To a certain extent, every career is a family project, and it is probably impossible to fully understand the events and meanings of a career from the viewpoint of every family participant. To draw just one small example from tonight's dinner itself, did it ever occur to you that your youngest grandchildren may now well be convinced that one of the ways to inspire a strong academic faculty that boasts a national reputation is to wear a succession of funny hats, one of which has a *dog that pees when you pull the string?* (Now, did you plan this? Can you blame them if they're confused?)

Let me now detail some other unintended by-products of your career.

What I learned as the Child of an Agricultural Engineer

1. Unlike fathers of other families, your father – *the Agricultural Engineer* — never goes to "work," he always goes to *"The Department"*. This is — mysterious. Also, *"The Department"* — is in — *"The Building"* (As in, *"Honey, I'm going to The Building"*).

    *   For many years, we thought Dad either worked for the CIA, or at a "department" store. We thought he was keeping something very secret from us, or else selling lingerie. (If you had worked in "Foundations" at Rothschild's, we would not have been surprised.)

2. As the child of an *Agricultural Engineer,* be prepared to spend long periods of time at the end of a hot summer day, in the car, with your Mom, waiting for Dad to come out of The Building, and drive you home.

    *   With all that time spent in front of The Building, we concluded that the Chairmen of The Department were two guys named "Ceres" and "Pomona." Why else would their pictures be carved in stone on the front steps of The Building?

3. At church, if Mr. Riley tried to give you candy, you had to accept it, even if you didn't like it.

- Mr. Riley was of course *the* Mr. Riley of Riley-Robb Hall fame. We went to the same church. We had a vague idea that he had something *special* to do with *The Building,* and with *The Department.* But we couldn't figure out how he fit in with Ceres and Pomona.

4.   Ceres and Pomona were apparently important, and Mr. Riley was some kind of wise man who had something to do with *The Building,* but the person who was really important, and who was obviously running things, was some guy named Sam Baughman.

- Sam Baughman's name was always mentioned with reverence. I later learned that, to an Agricultural Engineer, the only thing more important than *his Tools* themselves, is *Where They Are Kept.*

5.   At all times, be prepared for your Dad to leave to go to "Shay Zee."

- As in, *"I have to go to Shay Zee."* This was even more mysterious than Ceres, and Pomona, and Mr. Riley. There were three possibilities. "Shay Zee" was either:

    (1) a French restaurant (as in, *"Chez Zee"*);
    (2) a mysterious, secret place sort of like Treasure Island; or
    (3) a type of lawn furniture (as in, *"Honey, bring me the Shay Zee lounge"*).

We never got any further with that one. (This now reminds me that *"Picking Up The Fleet Car"* was part of the solemn ritual of *"Going To Shay Zee."*)

6.   If you have a need for any kind of *equipment* at home, and it's not *in the garage* at home, don't worry, because *Sam Baughman has it at The Building.*

- Let's say, for example, that you need a *portable, pressurized air tank* to inflate the tires on your station wagon. Again, there are three possibilities. First, you can use the air tank on Saturdays at The Building. Second, you can use it for a very short period of time at home before you have to return it to The Building; or third, and best of all, you can *keep the air tank in the car for an indefinite period of time.*

    i. I think that this is because when the air tank from The Building is *in the car,* you've never really taken it *home,* even if the car is *in the garage* at home, because *the car is by definition always on its way back to the Building.* Even when it's parked! I learned that this is one of the rules of Agricultural Engineers.

116

7.   If you are at The Building on a long Saturday afternoon working on a project with your Dad, using *The Department's Equipment* at *The Building,* and you get bored, you can always go into Sam Baughman's office and look at the calendars and postcards from all the tool companies on the bulletin board, which is always interesting because they are always festooned with shapely women sitting on all types of farm equipment.

- **Now I really understood why Sam Baughman was important!**

(But I never did find that farm.)

8.   If you observe your Dad having a problem at home with snow constantly drifting across your driveway in wintertime, don't worry, because he'll just have his grad students conduct an elaborate computer simulation of your house to determine where the snow fences should be put.

- That's why we had this tiny little metal model of our house — because Dad's Grad Students *had* to make it, or they'd *flunk.*

9.   While most people in the world pronounce it "agricultural enjineer," some of the engineers at the Department say it, "agricultural en-gi-neer" (with the "gi" pronounced as in "*git* me that Phillips-head screwdriver").

- Ken: "Dad, why does Dick Guest say "agricultural *en-gi-neer*"?
- Dad: "I have no idea."

10.   Expect your father – *the Agricultural Engineer* – to write a poem at regular intervals (say, once every forty years). (An extremely *short* poem.)

- When visiting your office one afternoon, which was (at the time) pretty small and (as usual) chock full of piles upon piles of technical-looking memoranda, assorted documentation and scale models of farm equipment, I spied this tiny ode written neatly in an obscure corner of a crowded chalkboard:

    **"One flake
    Does not a blizzard make.
    RF"[1]**

After finding that poem, I decided that Agricultural Engineers — including *my Dad, the*

---

[1]   Modern word processors cannot reproduce the way you actually write your initials.

Agricultural Engineer — really are something more than just practical, maddeningly precise, applied mathematicians. They are, in fact, Men of Letters. Now I could envision you dreaming up sonnets about Life At The Building, adjusting your laurel wreath even as you put the finishing touches on an heroic poem about controlled-atmosphere storage of fruits and vegetables.[2]

Speaking of poetry, I believe I have stumbled upon the only poem ever written that includes the words "agricultural engineer." The author is an actor friend of mine who lives in Chicago with his wife and two cats. It goes something like this:

"Three Blind Mice"

Three visually incapacitated *rodentia psychondra,*
Three visually incapacitated *rodentia psychondra.*

Observe their frantic method of perambulation,
Observe their frantic method of perambulation.

They pursued the spouse of an Agricultural Engineer,
Who severed their posterior appendages with a sharp-bladed culinary utensil.

Have you ever observed such merriment in your existence,
As three visually incapacitated *rodentia psychondra?*[3]

_____

That's my Dad. The Philosopher-King. The Agricultural Engineer.

Love always,

Your Son

cc: O.C French   Ceres
       Hollis Davis   Pomona

_____

[2]   Perhaps this is the Agricultural Engineer's understanding of heaven.

[3]   Copyright Jeff Steele. All rights reserved.

The Department
The Building
The Fleet Car
Shay Zee
Everyone (Anyone?) Who
   Ever Lived at Shay Zee
   (Wherever It Is)
Sam Baughman's Bulletin
   Board
All Painted Silhouettes of
   Sam Baughman's Tools
Dick Guest
My Big Sister
My Little Sister
Bill Irish
Barbara Irish
"The Irishes", as a "genre"
Barb Irish's Harp
The Sudan
Cheese Soup
All of My Adorable,
   Bewildered Nephews and
   Nieces
All of the unfortunate Grad
   Students
Bob Cooke
Norm Scott
The Dairy Bar
The Home Dairy
The Cornell Senate
The "Liberal Disguise"

Mr. Riley
Mr. Robb
Mr. Hall
The Department
Christmas Party
Sam Baughman
Sam Baughman's Tools
Cornell Hockey
Ned Harkness
Ed Marinaro
The Polo Barns
The Synchrotron
The Students
All Advisees
"Aye Zee" (As in, *"I'm going over
   to Aye Zee"*)
Bailey Hall
The Longhouses
"John and Diane"
Studded Snow Tires
Keith Kennedy
All Chicken Barbecues
   Held Anywhere in the
   Continental United States
Cornell Barbecue Sauce
Tower Road
The Alma Mater
The Big Red Barn
Taughannock Falls
Niagara Falls
Glens Falls

Dear Dad,
When I was just a little girl, I always looked up to you as the smartest, the strongest, and the kindest man in the whole wide world. In fact, it's safe to say you were my Hero

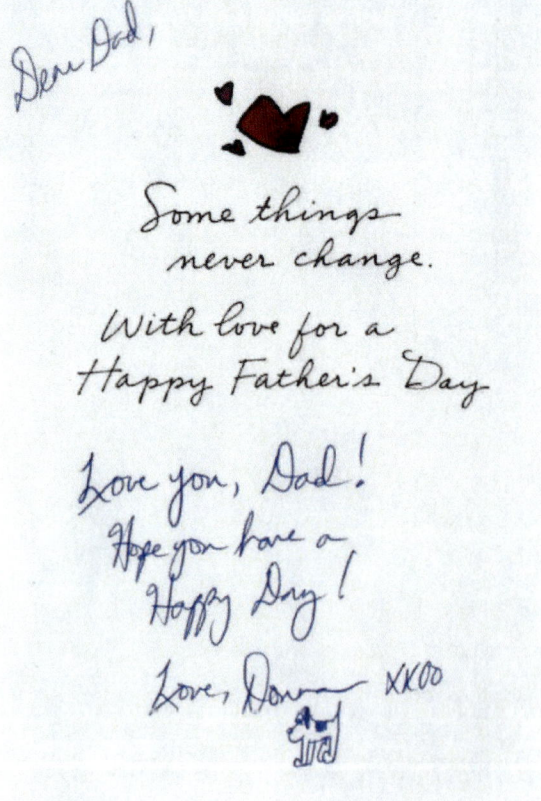

Dear Dad,

Some things never change.

With love for a Happy Father's Day

Love you, Dad!
Hope you have a Happy Day!

Love, Donna xxoo

FAMILY

If Ron has been in the department for 42 years, then I guess I've been in "the department" for 41 years, because my life is filled with memories of growing up in the Ag. Eng. family.

I remember Professor Riley, a very old man with a white beard and cane. I marveled at the stature of a man for whom a building was named. I remember department family Christmas parties and picnics with the famous Cornell chicken barbeques, to say nothing of hockey and football. I remember picking Dad up at the office when we had only one car. There were conventions on the campus when the children spent hours riding up and down the elevators. But what most impressed me as a child was the remarkable fact that my dad had a key to the faculty lounge and to the restrooms within!

I doubt that Ron knew when he came to Cornell as a freshman in 1949 that Cornell and Ag. Eng. would become such a family affair. He couldn't have foreseen that his undergraduate Ag. Eng. friend Dave Dirksen would marry his sister Joanne and become his brother-in-law. He couldn't have guessed that his daughter would marry Bill Irish's son. Nor could he have guessed that in his own family there would be nine degrees earned at Cornell University.

But throughout the years, Ron has set a standard, at home and at work, of excellence and caring. We have all benefitted from his example, and we strive to repeat it in our own lives. We truly appreciate you, and we thank you, Dad

Suzanne L. Furry-Irish

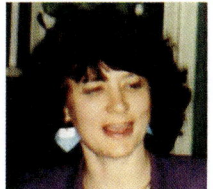

Cornell
University

Wednesday, November 22, 1995

Dr. Ronald B. Furry
Department of Agricultural and Biological Engineering
CAMPUS

Dear Ron:

It was a pleasure and privilege to participate in the ABEN celebration of your retirement — both because of our long friendship and because of your selfless service to Cornell. Your demonstrated commitment to 'citizenship' is unsurpassed.

My remarks at the dinner were heartfelt, so I've simply appended my notes.

Best wishes to you and Anne in this new phase of your life. Please stay in touch.

Sincerely,

J. Robert Cooke

Comments Made at Turback's

In preparing this retrospective, I've been reminded of the genius of Cornell's tradition of independence with responsibility. Here we have a splendid reminder of the benefits that come from not trying to force everyone into a common mold. The whole is larger than the sum of the parts when each of us is allowed—no, encouraged—to bring his or her own special talents to a professorial role. Let me illustrate.

Forty-two years of service is hard for me to comprehend. For example, Ron was already busy as a full-time teacher of Cornell students while I was still in Junior High School. I know first-hand only a portion of his long record of forty-two years of service to Cornell.

After completing both a bachelor and a masters degree at Cornell, Ron earned his doctorate at Iowa State and returned to Ithaca. One of the major themes of Ron's career has been computing — both analog and digital. To put his pioneering effort in perspective, remember that FORTRAN was invented in 1957. Ron taught computing courses for many years, including the largest course ever taught by this Department. His experience spanned the changes from Hollerith cards and batch computing, to 'Instant Turnaround' (or was that really 'Infinite Turnaround'?), to remote access, interactive computing

Department of Agricultural and Biological Engineering, 214 Riley-Robb Hall Ithaca, NY 14853
Phone: (607) 255-2480 / Fax: (607) 255-4080

via dumb terminals, and on to standalone microcomputers and smart terminals. He introduced and was responsible for the computer graphics course and computer-aided design. His other courses have included Similitude Methodology, Orientation to Research for Graduate Students and Career Development for undergraduates.

His abiding interest in undergraduate recruitment has been a major, sustained effort for 17 years and, even if largely unnoticed by his colleagues, his nation-wide recruiting effort has been highly successful and has made life in these financially difficult times much less threatening to his colleagues than otherwise would have been the case. Ron, you have ample reason to be proud of your key role of the legacy of a well-populated undergraduate program.

There are numerous other instances of dedicated service as a citizen of our community. I recall having served with you in the University Senate during a particularly difficult time in the history of this University. You provided leadership and service to Alpha Zeta. Over the course of the life of the Cornell Federal Credit Union you played an active leadership role, serving most recently in its top leadership role and nurturing its service role.

Your building design experience has played a major role in the design of the dairy facilities at ASTARC in Harford and at the Miner Institute in Chazy. Most recently you led the programmatic design for the renovation of Riley-Robb Hall.

You led the graduate program for several years and most recently worked with a department that experiences a perpetual identity crisis. Throughout all these years you have provided the benchmark by which we can all measure service and citizenship. You are one of a kind.

Thank you for this notably long record of service. We can legitimately address you now as 'Professor Emeritus Ronald Bay Furry, Public Citizen of Cornell University'.

Please accept our warmest best wishes to you and Anne on this new phase in your lives.

CORNELL
U N I V E R S I T Y

Cornell Local Roads Program   Telephone: 607 255-8033
416 Riley-Robb Hall   Fax: 607 255-4080
Ithaca, New York 14853-5701   Internet: clrp_mailbox@
                                   cornell.edu

28 September 1995

Professor Ronald B. Furry
Department of Agricultural
 and Biological Engineering
234 Riley-Robb Hall
Cornell University
Ithaca, NY 14853

Dear Ron:

I could not possibly count all of my fond memories of our 23(!) years together as colleagues. I treasure each and every one. In the interest of brevity I will describe only one here.

Back around 1973, shortly after I arrived at Cornell, I adopted you as my advisor. I never gave you the chance to agree to this role, and you never refused to share your wisdom.

One day I had written a memo to Stan Shepardson, suggesting that our new environmental chamber should be placed in the Machinery Lab. I asked you to look over the memo before I passed it on to Stan.

After only a few minutes you came into my office and said it needed revision. You went on to point out to me that the proper technique was to offer three choices. Number 1, you explained, should be plausible and far more than I could hope for, but wonderful if it was approved. Number 2 should be the choice that I really wanted. Number 3, "And this is most important," you said, should be an unacceptable choice, obviously inappropriate, which would never be selected.

"That way the Department Chairman will feel like he is doing his job, and you will get what you want. With a little luck, you will get more than you want."

That was useful advice to give to an impressionable young professor. I have never forgotten the lesson. I was reluctant to use the technique (very often) while you were Department Chairman, because I was afraid you would recognize it. But the new Chairman is fair game.

Thanks for the good advice and for being a friend!

Yours truly,

Lynne H. Irwin

October 8, 1995

Dear Ron and Anne,

There is at least one thing I like about this retirement, Ron...your continuing presence in Riley-Robb means I won't have to say good-bye just yet. I hope to see you around the 'Robb for a long time to come.

My association with you goes back a long way...actually about 35 years, to when I was a freshman at Cornell in our department. I had just finished taking 2 semesters of mechanical drawing with O. K. Dart as instructor, and he offered me the opportunity to work as a teaching assistant for the course the following semester, Fall 1960. I had enjoyed the course so much, I jumped at the chance, telling him I was looking forward to working with him. That's when I first heard of Ronald Furry...Olin Dart told me he was leaving Cornell, and I would be working for you!

Well, I'm awfully glad it worked out that way. I assisted you in drawing labs for probably 3 years, then you went off to Ames and I continued to assist Howard in mechanical drawing classes as a graduate student.

When you came back from Ames with a Ph.D., I had begun working full time doing research in dairy cattle housing with Bill Irish. Later we went on to designing the new Animal Science Teaching and Research Center buildings in Harford, and eventually to many years of research in the controlled atmosphere storage of vegetables. They called you "Mr. Cabbage", while my 6 year old son told people his daddy "made cabbages" for a living! I must admit, I never dreamed I would come to have such an intimate relationship with a large, round, green vegetable called Brassica oleraceae L.!

I have many fond recollections from these past 35 years. I can still see you as "Chif Juj", standing on a table, explaining the rules of the student engineering design contest. And stretching out your arms as you demonstrated how your neighbor removed his "invisible" deer netting from his shrubbery. Those many hours we spent elbow deep in rotting cabbage (Botrytis cinerea), assessing each storage trial. And many days in travel to Brockport for visits to field research sites. Do you remember the day we cut cabbage in snow up to our thighs?

Anne, you have been such a delightful person to know. I think it's wonderful that you are retiring at the same time. I wish we could have had more opportunities to put our heads together and poke fun at Ron's obsessive "attention to detail"! Now my kids think I'm the same way...do you suppose some of it rubbed off from RB?

Hey, Ron...I loaded Windows95 on my computer this week! Are you ready to take the plunge yet? It won't be pretty!

Ruth and I wish you both many many years of enjoyable retirement. You both have a special place in our hearts. I hope you get in a lot of travel. When I retire, I want to sell the house and take off in a motor home, to explore the country at a leisurely pace. Unfortunately, this does not have universal appeal in my household...oh, well!

Wishing you all the best,

Marty

Martin C. Jorgensen

CORNELL
U N I V E R S I T Y

College of Agriculture and Life Sciences   Department of Agricultural   Fax: 607 255-4080
                                                    and Biological Engineering
                                                    Riley-Robb Hall
                                                    Ithaca, New York 14853-5701

October 2, 1995

Dr. Ron Furry
Agricultural and Biological Engineering

Dear Ron:

As your namesake and colleague, let me congratulate you most warmly on your
accomplishments through your career as faculty member and chair. I have felt a close tie
with you since the day Dave Ludington intended to call us "the two Rons," but instead
referred to us as "the two Furrys."

I recall sitting in on the first day of ABEN 304, your huge programming course. After
handing out a thick, multicolored packet of <u>one day's</u> handouts, you said something to the
class that was very important: that the students should not worry about having prior
computer experience. I think this had a calming effect on the students who were afraid of
the computer, and since then I have tried to keep that same student-oriented perspective that
you displayed.

Thinking back, the highest priority you've had as long as I've known you is undergraduate
teaching, and in a sense the rest of the Cornell community has finally caught up with that.
So you deserve to be recognized for focusing on that part of our jobs which is really most
important.

Having a last name that frequently gets wrecked when spoken, I appreciate other last names
that spell new words. So I liked it when one of our former students said that she felt the
best course she took at Cornell was "Dr. Fury's." Of course, her message about your
teaching was the important thing. Thanks again for everything you've done in the last
decades. I look forward to sharing experiences with you in the coming years.

With affection,

Ron

Ronald E. Pitt
Professor

CORNELL
UNIVERSITY

Cornell Local Roads Program   Telephone: 607 255-8033
416 Riley-Robb Hall   Fax: 607 255-4080
Ithaca, NY 14853-5701   Internet: clrp__@cornell.edu

October 2, 1995

Dr. Ronald B. Furry
Professor
Department of Agricultural and Biological Engineering
Cornell University

Dear Ron:

I am delighted to have the opportunity to congratulate you on the occasion of your retirement. You can count me as one of the ABEN staff who will miss you.

Your support of our program activities and of my efforts to maintain our course in Lynne's occasional absences, were most appreciated. I always felt that I could come to you for advice and you would make time for me.

From my perspective, the most important thing you brought to the leadership of the department was openness. Even when you knew precious little about what budget cuts were coming or what changes could be expected, you told us what you knew. You gave us a sense of being part of the big picture. We didn't have to learn of changes in the department or college through the grapevine. This was especially significant for what I call the "forgotten staff," those of us who are neither faculty nor support staff. Even your practice of random walks through the halls to say hello is something I still remember because it showed you cared about us.

Thank you for your leadership and please accept my wishes for a heathy, vibrant, enjoyable retirement.

Sincerely,

Toni

Toni Rosenbaum
Assistant Director

CORNELL
UNIVERSITY

Agricultural and Biological Engineering
Riley Robb Hall   Ithaca, NY 14853
607-255-2801 (voice) 255-4080 (fax) mbt3@cornell.edu (email)

September 28, 1995

DR. RON FURRY
Professor Emeritus

Dear Ron:

Congratulations on your retirement. Some of us don't ever get that far, and in my case, someone (like a disgruntled fish grower) may shoot me!

Ron, I want you to know sincerely that I appreciate all the help you've been to me during my career. From my first interaction with you in the Similitude Class (remember, I got an A!), to your days as department chair, dinner at the Ithaca Tower Club, your taking my PhD thesis to the graduate school, your calls to me at NCSTate just to see if I was doing OK, and on countless other times, I have always enjoyed our interactions and the help you have given me.

Someday, I may be able to deliver those shrimp you keep asking about, but until, then you'll have to settle for tilapia.

Enjoy...

Best regards,

Mike Timmons

Mike Timmons

CORNELL
UNIVERSITY

College of Agriculture and Life Sciences

Department of Agricultural
and Biological Engineering

Fax: 607 255-4080

Riley-Robb Hall
Ithaca, New York 14853-5701

October 1995

Dear Ron and Ann:

Congratulations Ron and you too Ann, on reaching that time in your lives when you can plan your daily activities without thought of Ron getting to Riley-Robb "on time". Ron you may have thought you pulled a fast one kicking the traces a wee bit early as far as your time in Ag & Bio Engineering is concerned in order to escape, "Riley-Robb renovation and facilities planning", but the joke is on you. Don't think that just because you reached the golden age of retirement you are going to do less "work"; most people work harder in retirement than otherwise and knowing you as I do, I am positive you will too. Certainly, on this festive occasion honoring your many years of service to Ag and Bio Engineering, early on Cooperative Extension, and Cornell University, Lu and I wish both of you the very best.

It seems only yesterday that I met you Ron, first as an undergraduate, then graduate student, then faculty and lastly Department Chairman. As you may recall your early teaching of mechanical drawing, then extension work. I was really happy when you completed your Ph.D. at good old Iowa State University and returned to take over the similitude course, you were an excellent Glenn Murphy advocate. Every time I have dessert pie I think of you and pi terms. I still believe that our students should have some teaching and knowledge of similitude; A powerful tool.

Ron, as you progressed through the academic ranks here in our Ag and Bio Engineering Department, I remained impressed with your attention to detail and never leaving anything to chance. You certainly are to be commended for your adherence to "advance planning". Research was another area where you demonstrated your expertise, your classic work on controlled storage, specifically, cabbage, was a god- send to our New York State Cabbage Growers. I know that even you were surprised at the quantity of cabbage used in your commercial, "pilot project." It could have resulted in a mammoth amount of Kim-chi- enough to last Korea for years. Your promotion to Department Chairman was indeed positive from all perspectives. In my opinion, you were one of the best department chairmans I ever had the privilege to interact with and enjoy. I personally don't think too many department members realize the tremendous contributions that you made to Ag and Bio Engineering.

Finally, Lu joins me in extending our very best wishes to both of you as you move on to another stage in your lives.

Wes and Lu Gunkel

129

CORNELL UNIVERSITY
AGRICULTURAL & BIOLOGICAL ENGINEERING
RILEY-ROBB HALL
ITHACA, NY 14853 USA
(Tel: 607-255-2802)
(Fax: 607-255-4080)
(dah13@cornell.edu)

October 5, 1995

Ronald B. Furry
Riley-Robb Hall
Cornell University
Ithaca, NY 14853

Dear Ron:

It is very difficult for me to think of your retirement. You have been an important part of the department ever since I joined it, and it won't seem the same without you.

Your accomplishments were many, but some of the things I remember most were the times you volunteered for tasks others avoided, and subsequently turned the efforts into investments that paid enormous dividends for the department. Thus you agreed to teach an undergraduate computer course which subsequently, under your able teaching and organization, became the largest course the department has ever seen. How many of us realized that the number of credit-hours represented by this effort brought enormous credibility from CALS administration for our teaching efforts? An even better case is the determined and resourceful undergraduate recruiting program you created and then carried out for so long. We now take our large enrollments for granted, and you never trumpeted your role in these results, but where would we be now without them?

I also will never forget your work as Graduate Field Representative and Department Chairman. The fairness, hard work and dedication you brought to these posts were remarkable. You never pushed your own agendas, and the hallmark of your leadership was service - to the faculty, students and the people of New York State. You made my work easier, and also made me very proud to be a member of the department.

But my best memory is that semester when you sat in on all my course lectures. I was never quite sure why you did it, but it sure had an impact on me. I had only been teaching for a couple of years, and the idea of a senior faculty member listening to everything I said was intimidating. Eventually I realized that your presence was a validation of my teaching, and a useful resource. You never volunteered suggestions, but you always had some when I got around to ask. It was the kind of confidence building and learning experience everyone should have, and I feel guilty that I have never made a similar contribution in someone else's course.

Well, Ron, it won't be the same, and that's as it should be. Our newer colleagues will have to learn some of the same lessons we did, and they will make their own contributions. The department you helped to build and nurtured for so long is vigorous and healthy, and I guess that is the best memorial.

Douglas A. Haith
Professor

130

CORNELL
UNIVERSITY

College of Agriculture and Life Sciences

Department of Agricultural
and Biological Engineering
Riley-Robb Hall
Ithaca, New York 14853-5701

Fax: 607 255-4080

October 9, 1995

Dear Ron and Ann,

Knowing the two of you for the past 30+ years has been a very enjoyable experience. We have very pleasant and fond memories as a result of your friendship.

Ron, I must say that you have been one of the easier individuals to work with in the department, even though some of your projects were "It would be nice if I had it this afternoon, on yellow paper or was it buff paper".

During your professional career you have seen many changes in technology and the department which we shared. You made it a point to keep abreast of the latest computer technology. It sure has been a change from the punch cards that we used in your class to the desk PC. Sometimes I think the computer has created more work for me and I know that some of my work can be done faster on the drawing board.

Jan and I wish you and Ann a very happy retirement and enjoy life to its fullest.

(Kvisek)
Dick

October 6, 1995

Dear Ron,

I'm very sorry that we are not able to attend the celebration of your long and productive career in Ag Engineering. I'll be in Kansas to attend a "regional" ag engineers meeting.

It is an honor for me to have had you as a colleague. Your commitment to the department is unprecedented. You truly have given all of yourself to our department. Your extraordinary optimism in times of trail is an example to all of us of how to look on the bright side, quit whining and get on with making the most of what we have. And you have also been the one to recognize all that we do have, especially in our departmental human resources. As department chair, and more as a colleague, I want to thank you for all you've done for and given to ABEN.

Most of all, Ron, I want you and Ann to know how great it is to have you as friends. You are very special people.

Warmest Regards,

(Walter)
Mik

131

Gerald E. Rehkugler, Ph.D., P.E.
Rev. Nancy C. Rehkugler
P.O. Box 1034
34 Church Street
Moravia, NY 13118
Phone - 315-497-1412

5 October 1995

Dr. Ronald B. Furry

Dear Ron:

Congratulations on staying the course for 42 years of service. Wow!! That a few years. As I reflect on our association, I am reminded that our relationship goes back many years. I think my first recollections are the drawing course in Stocking Hall. You sure set some high standards for us "wet behind the ears" farm boys. You also exposed us to a unique sense of humor - that we didn't always appreciate - but grew to understand?

And then we shared the days at Iowa State in our overlap of PhD studies. I am not sure that Ag Eng at Iowa State ever got over your ability to move through the system in spite of the rules. I am also grateful for your pioneering effort that enabled me to take advantage of what you had set up the year before. Because you showed me that it could be done, I am sure that it helped me to finish in the two year time span.

In the intervening years we sure have kept busy haven't we? I trust that now you will be able to slow down and smell more roses, take more trips and listen to more of Ann's music. Best wishes to both of you for a great things in the years to come.

Sincerely yours,

Gerry Rehkugler

Ron - Enjoy your leisure!!! Joy & good health! God Bless - Nancy

Kifle G Gebremedhin
39 Horvath Dr.
Ithaca, NY 14850

October 6, 1995

Dear Ron:

Forty two years of service!!!! This is remarkable. I have done only one-third of yours and I see a lot of gray fur (smile!) on my head. Ron, do you know what you and I have in common? The red pen. I will think of you whenever I use it and I use it a lot.

Ron, I want you to know how much I very much appreciate your encouragement and help in my activities, especially in my capacity as the Coordinator of Instruction of our Undergraduate Programs. It was a pleasure working with you on our Undergraduate Programs during your tenure as the Department Chair. Thank you for the experience.

Ron and Anne, CONGRATULATIONS! on your retirement. Enjoy it. Ron, I will be checking on you in Riley Robb Hall.

With Best Regards,

Kifle G. Gebremedhin

October 3, 1995
4680 So A1A
Melbourne Beach
FL 32951

Dear Ron,

Time has flown by and you are retiring! 53 years - we can't realize it.! We would thoroughly enjoy attending your party, to Congratulate you in person. I appreciated your diligent work on drawing classes and on storage structures for apples and cabbages. You were, also, an excellent teacher. The extra time you spent with students should be especially recognized. Happy Retirement

Orval French

To Anne from Helen

Engineers never retire! If they see something to fix, they will try to fix it whether they can or not. Now, they can blame the computers. I've noticed that wives usually figure out and fix things too simple for an Engineer. It has to be more of a complicated problem for an Engineer to put their minds to fixing it or wondering why they can't do it. I have a picture of our daughter, Nina, reading instructions and putting together a kids sail boat while very smart Engineering sons and husband stand & watch. Concerning engines, especially cars, the engine must go until the guage shows near empty. They think of Retirement after they fall off of a roof or ladder or end up in a ditch out of gas, nor can fix things.

Remember our 25 anniversary party. 1957 My biggest dinner party, 125 in the Seminar Room You sang 'Buttons & Bows? Thank you

God Bless You Both. Helen French

CORNELL
UNIVERSITY

College of Agriculture and Life Sciences

Department of Agricultural
and Biological Engineering

Fax: 607 255-4080

Riley-Robb Hall
Ithaca, New York 14853-5701

October 20, 1995

Dear Ron & Anne,

I am really sorry that I missed your retirement party. I never knew about it until October 16 while talking with Bill Irish and Bill Millier. Apparently there was some foul-up with the computer lists, and double checking with knowledgeable people.

Anyway, you have had a pretty good tenure here all these years - from the bottom to the top! Did I suspect that while teaching you as an undergrad? - No way! So you see you did not get any of that pizzazz from me - it had to come from you - with Anne's help of course.

So now the thing to do is to get deeply involved in enjoying retirement. You will find that it is great!

Best regards to you and Anne. Keep healthy and happy.

As ever,

Stan and Mary Shepardson

135

Memorandum

TO: **Ron Furry**

FROM: **Sue Fredenburg**

RE: **Accolades for RB**

He always knows just what to say to make us all stay cool

When there's news just pass it on and let no one play a fool.

"Whatcha do'in," "can I help," he pleads and means it too

He always quickly lets you know, there's nothing he can't do.

He never lets a chance go by to tell you where he's at

You always know just *when* and *where*, and *if* and *what* and *that*.

And when he's on the run he yells, "see you when I'm back,"

It's then you know there's more to do before you want for lack.

Hats a plenty that's what he has and what he's always been

For no reward is better than a turn to play again.

Another role, another chance to make the world some better

And in the process, just who knows, he'll tell you in a letter.

Serious matters have their place but he always makes them lighter,

A touch of humor always helps, he's a happy fighter.

We'll miss the puns, the wit, the charm that RB brought to all

For we know, as warriors go, he's truly very tall.

CORNELL
UNIVERSITY

College of Agriculture & Life Sciences

Office of Academic Programs   607/255-3081
140 Roberts Hall   FAX: 607/254-4613
Ithaca, New York 14853-4203

October 6, 1995

Ronald Furry, Professor
Ag & Biological Engineering
234 Riley Robb

Dear Ron:

I wanted to convey my congratulations on your retirement and express my appreciation for the positive interactions that we have shared over the years. Our mutual interest in computing led us to serve on several committees together. It was always a pleasure to work with you. You have been a positive influence in your department, the college and the university.

We are not saying good bye because you will always be our friend and colleague.

Sincerely yours,

H. Dean Sutphin
Associate Dean
for Academic Programs

file: commu/furry/10.95

University of
Nebraska
Lincoln

Institute of Agriculture and Natural Resources
Agricultural Research Division

Northeast Research &
Extension Center
Concord, NE 68728
(402) 584-2261
FAX (402) 584-2859

Direct Phone: (402) 584-2855
E-mail: NERC009@UNLVM.UNL.EDU

January 10, 1996

Dr. Ronald B. Furry
Agricultural and Biological Engineering
Riley-Robb Hall
Cornell University
Ithaca, NY 14853

BEST WISHES

Ron, although this is somewhat belated, it is none-the-less sincere.

I want to wish you the very best on your retirement from Cornell. The courses that I had with you were certainly among the most useful of my academic training. (I still refer to the "Agricultural Process Engineering" textbook with some frequency.) While I didn't think so at the time, I have come to very much appreciate the high expectations you had of your students, and find myself with similar expectations.

One brief "story" - Nearly every time I tear the perforated portion off tractor-feed computer paper, I recall how adamant you were about laboratory reports being free of those perforations. Unfortunately, we no longer use tractor-feed letterhead, as I really wanted to leave the perforations on this letter!

My very best wishes to you.

Dave Shelton

David P. Shelton
Professor, Biological Systems Engineering and
   Extension Agricultural Engineer

University of Nebraska–Lincoln   University of Nebraska Medical Center   University of Nebraska at Omaha   University of Nebraska at Kearney

SUNY
Cobleskill

Office of the President

State University of New York • College of Agriculture and Technology • Cobleskill, New York 12043-9986 • 518-234-5111 • Fax 518-234-5888

October 20, 1995

Professor Ronald B. Furry
Department of Agricultural and
  Biological Engineering
234 Riley-Robb Hall
Cornell University
Ithaca, New York 14853

Dear Ron:

On the occasion of your retirement from the Department of Agricultural and Biological Engineering, I write to express my appreciation for all the marvelous things you have done for and to the Department, the College of Agriculture and Life Sciences, Alpha Zeta, the Cornell Federal Credit Union, the Ithaca area, and the people who have had the pleasure of knowing and working with you. Yes, that was a long sentence, but it only scratched the surface of what needed to be said.

Except for some brief periods, we shared the joy of Cornell - from the "old" Agr. Eng. shops to the new Riley-Robb (next to Wing Hall, on Wing Drive!); and from the "old" Alpha Zeta to the new chapter house; and from the "old" Zinck's (all three of them) to the new, albeit ephemeral, Zinck's night'; and more. So many memories - so little memory!

Thank you for all you did, and for the joy you brought to me. I expect you to have a very long and very happy retirement!

Sincerely yours,

Ken

Kenneth E. Wing
President

KEW:ivd

ALS

ALUMNI ASSOCIATION

Certificate
of
Recognition

Presented To

Ronald B. Furry

For academic leadership through
teaching, research and extension activities for
the College of Agriculture and Life Sciences
at Cornell University

We proudly acknowledge your many achievements
and wish you all the best in your retirement

Dean, College of Agriculture and Life Sciences   President, ALS Alumni Association

June 8, 1996

The Alumni Association of the
College of Agriculture and Life Sciences
Cornell University
Ithaca, New York

College of Agriculture and Life Sciences

Cornell Federal Credit Union

1030 Craft Road
Ithaca, NY 14850-1016
(607) 257-8500

October 6, 1995

Dear Ron:

You've shared your expertise with Cornell for forty-two years and with us Credit Union folks for about the same. I'm sure you were better compensated at Cornell, but no more appreciated. Cornell has grown tremendously during those years, as has CFCU.

Ron Furry counseled CFCU through new branches, issuance of share drafts, introducing ATMs and VISA and the planning for our administration building on Craft Road. From your account # 1017, we've grown to a membership of 44,000.

Your loyalty is valued . . . and you've been a good friend.

Sincerely yours,

Robert O. Witty
President and Chief Executive Officer

With branches at East Hill Plaza, Triphammer Mall, Bailey Hall, and Ithaca College/NCR

CORNELL FEDERAL CREDIT UNION

NEWS NOTES

Basement Bailey Hall   Telephone X 3806

Vol. 1   No. 1

Your Education Committee has suggested that you receive some News Notes each quarter. We are anxious that you be kept well informed about your Credit Union and this appears to be a convenient way to do so. If you want a meeting with employees in your area of the campus, to learn more about the Credit Union, call any member of the Education Committee.

* * * * * * * * * * *

For the first quarter of 1958 we have 950 members compared with 932 members a year ago; total loans are $221,109 compared with $146,782; the share balance is $256,504 compared with $167,485 and the earnings are $3,247 compared with $2,199 a year ago.

* * * * * * * * * * *

Your Board has loaned $20,000 to the Valley Stream Teachers' Federal Credit Union for six months at 4%. We are in the position now of profiting by increased savings. You can help by telling your friends about our dividend rate history. It seems likely that we can expect 4% or more in the years ahead.

* * * * * * * * * * *

The policy of charging 3/4 of 1% interest on the unpaid balance each month on all new car loans is in effect. The car must be new and the loan backed by a chattel or other acceptable security.

* * * * * * * * * * *

The members of the present Board of Directors are as follows: Bruce M. Payne, President (Assistant to Vice-President of the University), Day Hall; Paul C. Kilby, Vice-President (Administrative Assistant, Finance and Business Office), Roberts Hall; Richard G. Karch, Secretary (Superintendent, Division of Utilities, Building and Property Service) Service Building; Richard F. Fricke, Treasurer (Professor Emeritus, Agricultural Extension Service); and Fred B. Morris (State Leader of County Agricultural Agents), Roberts Hall.

We will give you the names of the other committee members in subsequent letters.

* * * * * * * * * * *

Fred O'Connell resigned as Treasurer as of May 15th. Richard F. Fricke is the new Treasurer, and Richard Stringham, a Cornell graduate and resident of Groton, is the office manager.

* * * * * * * * * * *

We will ask and answer some questions about the Credit Union in each News Letter. You may wish to file these letters for future reference.

Q. How are dividends paid?
A. They are paid at the end of each year at a rate determined by the members at the annual meeting on the recommendation of the Board of Directors. The amount of your dividend depends upon the length of time your money has been on deposit. This amount is credited to your account.

Q. Who is eligible to use our Credit Union service?
A. All employees of Cornell University, members of their immediate families and organizations of such persons.

* * * * * * * * * * *

The enclosed pamphlet will answer your insurance questions. Please pass it on to your friends.

Your Educational Committee: Fred B. Morris, Chairman
                Rollin Perry   Joe Thomas
                Ronald Furry   Earle Tallmadge

Office hours for your convenience are as follows:

Monday through Friday   9:00 a.m. to 1:30 p.m.
                                            and
                                  2:00 p.m. to 5:00 p.m.

DIRECTORY

Cornell Federal Credit Union

SEPTEMBER 1958
* * *

Board of Directors:
    Bruce M. Payne, President . . . .   Asst. to Vice President- Business
    Paul C. Kilby, Vice President . .   Finance & Business Off. - State Colleges
    Richard F. Fricke, Treasurer . .   Retired
    Richard G. Karch, Clerk . . . . .   Division of Utilities - Building & Property
    Fred B. Morris . . . .   Extension & State Leaders

Credit Committee:
    Michell J. Sienko, Chairman . . .   Chemistry Department
    Richard E. Hufnail, Secretary . .   Controller's Office
    Frederick S. Hoefer, Jr. . . . .   Dairy Industry
    Walter R. May . . . .   Electrical Engineering
    Howard L. Williams . . . .   Buildings and Property

Supervisory Committee:
    Harry G. Henn, Chairman . . . . .   Law School
    Kenneth Georgia . . . .   Finance & Business Off. - State Colleges
    R. A. Saunders . . . .   University Development

Education Committee:
    Fred B. Morris, Chairman . . . .   Extension and State Leaders
    Rollin Perry . . . .   Arts & Sciences
    Ronald Furry . . . .   Agricultural Engineering
    Joseph E. Thomas . . . .   University Laundry
    Earle Tallmadge . . . .   Campus Stores

Employees:
    Richard Stringham, Asst. Treasurer   Office Manager
    Doris (Mrs. Arthur) Davis . . . .   Part Time Office Work

Cornell Federal Credit Union

1030 Craft Road
Ithaca, NY 14850-1016
(607) 257-8500

October 6, 1995

Dear Ron:

How quickly time passes. But when I think about it, it was 35 years ago that I first met you down in the catacomb of Bailey Hall. You were chairman of the Education Committee at that time and CFCU had 1,650 very loyal members.

I believe you were responsible for CFCU's first NEWSNOTES. I have included a copy. You certainly have contributed many wonderful years and great insight to the Credit Union. Our parties were special during your tenure--we never knew what to expect--special prizes such as ATM (at table money), spoon on the nose act . . . and I'll never forget, much to our chagrin, Bob and me failing the magical rope trick.

Over the years you and Ann have added something special to our Credit Union . . . and you remain loyal to our yearly narratives. You even helped us improve on those. I know you will enjoy added time for your own pursuits and those of your family.

Enjoy!

Sincerely yours,

Mary

Mary B. Oberhaus
Executive Vice President

7830 Plainville Road
P.O. Box 289
Plainville, NY 13137-0289

What turkey should be!

Telephone (315) 638-0226

October 8, 1995

Ronald B. Furry
143 Brook Way
Ithaca, NY 14850

Dear Ron,

About 44 years ago I met a potential Alpha Zeta pledge for the first time by the name of Ronald B. Furry. We interacted as fraternity brothers for about a year, and then he disappeared. (Or, perhaps it was I who disappeared.)

About 5 years ago we both reappeared at 214 Thurston Avenue working together on a project whereby we might give to others some of what had been given to us.

Ron, I was and am impressed with both the dedication and excellence you have always exhibited. It was an opportunity and an honor to interact with you.

Your retirement will be a loss to the Agricultural Engineering Department at Cornell. I sincerely hope it will give you the opportunity to do some things, that will bring you enjoyment, you have had to postpone in the past.

The Bitz family wishes you and yours, good health and happiness for many years as you continue to move along life's path. We are sure that whoever you may meet along the way will be enriched by having known you.

Sincerely,

Bob

Robert W. Bitz

RWB/rad

145

Bad News and a Ruse

When I was appointed Department Chair in 1990, the New York State College of Agriculture and Life Sciences was in a condition of continued decline in support from the State University of New York (SUNY), and was transitioning from being a State supported College to a State assisted College. Budget cuts were continuing and salaries were stagnant. Our Department had lost virtually all of our funding for secretarial and other support staff, and morale was declining. Worse, our Multilith Copy Center Manager was having marital problems, but one Friday happily confided in me that he saw things greatly improving between him and his wife. Unexpectedly, on Monday we learned that he had shot himself in the head and died. He was very well liked and that set in a new state of gloom. I held a memorial service for him in our packed Seminar Room and folks spoke of his dedication and service. Later, at the funeral home I was shocked to see him standing at the door to the viewing parlor greeting visitors. I did not know that he had an absolutely identical twin who also dressed like him. To break the cycle of despair, I instituted a weekly Chit-Chat on Fridays at 10:00 AM. I supplied refreshments and snacks and then held informational meetings for all faculty and staff combined to inform them of the current state of departmental affairs and likely future events and have them interact with one another. The folks responded very favorably; it was well received and successive Department Chairs have continued the practice into this, the 28th year, with increasing involvement of faculty, staff and graduate students.

After some time had passed, on one of these occasions I decided to add a little twist to the gathering. I sent notices out announcing that I had invited an expert from the State Capitol in Albany to visit us to give us an evaluation of the "State of the Department." I detailed his credentials and presented his business card as Prof. Geheimnis Sharpstein. On the morning that he was due to arrive, we were assembled in the Seminar Room on the 4th floor for the usual Chit-Chat and everything was set for his presentation, but it was 10:00 AM and he had not yet arrived. I told the gathering that since he had not been to campus before that I was going down to the first floor entrance to show him the way to the meeting room. I left the Seminar Room, but dashed out of sight to the Seminar Kitchen where I had previously stashed a disguise. I put on a different shirt over the one I was wearing, donned an oversize suit on top of the clothes I was already wearing to make me look pudgy and changed my tie and shoes. I put on a black wig having a pony tail and added a slim mustache and a small goatee. Then I removed my wedding ring from my left hand, and placed a splint on the 3rd finger of my right hand to give the impression that I had a broken finger. Finally, I folded an old tan raincoat over my left forearm, picked up an old leather briefcase and held a black, folded umbrella in my right hand. When I entered the Seminar Room, I looked right and left as if trying to figure out my bearings, finally saw

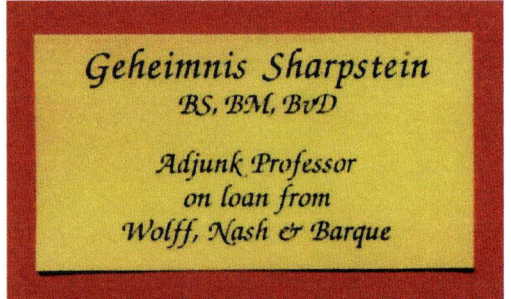

a movable coat rack to my left and moved to hang up my raincoat and umbrella. I "accidentally" dropped the umbrella on the floor and stooped to pick it up; everyone turned my way to see what had happened. I went to the front of the room, opened my briefcase, took out 8½" by 11" overhead projector frames and briefly pretended I did not know where the switch was to turn the projector on. Next, I moved to the lectern that was set up to the left of the overhead projector and introduced myself and my topic, thanking the assembly for the invitation and using a slightly disguised voice. During this introduction, I purposely dangled the fingers of my left hand over the front of the lectern to expose my ringless finger, and then switched to doing the same thing with my right hand, exposing my "broken" finger. Finally, I delivered my talk using the overheads, covering a litany of data and financial information that looked real but was actually nonsense. My conclusion at the end of the talk was that the State of the

Department was NEW YORK! It was obvious that the folks didn't know what to think. I immediately stepped in front of the lectern where I proceeded to take off my disguise, starting with my jacket, pants, tie, extra shirt and then the wig, mustache, goatee and finger splint, and put on my wedding ring. First impressions crowd out our logic: my personal secretary, Ruth Stanton, sat 5 feet in front of the lectern during the whole event and even after I had taken off my whole disguise and returned to my normal state, *she did not know me*! I was totally amazed!

It was lots of fun! So much in fact that Anne and I decided to perform a similar stunt on my sister's birthday, October 26, in Monroe, Ohio. We informed her children that we were going to surprise her on her birthday and asked them to set up a birthday outing for her at one of her favorite eating places, which happened to be a Japanese restaurant. We drove to Monroe, Ohio, and secreted ourselves in a hotel until that evening, when one of her kids picked us up and drove us to the restaurant before the birthday revelers arrived. I had dressed in my Geheimnis Sharpstein disguise, and Anne had dressed as a blonde floozy, with sunglasses, black hat and coat and plenty of lipstick. The restaurant had a large bar area with tables to the left of the entrance and overhead floodlights, in a dim interior. I put one of the tables directly under a flood light, got two beers and placed them on the table in front of us, and positioned us at an angle so that we could be readily seen by anyone entering the front door. Shortly thereafter, Joanne and her party entered the restaurant. Joanne looked into the bar, swept her eyes around the area, glanced at us, and then quickly moved to the rear of the restaurant where the hibachi service was located. After a few minutes Anne and I left the bar, went into the dining area and sat next to Joanne at the hibachi bar. She would not look at us, and was disgusted that these bums would sit at her table! I first took off half of my mustache, then my goatee, and eventually my entire disguise and she still did not look at us. Then Anne started to reveal herself. Joanne gave her a glancing look, looked away and would not look back. The folks at the table were hardly able to keep from bursting out

Joanne, Anne and Ron at a hibachi-style surprise birthday party for Joanne in Monroe, Ohio.

laughing, and were taking photos to boot, but Joanne didn't tumble. We were out of place in her mind; she had formed an opinion of us when she first entered the restaurant and could not give it up! After Joanne finally came around, other customers in the restaurant came up to us and wanted to know if we were famous people who were in disguise because we wanted privacy and didn't want to be recognized! By the way, Geheimnis is German for "secret." I couldn't remember the translation and had given Donna my English/German dictionary, so I called her and she remembered the equivalent instantly without using the dictionary even though it had been decades since she used the word!

Off to Egypt

The New York State Colleges of Agriculture, Home Economics and Veterinary Medicine at Cornell University used to hold a common annual 5-day open house in March for farmers, homemakers and any other interested personnel, including large numbers of rural students. Specially prepared presentations included an extremely wide array of topics and subject matter in lecture, demonstration and discussion formats, including live exhibits. Three colleges were involved, so a great deal of talent and facilities were available for programming. The 49th of these Farm And Home Week productions was held in 1960, when I was an Assistant Professor working as an Extension Agricultural Engineer. For this event I decided to present a look into the future for dairy farming and developed a concept that I called The Pentairy, from penta (five) and airy, from dairy. The Pentairy was a climate controlled dairy housing system consisting of five 100-cow housing units for twice a day milking that could be increased to 1,000 lactating cows total to accommodate a 3-times-a-day milking schedule, all connected to a central rotating farm milking plant that lines up periodically with enclosed dual-cell travel ways to the respective housing units. I wrote publications describing the various aspects of the system, from its size and physical needs, through the specialization that I envisioned to support and operate it, to the attendant external off-site necessary accessory needs and services. I also envisioned solar roof collectors and the use of novel structural materials, such as a special plastic membrane over a geodesic support structure, with clear hemispheres facing north to radiate heat to the sky to assist interior environmental control; as well as liquid manure, forage and other material handling systems.

Overview of the Pentairy, facing north. The 5 light hemispheres are the cow housing units, each connected to the central milking plant by dual cell travel ways. The attached dark horizontal hemispheres are the feed storage units. The milking facility wastes are processed in the unit to the south of the milking plant in the center. The milking parlor inside the model actually rotates in a timed sequence.

This presentation was developed consistent with educational objectives familiar to Extension personnel and based on historical data and current circumstances in the dairy industry, with a look into the future. In other words, I intended it to be an eye-opening teaching moment. Somehow, word of the Pentairy got out to Lisle L. Longendorf, U.S. Project Leader for the International Agricultural Exhibition to be held in Cairo, U.A.R. March 21 to April 20, 1961, and I was invited to send my model to Egypt to exhibit it in the U.S. Power to Produce for Peace theme section. So, I designed a special wooden and plywood crate to hold the model, which I had designed to come apart in two sections. After the usual government paperwork and insurance had been processed, the 250-pound crated model was sent to Egypt where it received amazing attention, since most people had not seen much of our conventional milking systems, let alone an advanced but doable concept such as the Pentairy. The U.S. representatives told us that 23 countries participated in the fair, and that 22,000 people per day came through the display area, with a total of 750,000 viewing the model system. That's a whale of a lot more folks that saw it than those who viewed it at Farm and Home Week! I didn't send my Pentairy cow, MOO-NIK, along to Cairo, though. I thought she might be a way too advanced concept!

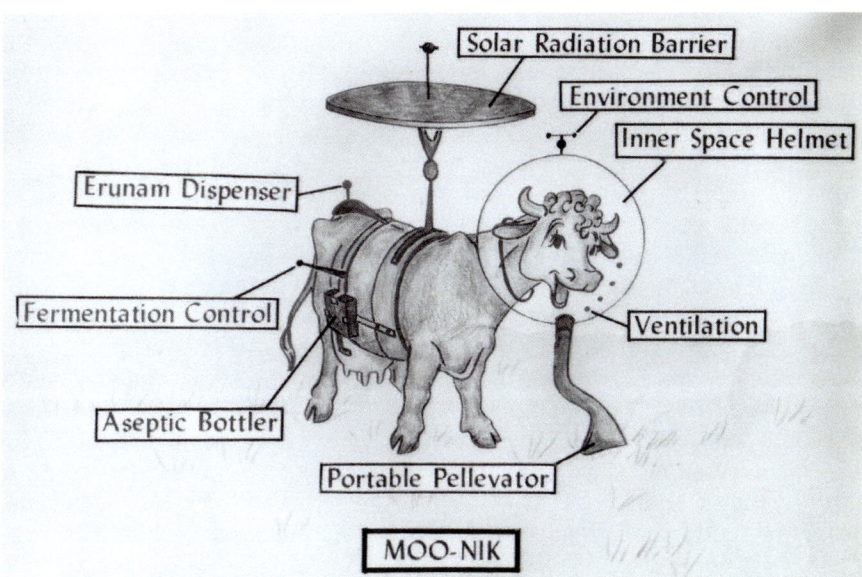

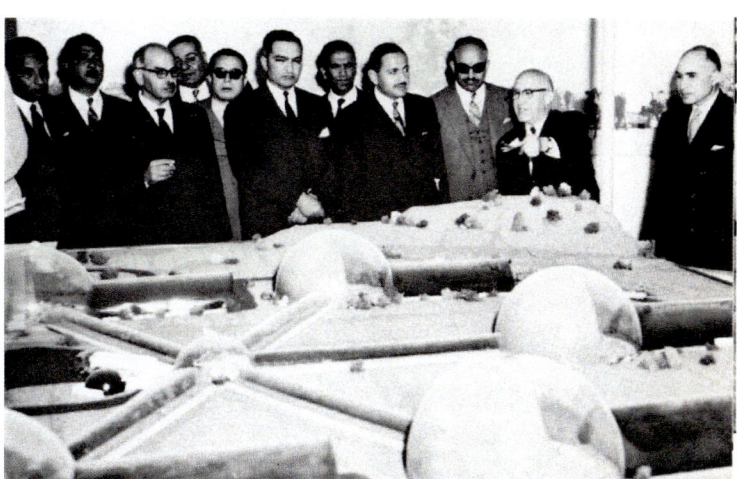

Exhibits sent to international agricultural fairs, such as this one in Cairo, help to tell the story of new methods and technology. The Cornell exhibit above, showing what dairy buildings of the future may be like, is being viewed by cabinet members of the United Arab Republic.

149

Willard Straight Hall Takeover April 18, 1969

On Friday, April 18, 1969, members of Cornell's Afro-American Society (AAS), led by Tom Jones, took over Willard Straight Hall, the Student Center on campus, forcing parents who were staying there for Parents Weekend out of their rooms, along with most of the building's staff. This action was a result of a year-long series of disputes by the AAS to get President James Perkins' Administration to give concessions to AAS demands for (1) the establishment of a radical black studies program, and (2) amnesty for some AAS students who had just been found guilty by the University Judicial Board for violating University rules. When students from Delta Upsilon fraternity tried to retake the Straight but failed, some of the occupying students fearing a further attack left the building and returned with firearms. This alarmed students, Faculty and local residents, some of whom armed themselves. Scores of police deputies from across New York State waited off campus in case of violence as anxiety and fear built up from intimidation and threats. David Burack and his followers from the Students for a Democratic Society (SDS) ringed the Straight as a protective shield for the occupiers. The AAS added a third demand, amnesty for the occupiers, but this required a Faculty vote, and it was rejected. The SDS then took over Barton Hall in support of the AAS demand for amnesty, and thousands of students on both sides of the issue became involved in a sit-in with almost continuous speeches from a podium and group discussion circles. Fearing vandalism, campus buildings were locked down and patrolled by Faculty day and night. The Seminar Room in Riley-Robb Hall on the upper campus was wired as the University's communication center, bypassing the Day Hall Administration Building on the lower campus. After days and nights of no sleep, time seemed to stand still. And business as usual came to an absolute standstill. Classes were abandoned and "orderly chaos" seemed to reign, with impromptu gatherings all over the campus, both inside and outside, where people were airing their gripes and displeasures that had nothing to do with the takeover. It was random and noisy but inclusive. Say what you want; and a lot was said, hours and hours of it.

Perkins eventually capitulated to the AAS demands, and the AAS left Willard Straight Hall carrying their guns. The Faculty, fearing threatened violence, reversed its previous day's vote against amnesty under great duress. Many disagreed with the reversal; Government Professors Walter Berns, Allen Bloom and Allan Sindler immediately resigned from Cornell. Our Agricultural Engineering Faculty was especially supportive of Walter Berns, and I wrote and delivered a signed petition to him fervently requesting him to reverse his decision, but he subsequently moved to Canada. Perkins resigned 2 months later and Dale Corson became President.

This event at Cornell affected universities all over the United States, and even some abroad. Alan Keyes (former presidential candidate, and Assistant Secretary of State), who was a Cornell student at that time disagreed with the AAS and had to be moved to Harvard for his own safety to complete his degree. The mission and philosophy of what a university stood for had changed.

Years later Tom Jones wrote letters to both President Perkins and Walter Berns apologizing for his actions. Perkins accepted the apology. Berns did not reply, due to his having received death threats during the incident. Tom Jones became successful in international finance, public accounting and management consulting, and was elected a Cornell University Trustee. AP photographer Steve Starr's Pulitzer Prize–winning photo (left) of Evans and another student leaving Willard Straight hall with weapons in hand was on the front page of virtually every newspaper in the United States the morning after the Straight was vacated. Great debates ensued on campus and eventually a Constituent Assembly recommended a shared governance system, and on March 17, 1970, the Board of Trustees instructed the Administration to form a University Senate. The present Assemblies system of governance was formed 11 years later. Professor J. Robert Cooke of my Department was the first Speaker of the Senate and I was a Senator. I also served as a College of Agriculture and Life Sciences Representative on the Cornell Faculty Council of Representatives (FCR) in the late 1970s. It was an interesting and instructive time, to say the least.

This view of Willard Straight Hall was taken in the 1950s when gorgeous giant Elm trees lined the streets. I can remember walking down the sidewalk in front of the Straight with the Elm branches from trees on opposite sides of the road reaching in both directions across the road until they touched each other. They provided delightful shade on a hot day. I took many photos of the campus and the picturesque framing that the elms provided. The Elm trees lost their battle with the Elm bark beetle, causing a decided change in the landscape, including our own property on Brook Way. They were magnificent.

Genealogy: The Furry Connection

Ronald Bay Furry's Genealogical Link
to
Lawrence Furry
from
Pennsylvania

For many years during the middle half of the Twentieth Century, my cousin, Eleanor Pilger, collected information on the Furry family at annual Furry Family Reunions held each July in Lowbanks, Ontario, Canada, where many Furrys had farms when they settled on the north shore of Lake Erie in the Eighteenth Century, approximately 30 miles southwest of Niagara Falls, New York. Eleanor compiled records on 8 generations, starting with **Lawrence Furry** from Pennsylvania, whom she believes settled in Lowbanks in 1772, and who had three sons, **Jonas**, **Lawrence** and **Silas**. When she retired, she gave her records to the Dunnville District Heritage Association, Dunnville Public Library, 317 Chestnut Street, Dunnville, Ontario, Canada N1A 2H4. During the years preceding her retirement, Eleanor gave me copies of most of her records, and using those records I've compiled a list that links me directly to Lawrence Furry from Pennsylvania as shown below (note the color coded and bolded links between families).

Head of Family and Children	**Spouse**
1. **Lawrence Furry**	Unknown
Born in Pennsylvania; settled in Lowbanks, Ontario in 1772	
Children:	
Jonas 5/23/1763 (or 1767?) – 5/23/1855	Barbara Seger
Laurence (or Lawrence) 1/30/1772 – 11/2/1849	Barbara Sevitz (or Zavitz)
Silas (a Pennsylvania preacher) ?/?/? — ?/?/?	
2. **Laurence (or Lawrence) Furry**	Barbara Sevitz (or Zavitz)
Born 1/30/1772 in Pennsylvania – Died 11/2/1849	
Children:	
Mary (Polly) 4/7/1798 – 1/12/1876	Moses Dodge
Henry 3/7 (or 9/8?)/1800 – 6/26/1887	Mary Montague
Jesse ?/?/1801 -- ?/?/?	
John ?/?/1803 – 12/13/1877	Elizabeth Leady (or Leidy)
Samuel 11/12/1804 – 9/15/1854	Elizabeth McKay
Jonas 2/2/1811 – 10/4/1874	Ruth Doan, & Ann McGowan
David 8/2/1812 – 3/9/1900	Susan C. Cook (Galbraith)
Sarah (Sally) ?/?/1814 – 8/20/1877	Thomas Montague
Laurence ?/?/1816 – 7/27/1891	Rachel Minor
Hannah ?/?/1818 – 11/10/1891	William W. Eyers
George Ermanville 1/1/1823 – 1/5/1905	Louisa Kinnard
Susan ?/?/1825 – 8/13/1859	James Campbell
William Emery 8/11/1827 – 10/27/1891	Susan M. Minor
3. **Henry Furry**	Mary Montague
Born 3/7 (or 9/8?)/1800 – Died 6/26/1887	
Children:	
Ann 3/8/1829 (or 1834?) – 3/29/1917	Audriff Burkett
William Henry (Hank) 12/3/1830 – 7/26/1911	Naomi Rozella Dodge
Lawrence 4/12/1832 – 6/24/1936	Kate Woods
Joseph Mailand (Mahlon) ?/?/1833 -- ?/?/?	Sarah (Catherine) Lapp
Marilla ?/?/1836 -- ?/?/?	Sylvanus Furry
Mary Catherine 8/19/1845 (or 1846?) – 4/1/1928	Burton Minor
4. **William Henry Furry**	Naomi Rozella Dodge
Born 12/3/1830 – Died 7/26/1911	
Children:	
Mary Ann ?/?/1853 -- ?/?/1906	
Barbara Aliza 8/13/1855 – 3/27/1952	William Nelson Furry
Sarah Almeda ?/?/ 1858 -- ?/?/1880	
Matilda H. ?/?/(1860?) -- ?/?/1945	John A. Stringer

Lozilla Jane 7/22/1860 – 7/6/1949	Henry Milway
Louisa ?/?/1861 -- ?/?/?	Sanford Stringer
Martha ?/?/1863 -- ?/?/?	
David Anson ?/?/1865 -- ?/?/1952	Etta Neff
Roland Hugh -- 8/25/1867 – 5/28/1949	Eliza Emma Ann Stevens
Hannah ?/?/1868 -- ?/?/?	

5. **Roland Hugh Furry**   Eliza Emma Ann Stevens
   Born 8/25/1867 – Died 5/29/1949
   <u>Children:</u>

Wesley Bay 12/12/1902 – 11/15/1955	Edna Louise Brown
Vivian Irene 2/14/? -- ?/?/?	Elwin Taylor
Mae 5/13/1897 -- 3/17/1978	James Wesley Frank
Roland Hugh 4/21/1917 – 12/29/2004	Viola E. Camann (1)
	Ruth Abele (2)
Reginald	

6. **Wesley Bay Furry**   Edna Louise Brown
   Born 12/12/1902 – Died 11/15/1955
   <u>Children:</u>

Ronald Bay 10/22/1931 --	Lois Anne McClure
Joanne Louise 10/26/1934 – 4/21/2015	David Phillip Dirksen

7. **Ronald Bay Furry**   Lois Anne McClure
   Born 10/22/1931 --
   <u>Children:</u>

Suzanne Lynne 2/1/1954 --	Lloyd Paul Irish
Kenneth Bay 6/1/1956 --	
Donna Wynne 6/8/1961 --	Donald Vincent Tongue

8. **Kenneth Bay Furry**
   Born 6/1/1956 –

Look at what happened to Henry Furry (Number 3 in the list above), the grandson of Lawrence Furry who settled in Lowbanks in 1772. The following account is excerpted from pages 497-498 of the 1992 book *Grand Heritage* by the Dunnville District Heritage Association. This 552-page book chronicles the history of Dunnville and the townships of Canborough, Dunn, Moulton, Sherbrooke, and South Cayuga. Moulton and Sherbrooke are the towns where the Furry farms are located in Haldiman County, Ontario, Canada. The story goes like this.

Buried Treasure

"Several local residents hinted about a smuggler's cove in the hamlet of Lowbanks, but no one was able to pinpoint the site. Although there is no evidence that there was any pirate gold buried in the area, something made three men dig up Henry Furry's grave one moonless night in the summer of 1941.

"Furry was 86 years old when he died in 1887. Alvin Barrick, Jesse Furry and Reuben Neff were digging Henry's grave in the local cemetery in Lowbanks when the side of the opening caved in and a stone chest slid out. The men laid the chest aside until they had completed their digging, then put it back in the hole and covered it up before the interment took place.

"Later Neff, Reuben and Furry realized that the chest might have contained hidden treasure but it was too late to do anything about it. The men told their story about uncovering the chest and two legends came to light, indicating what the stone chest might have contained.

"The first was the "Yankee Story." Because the Yanks were not sure what the outcome of the Civil War would be, some of them brought their money across Lake Erie from New York and buried it about ten miles west of Port Colborne. After the war they returned to the area but were unable to locate the buried money.

"Another legend told of a Spanish pirate who landed a boat on the point west of the cemetery. They say that the Spanish "gentleman" buried a chest of gold on a farm he bought in the area. Sometime after he returned to Cuba, the local folk were informed that he had been hanged there. It was also said that a Lowbanks farmer sent him two lots of money, 400 English pounds in all, with the understanding that if the pirate didn't return to Lowbanks, the farm would belong to him.

"These stories were passed down through until that night in 1941 when the three men desecrated the grave. They came in two cars, which they parked at the east end of the cemetery. They dug for four hours and when they were finished the casket of pine and oak and Henry Furry's bones lay scattered about. It is not known if the ghouls benefitted from their gruesome work, but most old-timers felt that the men probably dug for the treasure in the wrong place."

I recall hearing about this when I was young, but there is a greater danger that lurks along the shore of Lake Erie at the site of this old cemetery — wave action! I remember when first my Grandfather, and then my Grandmother, were buried in the Lowbanks cemetery. I watched as they lowered their caskets in the graves, so I know they were there. Years later I went back to visit the cemetery but could not find either of their headstones or several others. I was told that the winds off Lake Erie in the winter sometimes blow so violently that huge waves are made that easily erode the shore. The cemetery used to be quite a safe distance from the shore and it was on a small hill. That hill is now gone, along with both my Grandfather and Grandmother Furry. My Father also told me that the shore along his Father's farm was originally a good distance away from the road; but you can see from the photo (that follows some pages away) of my Mother sitting near the shore that the gravel beach is nearly up to the road where the car is parked,

Ken gave me an original copy of the HISTORY OF JOHONNES FURRY, (OR FORRER) AND HIS DESCENDANTS TO THE END OF THE EIGHTH GENERATION AS COMPILED BY HENRY S. FURRY, 1910-11, READING, PA. This is a 4 ½" x 6" grayish-green, hard covered book with 68 pages, containing 9 photographs, 8 of which are of male members of the Furry clan across the early years, and includes a lengthy LIST OF REGISTRATION at the end. The opening 9 pages of this book follow.

"On October 16th, 1727, Johonnes Furrey (or Forrer), and forty-six **Palatines**, with their families, about two hundred persons embarked on the ship, Friendship, of Bristol, John Davis, Master, from Rotterdam, last from Cows, from whence the ship sailed on June 20th, 1727, and landed at Philadelphia.

"This John Furrey went to Tulbehocken, Berks County, Pa., and got a land warrant for 346 acres, October 11th, 1744. This land had been granted to a man by the name of Hoobler who forfeited the warrant.

"The patent is certified to be recorded at Philadelphia, now at Harrisburg, in patent Book A, Volume 17, page 374, dated May 12th, 1752.

"This Johonnes Furrey (or Forrer) had located about three miles northwest of Womelsdorf, Berks County, Pa., on the road leading from Womelsdorf to Mt. Ætna. This land is now owned by Dr. Horace F. Livinghood, of Womelsdorf, and tenanted by the Frantz brothers. The original spring house is still standing and is in daily use. The farm is one of the best in the County, the soil is rich and fertile and slopes toward a little ravine from the east and west.

"Some years ago all of the original buildings, except the spring house, which was about 500 feet away, burned down. These buildings were the old-fashioned log buildings, but now new and modern buildings are erected in their places. The original tract is now divided into four different farms.

"There are a number of Furrys in Lancaster, York and different other counties in the State, and as they all originated from the Palatines, which is a section in Germany, there is no doubt that the Furrys' (or however they may spell their name) ancestors came from the same place in Germany.

"Ten persons bearing the name immigrated from the Palatines and Hugenots, which is a County in France, close to Germany.

"In years gone by people were not so exact in spelling names and this no doubt accounts for the different ways of spelling this name.

"The following persons immigrated to America in the following years:

NAMES	YEARS
Johannes Forrer, or Furrey	1727
Lanhart Furrer	1739
Hans Casper Furer	1747
Jacob Furrer	1750
Christian Furrer	1750
John Rudolph Furrer	1752
Christian Fuehrer	1754
Daniel Fuerhere	1754
Johonnas Forrer	1754
Peter Farry	1768

"What makes it certain that this branch of the Furrys is from the one that came to America in 1727, is because the first land taken by that name, in Berks County, was on October 11th, 1774, and we also know that this branch comes from Berks County, Pa.

"We find that prior to the year 1716 a family by the name of Ferrie or in German (Vere), was living in a town called Lindan, not far from the River Rhine in the Kingdom of France. This family consisted of himself, his wife, three sons and three daughters.

"The names of the sons were Daniel, Philip and John; those of the daughters were Catharine, Mary and Jane. Their religion was Calvinistic. The husband died and the widow with the rest of the family immigrated to America and first located in New York State. Later they moved to Lancaster County, Pa., where she died in the year 1716 and is buried in Conestoga Township, Lancaster County, Pa. Her maiden name was Mary Waronbower.

"We find that quite a number of prominent people have sprung up from this family. First their name was Ferrie, then Forry, and now Furry. We also find that some became ministers of the gospel, some doctors, and some attorneys. They claim relationship in America with the Furrys from Germany.
"The Furry family is an old and prominent family; we find that some have taken an active part in the Revolutionary war and also in the war of 1812. Some also took an active part in State affairs. They can be traced all over the United States. It is impossible to give an account of when the old people died and where they were buried."

The **LIST OF REGISTRATION** at the end of the book contains 362 names, 124 of which have surnames spelled Furry or Forry. Various alternate surname spellings appear within the book, i.e., Forrer, Furrey, Furry, Forry, Ferrie, Furrer, Furer, Ferrer, Fuehrer, and Farry, but the only surnames that appear in the early **LIST OF REGISTRATION** are Furry and Forry. Another interesting aspect related in this book appears on pages 7 and 8, where reference (see above) is made to the Ferrie family from Lindan, France that immigrated to America, located in New York State, and then moved to Pennsylvania where the wife, Mary Waronbower Ferrie, died in **1716**. I wonder what happened to them – they appear to be the first to have arrived!

A story about the kidnapping of John Furry's son, Henry, by Oneida Indians, described on pages 12, 40, and 41 in the book, holds real interest for me because I heard that story told by my Grandfather, Roland Hugh Furry and Father, Wesley Bay Furry, when I was a young boy in the 1930s! How they came by the story I do not know. I don't recall anyone in our families ever talking about Henry S. Furry's **History of the Furry Family**, nor do I remember ever seeing a copy of the book in their homes.

In the book **History of the Furry Family** by Henry S. Furry (1910-11), there are references to the name "Lawrence Furry" on pages 11, 24, 26, 40 and 41. There is a direct relationship to the families listed on the pages above, and the following March 1893 announcement concerning the death of Mrs. John Leslie, Henry Furry's daughter, Harriet, confirms it. Note that the March 23, 1893, article contains a spelling error. **Jones** should read **Jonas**, one of the three Furry brothers, Henry, Jonas and Lawrence, who settled in Canada.

Mrs. John (Harriet) Furry **LESLIE** 1893

March 24, 1893

Mrs. Leslie, mother of John and Charles Leslie, who recently fell and broke her hipbone, is very low. Her age is four score and over and recovery is considered very doubtful.

March 31, 1893

Mrs. Leslie, Sr., of High Banks, whose illness was noted in last week's Tribune, died on Thursday of last week. The remains were interred at Lowbanks on Saturday last.

March 31, 1893

At Highbanks, on March 23, 1893, Mrs. Leslie, Sr, aged 89 years.

MRS. JOHN LESLIE

Harriet Leslie died March 23 at her home in Sherbrooke Township, aged 88 years, 7 months and 5 days. She was born in the City of Montreal in 1804. She was a daughter of Henry Furry, who was born in Pennsylvania and taken from there by the Indians and sold at Montreal for a loaf of bread and a bottle of brandy, it is said. Before being carried away the Indians burned the village in which he lived and his parents were scalped. In Montreal he married a Miss Hewson, mother of the deceased Mrs. Leslie. Mr. Furry learned the shoemaker's trade in that city. From Montreal Henry Furry came to this county, where he learned from a man named Talbot that his brothers, Jones and Lawrence Furry resided. The family then settled down near where John Scholfield now lives but moved finally to the mouth of the Grand River and there, at the age of 17, the deceased married John Leslie, who died in 1839 at Belfast, Ireland. Leslie was a member of Her Majesty's army and was moved from pillar to post for many years, part of the time being located at Kingston and Quebec, and finally being honorably discharged in Ireland, receiving a pension until death. Eight children were born of this marriage; Ann, Mary Jane, John, Henry, James and Charles living and George and Robert who died in Ireland. All the legion of Furry's that populate this part of Canada have sprung from three brothers – Henry, Jones and Lawrence Furry. The late Mrs. Leslie lived in Ireland about 35 years and at the time of her death had been a widow for 54 years.

Unlike in Henry S. Furry's time, current technology makes it very easy to include photographs in documents and the following are presented to illustrate my progress at various times in my life.

1949
High School
Graduation

1953
Cornell University
Graduation

Ronald and Anne Furry in 2005

When my Grandfather Furry sold his farm in Lowbanks, Ontario, Canada, he kept a small parcel of lakeside property that he later deeded to my Father and his younger brother, Roland Hugh Furry.

The original farm from which this property was taken was jointly owned by my Grandfather, also named Roland Hugh Furry, and his older brother, David Anson Furry. The lot was very deep, 300 feet, but only 50 feet wide, and ran perpendicular to the Lake Erie shore. It was recorded on June 14, 1946 as Lot No. 11, First Concession, Township of Moulton. My parents' intention was to someday build a cottage on the property, and my Father and Mother kept items "for the cottage" for years, but there were never sufficient funds to follow through on this desire. In addition, zoning laws had been enacted later that changed the minimum lot size that was allowed for cottage construction. After my Father died in 1955, Hugh and I sold the lot to Christopher J. Fildes who at that time lived in Grosse Pointe Farms, Michigan. Before that, my parents and Joanne and I occasionally drove to the lot for a day's outing, sat on the shore to watch the water, and had a cookout. For swimming, there was the Furry Sand Beach, owned by relative Robert Furry, down the road a bit; it had a huge sand beach that ran for a great distance out into the lake at a very gentle slope. And it was nice and warm! We really liked it. An interesting feature of this area was that if a natural gas line ran across the property, the owners were given free gas forever. I can remember the gas mantles on the light fixtures glowing white hot during the day and evening and then orange at night if it was a sleeping area. My Dad said they never turned the light fixtures off.

157

My mother, Edna, liked to sit on the shore and watch the waves in the bay.

The Canadian Register of Historic Places (CRHP) formally recognized the Furry Tavern, located at 2511 North Shore Road, Haldimand County, Ontario, N0A, Canada as an historic place on November 8, 2004. A recent photo of the tavern is shown below, followed by the CRHP description.

"Description of Historic Place

The Furry Tavern is a two-story frame building with a gable roof, originally, built as a residence. Located in the former Moulton Township, in the current village of Lowbanks, Ontario, it is a reminder of the area's earliest settlement.

Haldimand County designated it for its heritage value under By-law 548/04.

Heritage Value

Lawrence Furry and his family were some of the first settlers along the lakeshore of Moulton Township. The Furry Tavern was built, in 1821, of sawn lumber, at a time when most buildings in Haldimand County were made of hand-hewn log. The size and architectural conventions employed in constructing the Furry Tavern reflect the wealth and history of the financially secure citizens of colonial Pennsylvania. Lawrence Furry's descendants still live in the region.

Although the Furry Tavern dates from 1821, it is remarkably well preserved. It is a two-story structure built of sawn lumber and notable because local saw mills were not yet operational. The building still displays some of the decorative stenciling on the original walls, and remarkably, a plank in the attic still remains, bearing the date of construction. Exterior windows are trowelled glass. The first floor windows have sashes of 12 over 8 and the second floor windows have sashes of 8 over 8. Interior flooring is pine throughout. Many of the interior doors have original transition latches and hardware.

Source: Designation By-law 548/04. Identifier: HPON07-0191

Character-Defining Elements

Character defining elements that reflect the heritage value of the Furry Tavern include its:
- dated roof plank (1821) located in the attic
- remarkably well preserved structure
- sawn lumber material notably sawn before local saw mills were operational
- original pine flooring throughout
- beaded board walls in the hallway above the first flight of stairs
- its original doors and hardware"

As of this writing, the tavern is nearing its 200th birthday!

It would be nice if one of my descendants visited it someday.

Genealogy: The Brown Connection

The following summary of the early years of the **Brown** family is based upon the compilation by **Marion B. Hague**, who at a Brown Family Reunion in 1934 agreed to record the family's history, and eventually succeeded in acquiring sufficient data from descendants to present a generational report in 1972, following her retirement. We owe her a great deal for her efforts. Thanks Marion!

The Zeroth and First Generations:

- **Bartholomew Brown** (either **Irish** or **English**) emigrated to Germany — date uncertain — and changed his name to **Braun** (which in German means Brown).
- **Bartholomew** married and had two children, first **Phillipine**, and later, on March 27, 1828, **John M. Braun** was born. Regrettably, the children were orphaned at an early age.

- **John M. Braun** lived in Reutlinger, Germany, where he learned the milling trade, and delivered flour to homes.
- At one home he met **Louisa Roessler** (b. 1832 in Kolb and reared in Ulm). A friendship developed and they discussed their troubles and ambitions.

- Discontented with conditions in Germany, in 1852 the two friends emigrated to America on a 90 day boat trip during which their friendship ripened.
- They landed in New York City, and after working a few months were married.
- Their first child, **Kate**, was born in New York City on December 5, 1853.

- Because of better work opportunities in a millstone shop, the family moved to Utica, NY, where **John Brown, Jr.,** was born on March 16, 1856.
- The next move was to Clyde, NY, to work as a miller where their daughter **Phoebe** was born on July 20, 1858.

- Due to insufficient pay, the family returned to Utica and **John** to his former job.
- His sideline attempts to improve the sifting or refining of flour finally bore fruit and he received patents for the process in both Canada and the United States.
- He then moved to Jewsburg (Clarks Mills), Canada to equip Schneider's mill with his new equipment.

- A son, **Charles C.,** was born October 6, 1860, in Utica, and another girl, **Wilhelmina** (Minnie) was born in Clarks Mills on April 23, 1863.
- His flour-sifting devices proved to be very successful and in demand, and he moved to Dundee to set up a mill. His son, **Fred**, was born in Dundee on April 11, 1865.

- The family returned to the U.S. in 1865.
- He entered into a business deal with the firm of Hart and Munson to manufacture his flour processing system, but the firm failed. He changed his name to John Brown for business purposes.
- One mill using "John Brown's Patent" was Thornton and Chester in Buffalo, NY. This mill was rented from Schoelkopf and the 10-year lease expired, initiating a negotiation.
- A contract between Schoelkopf and **John Brown** gave **John** $4,000 per year and 4% of the profits. (Imagine, this was just after the Civil War!)
- In 1867, **Mary Brown** was born, and **Louis George Brown** was born February 28, 1869.
- Their next move was to Buffalo, NY, to work with Schoelkopf.

- Due to bad health, **John Brown** declined Schoelkopf's offering of a supervisory position and half interest in the Hydraulic Power Co.
- The Schoelkopf position brought the family to Black Rock, where on March 4, 1871, the last son, **Arthur Henry Brown** was born. (This is my *Grandpa Brown*!)
- In 1876 they moved to Ebenezer, NY, to the old homestead where John Brown, Jr., ran a flour mill.

- At contract renewal time with Schoelkopf, the document could not be found, John Brown signed off, and he died in 1881 due to Miller's Consumption.
- Ironically, two weeks after his death, his wife found the Schoelkopf contract. She died in 1885.
- **John M.** and **Louisa Brown** are buried in Forest Lawn Cemetery in Buffalo, NY. A small monument bearing a Masonic emblem marks **John M. Brown's** grave in Section O, Lot 5. The graves of **Minnie** (Pleister) and **Fred** are beside them.
- **John Brown's** sister, **Phillipine Braun**, came to the U.S., married a Mr. Streib, lived in Rochester, NY, and had two sons, one called Robert.

The entire second generation:

Kate (b. Dec. 5, 1853 -- d. ~1930) Married Otto Richt; 3 children

John, Jr. (b. Mar. 16, 1856 – d. ~1934) Married Jenny Andersen; 4 children;

Phoebe (b. July 20, 1858 – d. March 4, 1953) Married Frank Witzig; 3 children

Charles C. (b. Oct. 6, 1860 – d. ~1935) Married Julia Wendling (d. ~1934); No children

Wilhelmina (Minnie) (b. Apr. 23, 1863 – d. 1932) Married Frank Pleister; Frank had a daughter.

Fred J. (b. Apr. 11, 1865 – d. Mar. 27, 1889) Married Christina Menzies (d. 1951); 3 children

Mary (b. 1867 – d. 10 months later)

Louis G. (b. Feb. 28, 1869 – d. Mar. 26, 1948) Married Ada Carr June 21, 1905 (d. Mar. 17, 1957); 3 children. [Riverdale Cemetery, Lewiston, NY]

Arthur (Art) Henry Brown (b. Mar. 4, 1871 – d. Sept. 29, 1938) [My Grandpa] Married **Catherine (Kate) E. Doeseckle** (b. June 10, 1871 – d. Sept. 9, 1957); 7 children. [Riverdale Cemetery, Lewiston, NY] Catherine's Father was Frederick Doeseckle, her Mother was Ellen Brennan of Ireland.

Some of the Brown and Doeseckle family members in 1927. Bill Brown kneeling on left, Catherine Doeseckle Brown standing on left with her brothers.

Five of the Browns, including John, Kate, Fred, Minnie and Phoebe, and friends in masquerade with the usual dogs (there are two of them in the photo).

100 years after the photo above was taken, Ron and Anne dressed in costume to attend a Halloween party given by his Department Chairman, Norman Scott. No one knew who we were in spite of the fact that "Anne" made political type promises, and "Ron" expounded on his research on controlled atmosphere cabbage storage. Ron is on the left, and Anne is on the right. It's amazing how much first impressions cloud a person's ability to see the true picture.

Arthur Henry Brown (center, with dark mustache) and his co-workers at the Central Milling Co. in Niagara Falls, NY. Milling was a big industry because of the ready supply of water for power. Flour dust from the milling operation could cause asthma, rhinitis, conjunctivitis and a host of other problems. It can also form a dust cloud that could be ignited and cause an explosion.

View of the Niagara Gorge on the American side when waterpower was King. Nikola Tesla invented the first alternating current (AC) motor and developed AC generation and transmission technology that changed the world. Nikola Tesla and George Westinghouse built the first hydro-electric power plant in 1879 in Niagara Falls, New York; it is still there.

Arthur Henry Brown at his workbench in the Central Milling Company in Niagara Falls, New York. His Father held several patents for the sifting or refining of flour, and he received patents for the process in both Canada and the United States.

Catherine (Kate) E. Doeseckle and Arthur (Art) Henry Brown in the side yard of the Brown home at 167-60th Street, Niagara Falls, New York. Their home was in the Village of LaSalle, which was later incorporated into the City of Niagara Falls, New York in 1927. (Note the sturdy bumper on the car behind Kate and Art in the picture!)

Catherine E. Doeseckle, shown here in 1893, was born on June 10, 1871 in Merriton, Ontario, Canada. Her middle initial stands for Eucheria.

Arthur Henry Brown was born in Black Rock, NY on March 4, 1871.

My Uncle Bob Brown, neighbor Rich Manchester, my Aunts Florence and Margaret, and Uncle Bill Brown, and always a dog.

The entire third generation. On average, Catherine Brown had a baby every two years:
John F. (b. 1/8/1898, d. 11/20/1960) Married Florence Taylor; Children: Jack, Barbara
Charles Roessler (b. 1899, d. 1908)
Edna Louise (b. 2/14/1902, d. 7/25/1984) Married Wesley B. Furry; Children Ronald, Joanne
Florence K. (b. 3/14/1904, d. 5/16/1971)
Margaret (b. 1/13/1906, d. 3/13/1931) Died of appendicitis.
Arthur William (b. 5/1/1908, d. 8/27/1981 Married Helena Blum; Children: Salinas, Sharon
Robert Raymond (b. 6/29/1910, d. 3/11/1985) Married Marion Alice Beaber; Children Kay, Mary Ann

Their lifespans (average lifespan 56 years):

John F.	62 Years
Charles Roessler	9
Edna Louise	82
Florence K.	67
Margaret	25
Arthur William	73
Robert Raymond	75

Robert Raymond Brown in second grade in Evershed Grade School, Niagara Falls, NY.

Arthur William Brown in the backyard garden at 167-60th Street, Niagara Falls, NY. At one time Bill played semi-pro baseball.

166

A rare event — the surviving children of Catherine and Arthur Brown meet at Robert Brown's farm in Pekin, NY, in the late 1940s: From the left, Bob, Florence, Edna, John and Bill.

Marion Brown (Bob's wife), Ken and Helena Brown (Bill's wife).

This was my Grandmother Brown's dog. He was my favorite pal when I was growing up in the 1930s. Of course, his name was Brownie! He had a speckled. coat. I like dogs with a long nose, long ears and a long tail.

Photo Gallery

Furry Related…

Eliza and Roland Furry — 50th Wedding Anniversary

Sister Mae Furry with Wesley Bay Furry
at his 1903 Christening

Sisters Mae and Vivian Furry with
Wesley Bay Furry

Back: Wesley Bay, Roland Hugh, Eliza Emma Ann, Edna Louise, Viola E.
Front: Ronald Bay, Dawn, Joanne Louise, Diane — all Furrys, plus Grandfather's dog, at Grandfather Furry's farm in Bergholtz, New York.

Wesley Bay and Brother Hugh Furry

Bay in a 1924 Hupmobile Club Sedan. Hand-cranking was required!

When I was old enough to appreciate fireworks, my folks would let me have baby paper crackers, cherry bombs, and sparklers. The cherry bombs came packed in sawdust in a cardboard box. Each piece of potassium perchlorate was encased in a spherical paper shell wrapped in crinkly aluminum foil. If you shook them gently, you could hear them rattle inside their shells. They were shock sensitive, so to make a noise all you had to do was throw them down on a hard surface, such as a concrete walk, which I did. I also found out that they made a noise and a nice big gray splash pattern if they were thrown against the door of my Father's car. That was not appreciated, and my supply was not replenished! My Uncle Bob was a real fireworks enthusiast. I remember one 4th of July when he used his Mother's big cooking pots for targets. He would lie down on the ground, light the fuse of a firecracker and then toss it overhand into one of the pots. These were huge firecrackers, and they damaged the pots, both with powder burns and dents. Grandma did not like it at all.

Running boards made getting in and out of cars easy. They also made good seats for a rest. Here's Joanne and I in 1938 in our woolen snow suits taking it easy. Note the back doors hinged at the rear as used in horse drawn carriages — called suicide doors because they were deemed unsafe. A 2-seat 4-door car was needed because of increased family size — Joanne and I. Still had to crank it.

Edna in a "modern SUV"!

Wesley Bay and Roland Hugh Furry ca. 1948 in the backyard of Roland's Bergholtz Farm. Do you see the cat?

Brown Related…

Portrait of Florence Brown in 1926

Robert Raymond Brown — World War 2

My Mother's oldest brother, John Frederick Brown, also worked at the Shredded Wheat Company in Niagara Falls. He played the drums and also belonged to the Mandolin Club. He's in the top row, far left, next to the brick column in the Shredded Wheat Band photo above, and in the top row, far right, smoking a cigar in the photo on the next page. The band was formed in 1926. The Carborundum Company decided to use the band in its advertising and it was then known as the

Carborundum Band and was featured weekly on nationwide radio for 13 years. When the radio programs came to a close in 1939, the band became known as the Niagara Falls Concert Band.

The Niagara Falls Concert Band is still active. The bands recent welcoming statement follows:

"The Niagara Falls Concert Band performs a varied repertoire of music including marches, show tunes, big band, rock, classical, Broadway, Disney & pop tunes. We are a community concert band made up of musicians of all ages and backgrounds from the Niagara region attracting musicians from Niagara Falls, New York. The level of musicianship ranges from intermediate to advanced, to semi-professional and professional musicians all working together to create a relaxed and fun atmosphere to perform music. We perform at seniors' residences, civic events, parks and festivals."

John Brown would be very pleased and right at home on these drums!

Championship Hockey Team — The Niagara Falls Celtic Hockey Team
won the 1926-27 Western New York Suburban League title.
Robert Raymond Brown, 2nd row, 2nd from left.

Wesley Bay Furry and Edna
Louise Brown in 1929

Edna in backyard
at 167-60th Street

Wesley Bay on Three Sisters
Island at the Falls in 1929

Edna and Bay met while ice skating. Bay played semi-pro hockey for awhile.

Cousins and such…

Front: Steve Foehner, Doug Foehner, Andrew Foehner
Back: Sue Furry-Irish, Ken Furry, Donna Furry Tongue

Anne Furry, Miki Crandell, Barbara Foehner, Lois McClure Hough in 1985

Kay Brown and Peter Keckel Wedding in 1971

Mary, Marion and Kay Brown

Mary and Kay Brown

175

Anne Furry, Kay Brown Keckel, Ken Furry, Sue Furry-Irish with Bradshaw Irish, Peter Keckel,
Peter Campione, Sharon Campione with Brian, Roland Hugh Furry and Viola E. Furry
assembled in Ohio for Debbie Dirksen's marriage to Paul Heck

Brown family reunion in Monroe, Ohio, October 16, 2004

Joanne Furry and Dave Dirksen's wedding, November 1, 1958. They were married in St. John de LaSalle Church where Joanne previously taught. From left: Ronald Furry with Kenneth Furry, Maryanne Connaly, Anne Furry with Suzanne Furry, Edna Louise Brown Furry, Joanne Louise Furry Dirksen, David Phillip Dirksen, Anne L. Dirksen (Dave's Mother), Bill Dirksen (Dave's brother).

Paul and Debbie Heck with Anne and Ron at the Hecks' home in Ohio.

The Dave (seated on left), David (standing on left) and Stephen (seated next to Dave) Dirksen Clan plus Anne (standing) at David Dirksen's home in Monroe, Ohio at the Brown Family Reunion in 2004. (Note the headless baby held by Mary Beth Dirksen!)

Barbara Brown Westley (right center in black dress) and family; John F. Brown's daughter.
Inset: David Westley and Barbara Brown at their wedding.

Jack Taylor Brown Family - Julie(30), Peter(35),Jack, Carol, Tim(39), Jeanne(37)

Jack Taylor Brown and Carol Brown Family; Jack is John F. Brown's son.

Lois Crandell McClure Hough and Seabury Hough on Honeymoon in 1963.

Paul and Barbara McClure Foehner Bither

Suzanne Furry was the only one of our children
that my Father saw before his death in 1955.

From left: Denise Beane (Ted),
Diane Weaver (Jack),
Dawn Sutherland (Jack)

A photo of Hugh and Viola
rests on the table.

Darlene Taylor Walck and
Elwyn Taylor Jr., Vivian Irene
Furry Taylor's children

Rotary Exchange Student Leslie Oorloff from New Zealand in January 1975. She attended Ithaca High School for her senior year, living with us on Brook Way. Leslie now resides in Hawaii, where it's warm!

Back on Brook Way for a visit.

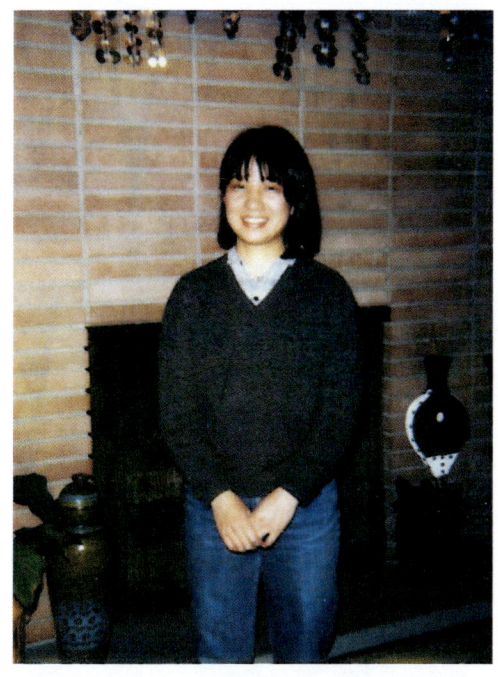

Sachi Anne, Emiko's daughter, at 2 years old. Sachi Anne is named after Anne Furry.

Rotary Exchange Student Emiko Aridome from Japan lived with us at Brook Way. She is now in Japan with her daughter.

181

Back: Joanne Furry Dirksen, Edna Furry and Florence Brown.
Front: Dave Dirksen, Sue Furry, and Anne Furry holding Ken.
Easter visit by Jo and Dave in 1957 to Ithaca, NY.

An old tintype photo:

Catherine E. Brown (sitting) and friends in a professional photographer's studio in the late 1800s. There is no tin in a tintype. The name derives from the tin shears used to cut up the thin iron plate upon which the photo was produced. It was like a Polaroid photo in that the print was available immediately.

And now our most recent generations…

Our **Generation Y** Grandchildren: Ginger Irish, Robbyn Tongue, Cece Irish, Bradshaw Irish and Meghan Tongue at the Tongues' home, 1993. They have all inherited the smile gene!

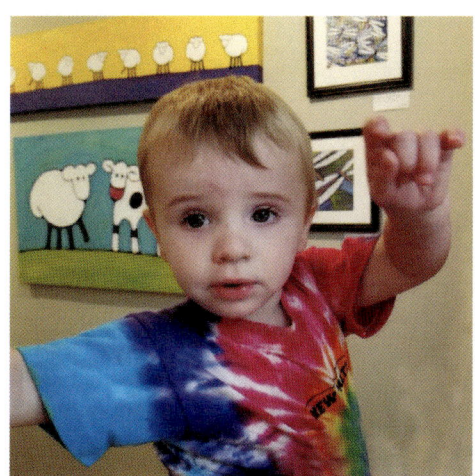

Cohen Ploof, 2018   Harrison Tongue, 2017
Our **Next Generation** Great Grandchildren are great!

Baby Boomers: Born between 1946 and 1954 **Generation Jones:** Born between 1955 and 1965
Generation X: Born between 1966 and 1976   **Generation Y**: Born between 1977 and 1994
Generation Z: Born between 1995 and 2012   **Next Generation**: Excelsior!
A generation is about 30 years.

Art Gallery

Here are samples of some of my artwork. Most of them hang framed on the walls of our home; yep, one is a drawing of a Terrier dog!

Woodworking by Ron

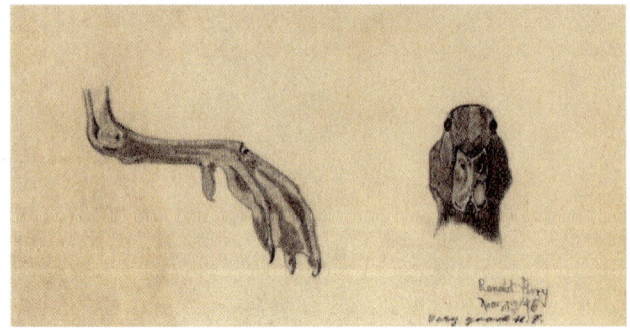

Ron by Ron

Anne by Ron

Perhaps this homemade book cover
that I made when I was a kid is what
started me on my artistic bent!

Terrier

Die Rote und Blaue und Gelbe Papageien

Tiger Lilies

Fruit Medley

186

Donna Tongue has the framed original of my rendition of Michelangelo's statue of Agony.

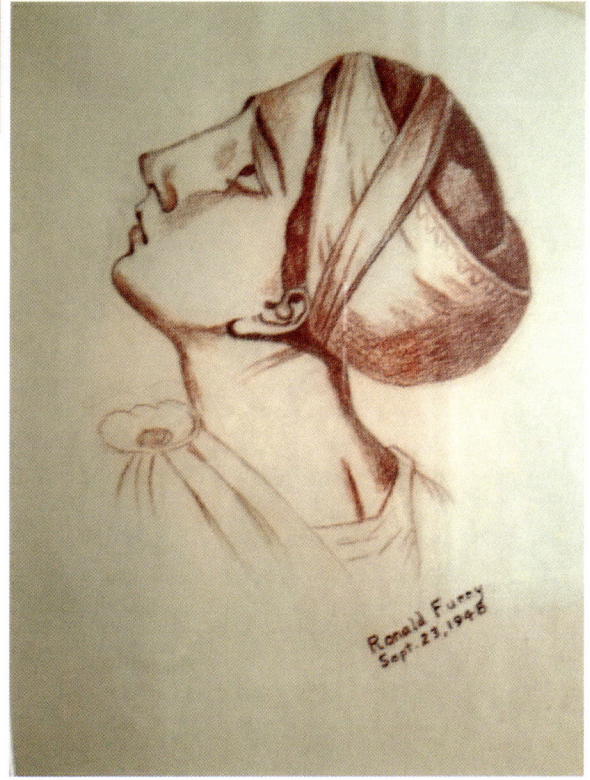

Sue Furry-Irish has the framed original of this Greek woman.

I call this photo my *Electric Tree*.
It's a digitally altered version of the
real world tree shown below.
This is the extent of my digital art!

This tree lives in Shelburne, Vermont,
where Sue and Paul Irish live. I love
this kind of tree and couldn't resist
this winter scene.

Shoulda, Coulda, Woulda

There are many things that I would like to do, such as tap dance, play a major sport, swim well, read music, paint in multiple media, play the piano and/or guitar, sing in a group or quartet, parachute out of a plane, ski, skate very well, sail my own boat, speak and write a couple more languages really well, and a few other activities. I promised myself that I would do some of these when I retired, but that didn't pan out because most were beyond my capabilities at that time. Not very good planning. I've discovered that musicians have all the fun because they can perform their whole life through, singly or in pick-up groups. I had a great pitching arm, so baseball would have probably been the sport for me, but my eyesight has been a problem all my life, so that was out of consideration, too. My size also kept me from some activities, and I didn't consider myself talented enough for others. But, that's life. I probably spent too much time at my work, instead of being with my family, especially my kids, and for that I am truly sorry. I plan to do better next time. There I go again.

Miscellany

My Mother found the following story and sent it to the male members of the Furry family in the days when the US was developing experimental hypersonic rocket powered aircraft. The X-15 set speed (4,520 miles per hour) and altitude (102,100 feet) records in the 1960s, reaching the edge of outer space. This particular Spoonerism is titled X-15 GETS AWAY.

"The news hasn't come out officially yet, but one of the pilots who's flying the X-15 let it get away from him sometime during the past month and shot beyond Earth's gravitational field. He soared helplessly, and finally effected a controlled crash on Mars. When he'd pulled himself together and climbed out, he saw standing there a fellow about 4 feet tall who looked more or less like an earthling except that he was covered by an exuberant growth of fur. All the pilot could see of what lay beneath were two beady little eyes regarding him intently.

> "Who are you?" the X-15 man asked.
> "I'm a Furry," the little man replied.
> "There are thousands of us here on Mars."
> "Gee, that's interesting," the pilot said.
> "Could you take me to your leader?"
> "My pleasure," said the Furry, and off he went across the powdery red dust with the pilot a few steps behind.

An hour later they came to a huge, dank cave. The Furry led the way inside, and drew up short before a massive throne. Perched on top of it was another little man who looked just like the Furry except for a large hypodermic syringe growing out of the top of his head.

The pilot glanced at his guide, then looked back at the throne.

> "Are you a Furry, too?" he asked.

> "Not exactly," said the Martian.

> "I'm the Furry with the Syringe on Top."

The Spoonerism of course is from "The Surrey with the Fringe on Top," a song in the musical "Oklahoma!" by Rodgers and Hammerstein. Here's a real surrey with fringe on top:

My Mother said, "Time is Nature's way of keeping everything from happening all at once." She also said that Hell is here on Earth!

Furry Funerisms:

A few of the sayings that I originated:

> Greetings and hallucinations.
>
> One flake does not a blizzard make.
>
> If you don't ask, the answer is always NO!
>
> The wave of the future starts with a little ripple.
>
> People interpret things to their own best advantage.
>
> Everything is caused by something, but nothing causes everything.
>
> The best way to keep faculty happy is to give them more than they need before they know they need it.

My Poem:

Movin' On

I'm a movin',
Oh, yes I am!

I'm a movin',
Fast as I can.

The only trouble
I've got today,

Is that I'm movin'
The opposite way!

Which way did they go, which way did they go?!?!
Ron and Jo in 1937.

Twisters:

Read it and weep

Weed it and reap.

The fecal finger of fate.

Road Signs:

STOP ONE WAY
AHEAD THE OTHER WAY

GO
AFOOT

Personal Philosophy:

If there is to be chaos,
Furry wants it…
   …organized, and
   …in color,
   …by 5 o'clock,
   …with 25 copies,
   …stapled.

Important Concepts of Mechanics:

$F = Ma$
You can't push on a rope.
Don't stand sideways on a ship.
Fried egg analogy.

Time:

Draw a straight line from left to right and let it represent time. Place a dot on the line somewhere to represent the present. If everything to the left of the dot represents the past, and everything to the right represents the future, how long is the present?

Saying from Our Trip to Japan:

"Never say 'kekkō' until you've seen Nikkō"

This means that one should see the place called Nikkō before you've decided to call something beautiful. The statement is correct; we checked it out on our trip to Japan.

Logic:

What is a used Kleenex called?
A DirtyY.

What is the favorite song that birds sing?
"Let Me Call You Tweetheart…"

Just What the Doctor Ordered

Living in an era devoid of antibiotics brought home remedies to the forefront, and one of those was the mustard plaster. My Grandmother would save goose grease from a roast and later combine it with powdered mustard seed to make a paste that was spread on cotton cloth cut to the size of the user (me, for example, as a young boy). A second cloth was placed on the remaining paste side and the whole of it was them placed on the affected site, my chest in this case because I was plagued with bronchitis for years. So there I lay in bed waiting for the mixture to work. A chemical reaction caused the poultice to heat up and I could tell it was working! A quick peek at my skin told my Mother that it was doing its job – my chest turned bright pink then red! The heat can cause severe first degree burns, so leaving it on too long was not recommended. I guess it worked, or else I was being tortured for some reason or other! Eventually my chest returned to normal color and temperature. This was standard treatment for congestion, arthritis, rheumatism, sore muscles and the like; no pills or needles needed.

Another problem I had was recurring nose bleeds. Sometimes they would just not stop. I remember one that lasted all day long and I think my Mother was almost in a panic as she treated me in bed. I was pretty weak for awhile. Some of my cousins had the same problem, but we are living to an old age, so it may not be a hereditary problem in our case. My nose usually used to bleed right from the time I got up in the morning. I recall one episode where I walked all the way to high school one morning, swallowing and spitting blood all the way, and went into the boy's locker room to tell Coach Chauncy Brown that I needed some help. He sat me straddling a bench and "volunteered" a student in the gym class to sit behind me and put pressure on my temples and both sides under my jaw. Every time a new class would start, he'd instruct a new student in the exercise. I sat there all day, right through lunch time. I was finally able to go to class about a half hour before school let out. Although my nose bleeds became less frequent, they did not stop. I still get one once in awhile but they are easier to control in my old age. In 2008 I had laser cautery of my turbinates that seemed to help reduce snoring, but didn't appear to help my nosebleeds.

Sometimes I seem to have been "born too soon", with a new advance coming in medicine that was much superior to that which I underwent. As an example, in 1981 I had in-hospital open eye surgery for the first of my cataracts; this technique made my vision very troublesome for a year and longer, compared with the later method of using self-unfolding plastic implants that are placed through a 2mm slit in the eye and allow the patient to go home in a couple of hours with improved vision. In 2004, I had a corneal transplant in my left eye, which allows me to say that I am now 99 and 44/100% "pure me"! It took years before I could see fairly well due to the mismatch in the curvature of the corneas. My brain knew it wasn't my own cornea and insisted that my left eye was outside my skull and several feet in front of me! In 1985 I had a Zenker's diverticulum repair of my esophagus from the outside, and a second repair in 2012 from the inside using 30 Titanium staples. The latter gives you a temporary sore lip, but the former is problematic for years due to the scar tissue around the esophagus itself making it difficult to swallow. I also developed prostate cancer, and in 1997 had a radical retropubic prostatectomy, resulting in ED. Nowadays it would have been done robotically, and saved me on recovery time with less pain and disfigurement. I've also had a bunch of colonoscopies with polyp removals. I didn't mind the colonoscopies at all; it's the preparation that's a pain in the…!

I've had my share of colds, ear infections, whooping cough, mumps, chicken pox, bronchitis, flu, insecticide poisoning, multiple pre-cancer moles, and the like, with attendant treatments, like a tonsillectomy, but in my first semester at Cornell in 1949 I developed an ear infection which you can read about earlier in the book in the "On to Cornell" section. Because of the 19-shot serial treatment of Penicillin I got at the Cornell Clinic, which had terrible side effects, I'm now allergic to Penicillin. I had another bad ear infection when I was at Wright Patterson Air Force Base in 1952, but it didn't require as severe a treatment. Lucky me!

In 2008, I was diagnosed with degenerative disc disease. In 2009 I had a total right hip replacement, with a titanium implant; it was not fully successful and I have chronic soreness 24/7/365. That coupled with a repaired hammer toe and broken foot on my right leg, lumbago and arthritis, and a unilateral inguinal hernia repair (right side) make me a wishful candidate for a whole new right side from hip to foot. That'll be the day! Other than that, I'm pretty good, with only Prednisolone Acetate drops for my eyes, and medication for my high blood pressure every day, since I was about 25 years old. C'est la vie!

Odds and Ends (Mostly Odds at the End)

When I was a little tyke, with no neighboring kids around, I would play outside in the backyard in good weather until it was pitch black at night. I even skipped meals to accommodate my imagination's activities. One evening my Mother called me for supper several times, but I ignored her. Then my Father came outside to look for me, so I ran to the back of the lot and turned left onto the undeveloped alleyway and headed as fast as I could go down the trail! He followed me, and I knew he would eventually catch me, so I looked for a place to hide in the shrubbery. I spotted a big pile of lawn clippings at the edge of a lot on the alleyway and lay down in the clippings, covering myself from head to foot, with just a peek hole. I stopped breathing when I saw my Father's legs walking along right across from the pile. He went right past me! My heart was racing. After a few minutes I got up, brushed myself off, and went home. Not a word was spoken about my escapade, but I ate a cold supper. To this day, I do not know whether my father saw my charade but let me believe the camouflage deception worked because he was amused by my ingenuity. Good old Dad!

My sister, Joanne, and I got along marvelously and never fought, but one day when I was about 6 years old and she was 3, we got into a shouting match in the backyard that became so loud that my Mother came out of the house to take Jo inside. She took her hand and pulled her inside the screened back door. As the door was closing, I picked up a small green apple that had dropped from the old apple tree where we were playing and heaved it at the door about 20 feet away. The apple went right through the inch-wide vertical gap as the door finished closing and hit Jo in the left eye. She let out a piercing wail that I can still hear. It didn't have any lasting effect on her, but I never forgave myself for that act. On an earlier occasion, I accidentally closed the closet door in our foyer not knowing she was behind the door and had stuck the middle 3 fingers of her right hand in the crack. My Father had to remove the hinges to release her fingers. Fortunately, at that young age it did not damage them at all. I'm terribly sorry for your suffering, Jo.

When I was in my teens, some of the kids in the neighborhood frequently played on the shore of the Niagara River where there were no homes or businesses. It was a rocky playground, and we would catch little fish that we called "grubs" and build a small puddle on the shore to keep them in until we couldn't find any more. When we were tired of playing fishermen, we'd put the fish back in the river. One day, when my friend Paul Holzle and I were leaving this river playground, we heard a very noisy crow coming up behind us. It was flying about 100 feet in the air to our right as it neared us. Paul dropped his bicycle, grabbed a stone, and threw it as hard as he could at the crabby crow. It connected with the crow in mid-air! The crow stopped its noisy tirade, dropped about 50 feet, and flew away. Some folks can't hit a bird with a shotgun!

In high school, I earned the nickname Dracula. This was due to my propensity to catch flies, remove one of the white cantilever dumbbells located under the wings on one side, and let the fly go. It would then fly wildly upward in tight spirals, unable to keep its normal orientation. This was because the dumbbells were part of the fly's gyroscopic control system that was activated by its moving wings. The fly rotated left or right depending on which dumbbell was removed. Yep, tried both off, too!

One evening when my Cornell freshman roommate John Chin and I were in our barracks dorm room, a big fly flew in, making rapid movements around the room and a loud buzzing noise. We tried our best at using improvised fly swatters but couldn't catch it. We finally decided to see if it would settle down, so we stood motionless in the room. It eventually landed on our tiny table near the lamp. I cautiously reached into my pocket, extracted a penny, held it between the thumb and forefinger of my right hand at the height of my right eye and moved ever so slowly toward the table. Standing upright and barely breathing, I was able to get directly above the fly and dropped the penny. Bullseye! It hit the fly, trapping it under the coin. Good bye fly!

On another occasion in our dorm room, I reached into my pocket to get some change, and a dime fell out and dropped to the floor. It bounced but continued to roll upright for quite a distance, crossing several cracks in the flooring, and eventually came to rest upright in a tiny crack between two of the floorboards. Not a good place to store extra change.

One day John Chin and I decided to have the thinning leather soles of our shoes resoled. He said, "OK, let's go find some cat's pour." I said, "Cats pour what? Water?" He said, "No, no, no!" I asked him to spell it. He said, "Cat's pour — *P-A-W*." My ears were not yet tuned to his New York City accent. Cat's Paw was a brand name for shoe resoling material.

Collegetown is a section of Ithaca, NY, that is directly connected to the south side of the Cornell University campus. Within Collegetown, one of the connector roads between College Avenue and Eddy Street is a short, steep section of Dryden Road that runs downhill in a lazy stretched-out reverse-S curve. It drops 50 feet in 500 feet. One miserable gray day in the early winter of 1952, I had just turned off College Avenue onto Dryden Road heading downhill to Eddy Street in my old 1941 Chevy to visit Anne, when the skies let loose with a furiously fast wet snowstorm — huge flakes — Ithaca's best! The relatively warm roads went from dry and snowless to slick and slippery in seconds! I was moving very slowly, but the rear end of the car slid to the right as I approached the first bend of the crowned road. I glanced ahead and saw that the far side of the T-intersection with Eddy Street was completely filled with parked cars — right where I was headed! I could almost hear the collision and visualize the mess that was coming up. I depressed the clutch to stop the rear wheels from driving the car ahead and simultaneously turned the steering wheel as far and as fast as I could to the left. The car swung completely sideways and travelled through the curve, rotating slowly until it was in the left-hand lane going backwards. It came to a stop pointing uphill in the left lane, resting tightly against the curb with only the rear bumper sticking out into Eddy Street. I started to breathe again, quickly put the car in first gear, let the clutch out and returned up Dryden Road. No more of this downhill stuff for me that day. Anne would have to wait.

When we built our house on Brook Way, my habit was to get a drink of water in the dark if I got up to use the bathroom. I knew right where the cup holder (our young daughter, Sue, called it the "cup's chair") was and would fill it and drink it straight down. For some reason, one night I decided to turn the bathroom light on, then grabbed the cup, peered inside and saw a huge black spider at the bottom. From then on it was lights on!

The dress code at work for men during the early part of my career was to wear a long-sleeved shirt, a tie and jacket. One hot, humid summer day I decided to wear just a short-sleeved shirt. I sat down at my desk, rested my arms on the edge and immediately felt a tingling sensation across my body. I discovered that the SteelCrest desk in the office was leaking current from a fluorescent desk lamp that was clamped to the chrome accent strip surrounding the desk top. With my long-sleeved shirt and jacket on, there was enough insulation so that I had not felt the current flow. Got a new lamp.

Some of the men at work in Riley-Robb Hall had the practice of growing beards in the fall and shaving them off in the spring. I tried that, too, and discovered that I had a very pronounced white oval of whiskers on my chin. No more beard. I then turned to growing long sideburns, then a mustache. One day I came to work, sat down at the desk, placed a white sheet of typewriter paper on the desk in front of me, reached for a pen, and saw a flea jump from my mustache onto the paper. I had transported a flea from our dog to work! We kept the dog and got rid of the mustache.

I think most people have stories like these, so this is a good place to end. Auf Wiedersehen!

My profile as created by a Chinese paper cutter on the Bund in Shanghai, China.
He gave me hair!